1864

1864

The forgotten war
that shaped
modern Europe

TOM BUK-SWIENTY

Translated by Annette Buk-Swienty

P

PROFILE BOOKS

Profile Books gratefully acknowledges the financial assistance of the
Danish Arts Foundation

DANISH ARTS FOUNDATION

Published in Great Britain in 2015 by
PROFILE BOOKS LTD
3 Holford Yard
Bevin Way
London
WC1X 9HD
www.profilebooks.com

Originally published in Denmark in 2008 by Gyldendal,
entitled *1864: Slagtebænk Dybbøl*
Copyright © Tom Buk-Swienty and Gyldendal, 2008, 2015
Translation copyright © Annette Buk-Swienty, 2015

10 9 8 7 6 5 4 3 2 1

Printed and bound by
CPI Group (UK) Ltd, Croydon, CR0 4YY

Typeset by MacGuru Ltd in Granjon
info@macguru.org.uk

The moral right of the author has been asserted.

A CIP catalogue record for this book is available from the British Library.

ISBN 978 1 78125 276 5
eISBN 978 1 78283 077 1

FSC
www.fsc.org
MIX
Paper from
responsible sources
FSC® C020471

For my parents,
who taught me to choose my battles wisely

Contents

'The scene ... had about it a strange beauty. On the face of Dybbol Hill, looking eastwards, the morning sun shone brightly. To the right, along the Sund, vast columns of smoke rose straight into the air from the burning cottages of Ulkebøl Westermark. On the left the cliffs of the Wemming Bund shores were enveloped in the haze caused by the ceaseless puffs of snow-white smoke which were belched forth by the Broager batteries. From the crest of the hill a belt of flame flashed constantly; and the clear blue sky overhead and the still blue sea underneath encircled the whole of this picture of fire and flame and smoke in a gorgeous setting. The noise was fearful, greater even than I ever yet have heard it.'

Edward Dicey, British war correspondent, Dybbøl, 18 April 1864

Dramatis personae

Prussia

Otto Eduard Leopold von Bismarck-Schönhausen (aged forty-nine): Prussian minister-president, Foreign Secretary and primary advisor to King Wilhelm I. Conservative and politically astute, Bismarck takes advantage of the Schleswig crisis to further his own political goals of strengthening the Prussian military and the Prussian Crown.

J. Bubbe (age unknown): A Prussian private in the 24th Regiment. He participates in the early battles of Mysunde on 2 February and Dybbøl town on 17 March, as well as the final assault on 18 April, where he is in the 5th assault column attacking Redoubt V.

Carl Bunge (age unknown): A Prussian captain in the 11th Regiment, who participates in the second wave of attacks on 18 April. He led his men towards Reboubt II, proceeding from there to the Danes' second line of defence, where they meet the Danish 8th Brigade. He also fights at the Battle of Mysunde on 2 February and the successful nightly attack on the remaining advanced Danish posts in front of the redoubts, conquering this ground.

Wilhelm Gather (aged twenty-six): A Prussian private in the 4th Regiment. He is selected for the 6th storm column on 16 April and participates in the attack on Redoubt V on 18 April. He was born and grew up in the Prussian Rhine Province. He hates the war and life as a soldier and dreams of returning home to his family farm.

Prince Friedrich Karl (aged thirty-seven): At the beginning of the war he is in command of the 1st Prussian Army Corps and from 1 March he is given command of all troops at Dybbøl. Initially somewhat indecisive and ineffectual, Prince Friedrich takes a firmer stand from mid April, by which time the siege bombardment has all but silenced the Danish cannon and destroyed most of the redoubts. He devises the Prussian strategy for the final assault of the Danish position.

Friedrich Heinrich Ernst Graf von Wrangel (aged eighty): At the outbreak of war Field Marshal von Wrangel – nicknamed Pappa Wrangel – is, as soon becomes apparent, far too old to command the allied forces successfully. Wrangel has a highly distinguished military career behind him, however. He entered military school at thirteen and rose steadily through the ranks, winning distinction in the Napoleonic Wars (1807–15) and the War of Liberation (1813). As commander of the 2nd Corps of the German Confederation, Wrangel won several engagements in the First Schleswig War (1848–51).

Denmark

Wilhelm Adolph Dinesen (aged eighteen): A second lieutenant in the 9th Regiment of the 8th Brigade of the Danish army and one of the youngest officers to serve. He arrives at Dybbøl on 14 April, and on 18 April participates in the 8th Brigade's suicidal counter-attack on the Prussian assault columns. Dinesen survives the battle and is later to become the father of world-renowned Danish writer Karen Blixen.

George Daniel Gerlach (aged sixty-five): Given high command of the Danish army on 29 February following the dismissal of Christian de Meza, who had been responsible for the withdrawal of the Danish army from its first main position at the Dannevirke. Gerlach had nothing to do with this unpopular decision, which in part explains why he, though a weak leader, was chosen to head the army.

Niels Larsen (aged thirty): An infantry reservist in the 22nd Regiment. He is a successful miller from Hellum, northern Jutland, and is married to Inger Marie. The couple have a son and a newborn daughter. On 17 April, Larsen is sent on duty in the most advanced redoubt line, stormed by the Prussians the following morning.

Johan Peter Larssen (aged forty-two): A corporal in the 4th Support Company and the oldest private in the Danish army. Inspired by news of the Danish losses at Dybbøl, he volunteers for combat duty in April, leaving his job as a skipper on a light vessel.

Carl Christian Lundbye (aged fifty-one): Former artillery officer and now Danish minister of war. He was on active duty during the First Schleswig War, but despite being an experienced soldier by the time the Second Schleswig War breaks out in 1864 he proves a pedantic, meddlesome leader guided by pride rather than rational argument, and seems curiously oblivious to the actual situation on the front. He is instrumental in the dismissal of Commander-in-chief General de Meza following the latter's decision to withdraw from the Dannevirke.

Christian Julius Frederik de Meza (aged seventy-two): Commander-in-chief when the war breaks out. Though a somewhat eccentric old man, he is a competent and decisive commander whose career flounders on the highly unpopular but ultimately wise decision to withdraw the Danish army from its first main position at the Dannevirke in southern Schleswig.

Ditlev Gothard Monrad (aged fifty-two): National-Liberal prime minister of Denmark, a bishop and one of the founding fathers of Denmark's constitution. He had been known for his strong work ethic, but by 1864 he is worn out and mentally ill. He has little comprehension of the actual situation on the front and therefore turns a deaf ear to pleas from his generals for a withdrawal.

Rasmus Nellemann (aged thirty-four): A corporal in the 2nd Regiment. The estate manager of Frijsenborg near Hammel, Jutland, he is a devoted family man who only reluctantly reports for duty. The surviving letters he sent from the front give a vivid description of life there. He is on duty in the trenches near Redoubt II on the morning of 18 April, when the Prussians attack.

Peter Henrik Claude du Plat (aged fifty-four): A general and commander of the Danish army's 2nd Division at Dybbøl, he is a well-educated gentleman officer, loyal, brave and fair. On 16 April he offers to take the blame for the Danish retreat from Dybbøl, though the wounded commander-in-chief, Gerlach, refuses to accept his gallant bid.

Ernst Schau (aged forty-one): A major and staff officer with General du Plat. Although known as a talented soldier and leader, Schau was plagued by premonitions of his own death. He writes home daily to his wife, Friede, whom he clearly loves dearly, and is on duty in the redoubts during the Prussian assault.

Others
Edward Dicey (aged thirty-two): British war correspondent from the *Daily Telegraph*. A seasoned and talented war reporter who had covered the first years of the American Civil War, Dicey was sent to report on the Danish–German war on the Danish side. Like all who participated, he was deeply affected by the horrors of the war, as is apparent in his reportage.

P. V. Grove (aged thirty-one): War correspondent for the Danish daily *Dagbladet*. The first real Danish war reporter, he stayed with the troops from the Dannevirke to Dybbøl and experienced the war first-hand. His coverage is vivid and spell-binding.

Charles William Meredith van de Velde (aged forty-six): One of two Red Cross delegates sent to observe and help out in the Danish–German war. He is stationed with the Danish army, while his colleague Louis Appia is on the German side. Van de Velde has a sensitive nature and has a tough time stomaching the sight of the severely wounded.

A note to the reader

In February 1864 war broke out between Denmark and the two principal German powers, Prussia and Austria, over an obscure duchy straddling the Danish border with Germany. The Danish cabinet had provoked the war in 1863 by passing into law the so-called 'November Constitution', which was the first step towards an annexation of the Duchy of Schleswig. Not only did Denmark's actions violate an international agreement known as the London Protocol, drawn up by Russia and Great Britain in 1852, but it outraged the German Confederation – over half of Schleswig's population were German-speakers.

Though it has been all but forgotten by history, the Danish–German war of 1864 was a major international crisis which captured all of Europe's attention. European heads of state were concerned that this minor conflict could spark a large-scale European war. Great Britain in particular feared an upset of the balance of power on the Continent, with Parliament debating whether to provide military support to the Danes. The war made the headlines in British dailies and several of their top war reporters were sent to the front. Their stories focused on the struggle of the underdog – the Danes – against the Goliath-sized allied Austrian and Prussian forces. Queen Victoria's sympathies, however, lay mostly with the Prussians, in part because the princess royal, Victoria, was married to the

Prussian Crown prince. She kept her prime minister, Lord Palmerston, on a tight leash, preventing any military engagement. Palmerston instead put his efforts into brokering a peace between the warring parties. A peace conference was held in London in May–June of 1864 but no agreement was reached. As it turned out, the complexities of the Schleswig-Holstein question eluded even intense British peace efforts. Palmerston later famously summed up the enigmatic and complex causes of the conflict as follows: 'Only three people … have ever really understood the Schleswig-Holstein business: the Prince Consort of Augustenborg, who is dead, a German professor, who has gone mad, and I, who have forgotten all about it.'

The war dragged on into the summer of 1864. Once all Danish resistance had been thoroughly crushed, a peace treaty was signed in which Denmark lost two-fifths of its territory and almost half of its population. With the Danish defeat, the map of Europe was about to be completely redrawn.

It was Bismarck's first war, and his successful campaign against Denmark set him on his path towards political greatness. Resultant squabbles over the control of neighbouring Holstein set in motion a string of events which led to the Austro-Prussian war of 1866, and which in turn ensured Prussian dominance over the German Confederation and, ultimately, paved the way for the unification of the thirty-nine German states under Berlin rule in 1871.

Seen in this light, the forgotten war of 1864 deserves more than a footnote in the annals of history: it was the pebble that started an avalanche of decisive political decisions which still affect us today. Some historians even posit that we can draw a straight line from the war of 1864 to the First World War.

For Denmark the war was certainly an earth-shattering

and deeply traumatising event. For several months, and against heavy odds, the Danes held out against a significantly more powerful enemy. The two-month-long bombardment by Prussian forces of the Danish positions at Dybbøl was, at the time, one of the most intense bombardments in military history. The siege culminated in a massive assault on the Dybbøl fortifications on 18 April 1864.

The following narrative is about this forgotten war and the men who fought it.

Preface

Many of the survivors who later described the Battle of Dybbøl recalled the weather as vividly as the exploding shells, screaming soldiers and mutilated bodies scattered across the blood-soaked, bomb-torn ground. In surprising detail, they remembered the hint of spring hanging in the air, the large moon lighting up the windless night, and the clear dawn breaking into a beautiful day. They recalled the soft hillsides and idyllic coves bathing in the sunlight, and the shimmering waters surrounding the Sundeved headland in southern Jutland, where the battle took place.

Remarkably, survivors also shared a recollection of hearing larks sing through the infernal noise of cracking musketry and booming cannon. Through the early morning and into the day of 18 April, 8,000 shells fell among the Danish soldiers, who took cover in the trenches, rifle-pits and redoubts of the Danish defensive line. Reportedly, the birdsong was especially prominent at exactly 10 a.m., when the Prussian shelling abruptly ceased. This moment signalled the beginning of the end for the Danish troops; seconds later, all hell broke loose and swarms of Prussian soldiers stormed the Danish position.

It has been argued that the recollections of birdsong may have been little more than figments of the men's imagination – a result of their stubborn humanity, longing for life and a refusal to accept the destruction and mayhem of their situation. It is certainly interesting that veterans of the Battle of the Somme – one of the bloodiest battles in history – also remembered birdsong and glorious weather on the battlefield on the first day of battle, 1 July 1916. The September 11 attacks in New York are further poignant examples, taking place on a sunny, crystal-clear day.

18 April 1864 was another day from hell. As at the Somme half a century later, both sides experienced intense fear, pain and adrenalin levels, suffered gruesome mutilations and heavy casualties; and had overburdened field hospitals. Nevertheless, the number of casualties on the Danish side far exceeded that of their opponents'; they were, in almost literal terms, butchered. By 1864, Denmark had seen its share of major battles – most notably the many wars against its neighbour Sweden; the intense and bloody Battle of Copenhagen on 2 April 1801 against the British; and the Battle of Isted on 25 July 1850 against Schleswig-Holstein rebels (or freedom fighters, depending on your point of view). But nothing the Danish armed forces had seen before could prepare them for what would unfold at Dybbøl. On 18 April 1864, Denmark was up against an adversary of tremendous strength. On most sectors of the front, the Prussians outnumbered the Danes four to one. The loss of life on the Danish side was so heavy that whole companies were wiped out, whole regiments dissolved. Only about half of the 12,000 Danish troops made it back to their barracks on the island of Als that day.

The Battle of Dybbøl became a significant milestone in Danish history. At the turn of 1864, Denmark was a multi-national, integrated state; after the conquest of Als of 29 June its population was reduced by a million and its territory by one-third. Denmark became a Lilliputian monarchy of little political consequence. The Danes became mired in defeatist self-pity, a mood that lingers even now, although the country's recent involvement in the wars in Iraq and Afghanistan suggests Denmark may slowly be coming out from under the shadow of 1864.

For Prussia, the Battle of Dybbøl marked the beginning of a remarkable ascent to Continental supremacy. At the time, however, Germany was not yet unified but rather a loose political association consisting of thirty-nine large and small states, of which the largest were Prussia and Austria – both vying for power and dominance. The Prussian minister-president, later chancellor of Germany, Otto von Bismarck, was ambitiously planning to forge a unified German empire under Berlin rule. These were daring plans in light of the many influential liberal Prussians who were apprehensive about warfare and of a democratic mindset. In 1864, Prussia was still deeply marred by its crushing defeats in the battles of Jena and Auerstedt (1806) during the Napoleonic Wars. Though the Prussian army went on to play a central role in the final defeat of Napoleon at the battles of Leipzig (1813) and Waterloo (1815), these earlier defeats at Jena and Auerstedt had shaken its military leaders. And in 1864 it was still plagued by self-doubt and a deep lack of military confidence.

So it was by no means with a sense of a certain victory – as history would like to have us believe – that Prussia went to war with Denmark. Furthermore, Danes were perceived as aggressive oppressors of German liberty in the duchies of Schleswig and Holstein. Many Germans referred to Denmark with an equal measure of fear and contempt as *das Dänenthum*, which loosely translates as 'Dane-dom'. Even though Denmark was no great military power, it held a distinct naval advantage over

Prussia, and the Danish fortifications at the Dannevirke and Dybbøl were perceived to be formidable military strongholds.

Politically, however, Bismarck and King Wilhelm I were dependent on winning a decisive battle at Dybbøl, as a defeat, they believed, would crush their plans to unify all German states under Prussian rule. Thus, when, after a long and costly siege, the news of victory at Dybbøl reached Berlin, it was received with relief – although not by the kingdom's liberal classes. The successful campaign took the wind out of their sails, and set Bismarck on his path to political greatness, seemingly proving his famous saying that the questions of the day had to be decided with blood and iron. Without victory at Dybbøl, Bismarck would not have been able to secure the political backing he needed to wage war against Austria (1866) and France (1870–71) – successful campaigns that paved the way for the unification of Germany and the making of a world power. In that context, the battle of 18 April 1864 is a milestone not just in Danish and German history, but in that of the entire European continent.

Introduction: The veteran

As the steamship rounded Kegnæs – a tail-shaped point off the island of Als – the famous Danish poet and author Holger Drachmann gazed towards the horizon in the direction of Dybbøl Hill, which looked to him 'like a giant beached whale in its death throes'.

It was late afternoon on 18 April 1877. Drachmann was on his way to Sønderborg and Dybbøl to see the battlefield where, thirteen years earlier, Danish soldiers had fought hopelessly against a superior enemy. For Drachmann and his contemporaries, '18 April' and 'Dybbøl' were synonymous with destruction and humiliation.

Shortly after his arrival in Sønderborg, Drachmann went on a guided tour of the old defence works. A local veteran who had survived the heavy bombardments and the Prussian storming of the Danish position served as his guide. The veteran and his regiment had moved into position on the battered left flank of the Danish defensive line on 17 April 1864, and were thus fated to participate in the final, crushing battle of the war.

'So, what was it like? How did you feel in the hours before and during the offensive?' Drachmann asked. Clearly unaccustomed to being interviewed, let alone questioned about his feelings, the veteran replied, 'What a queer thing to ask!' Still, the question seemed to evoke a series of mental images from that day, during which he had in fact shut down all feelings. Hesitatingly at first, then in a torrent of words, the veteran began describing the incessant bombardments preceding the storm:

> We were almost at death's door and looked like we had been sleeping in a pigsty, which in a sense we had. Throughout the night we could hear the sound of the Prussians throwing up trenches only a few yards from our own defensive works. The day before, they had taken the sap trenches we had dug in front of the entrenchment, and we had not been able to beat them back. So they were really close, and we knew something was bound to happen soon, and we hoped it would. We could not stand the wait. We were just sitting there in the trenches, basically doing nothing, and were as dirty as filthy rags. No one would have confused us for Danish soldiers. My face was covered with the brain matter of a fellow soldier whose head had been shot off during a shoot-out. In the night, we fired our last shells targeting those Prussian trenches where we could make out the faint forms of crouching soldiers … We thought for sure they would attack, but they did not. They just pounded us. It was the worst bombardment yet. You cannot imagine the shower of shells that rained down on us. I cannot explain it, because you would not understand.

The veteran paused, as though searching for words: 'It was as if a grindstone kept churning inside my head, and, now that I think about it, I can still feel this grinding in my head.'

Drachmann and the veteran fell silent – the veteran's last sentence left hanging in the air. Quietly, the two men took in the landscape around them and the setting sun, casting long shadows on the now grassy Dybbøl Hill.

Drachmann was the first to break the silence. 'So, what was it like when the Prussians finally attacked?' A look of bewilderment settled on the veteran's face. 'I do not know.' Yet it was clear to Drachmann that his question had evoked another host of mental pictures. After a long, contemplative pause, the veteran began talking with great urgency:

They just burst out of the ground in long lines. Immediately bending forward, then running fast towards us; the first line with fixed bayonets, the next with their guns held crosswise against their chests … We levelled our rifles, aiming for their faces, but soon they were among us.

We tried to drive them back, but they came at us again, and again. They kept pushing onwards, and there were a terrible lot of them. I know, I looked them straight in the face, and yet I do not remember a single one. Some were howling like animals, others growling through clenched teeth, as I am sure we did too. But unlike them, we were not drunk. I swear to it. Though perhaps everyone behaves like drunkards in such a situation. I cannot really tell you more. It is all a muddle now. But we fought on the parapets and in the trenches. And as long as we had guns, we used them like real soldiers. I kept mine, but I saw others engaging in raw fist-fights and biting each other's throats. A big, handsome Prussian lad with wellington boots suddenly leapt at the chest of one of our men and crushed his face. I stabbed him with my bayonet; he fell on top of me, and I had to kick him hard to free myself. In fact, there was a lot of kicking, but I do not much care to think about it

… then suddenly it was as if someone hit me with a really big stick on the left arm … blood began trickling down my arm and hand … around me there was shooting, howling and hooting, but it was as if I was not really there. I was in a sort of trance.

Part One

THE DAY BEFORE

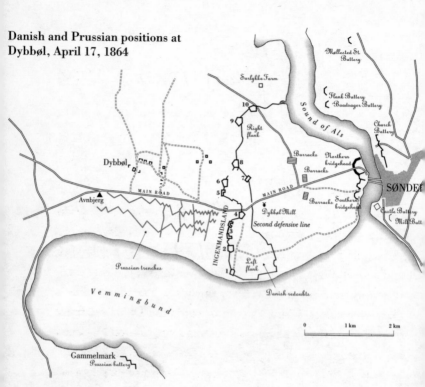

Danish and Prussian positions at Dybbøl, April 17, 1864

Møllestad St. Battery

Surlykke Farm

Sound of Als

Flank Battery
Buadsager Battery

Church Battery

10

9

Right flank

Barracks

Northern bridgehead

8

Barracks

Dybbøl

MAIN ROAD

6

5

7

MAIN ROAD

SØNDE

Avnbjerg

INGENMANDSLAND

4

Dybbøl Mill

Southern bridgehead

Barracks

Castle Battery

Mill Batt.

Second defensive line

Prussian trenches

3

2

Left flank

1

Danish redoubts

V e m m i n g b u n d

0   1 km   2 km

Gammelmark
Prussian battery

Sunday, 17 April 1864

Only a few hundred metres – in some places a mere 150 – was all that separated the opposing armies on 17 April. For several weeks the Prussians had advanced on their enemy with pick and shovel, digging a gigantic system of zigzagging communications trenches and parallel trenches, which spread like a giant web across no-man's-land towards the Danish defence works. More than a hundred Prussian siege cannon had been mobilised to wear down the enemy before a decisive assault. Powerless to defend themselves, the Danish troops had no choice but to seek cover from the relentless shelling and pray for a miracle, the men crouching in or behind anything that could provide shelter: parapet walls, powder magazines, trenches, shell-holes and rifle-pits.

The position was untenable. Yet on 17 April neither side knew what the other was planning. The Danes expected an attack, but were unsure when it would take place. The Prussians, in turn, were readying a large mass of troops to storm the Danish position the following day. They did not, however, know whether the Danes were preparing a sortie or perhaps even an evacuation of the position.

An international peace conference had been scheduled for 20 April in London, and both parties were eager to enter into these negotiations from a position of strength. In Berlin it was believed that a major victory would speak in their favour. Conversely, Danish politicians in Copenhagen believed sustaining a hostile attack would garner support for Denmark's interests – even if, as they phrased it to their generals, 'such a defence would result in massive casualties'.

The chosen one

'Am I going to die?' 26-year-old Wilhelm Gather of the Prussian army wondered while attending an outdoor service with his company on a cold but sunny April morning in 1864. He could hear the muted thunder of cannon in the distance as he received Holy Communion. With his head bent like his comrades, he thought about the prospect of dying in battle. 'Who among us here will soon depart this earth?' he silently asked no one in particular.

Wilhelm Gather belonged to the 4th Company of the 4th Regiment, quartered in the small village of Nybøl a few kilometres from the front line. Gather and his regiment had come in from Varnæs, near Åbenrå, twenty kilometres west of Dybbøl Hill, where they had been encamped for a few days. On 16 April they had been given their marching orders for Nybøl. And like everyone else in his company, Gather knew that this meant an attack was under way.

A week earlier the Prussian general staff had begun the process of selecting the regiments that would serve as assault troops. Gather's regiment was among the chosen ones, and he would be in the first line of attack. Essentially, assault troops were responsible for overpowering the enemy and thwarting any counter-attacks until reserves could be deployed. And everyone was aware that this assignment was extremely

A Prussian lieutenant from the 4th Company of the 4th Regiment
who were given the order to march to the frontlines on 16 April
and became part of the first wave of attack on 18 April.

dangerous. Assault troops always suffered huge losses.

Gather became overwhelmed with fear when on 13 April
he was told his company had been selected to spearhead the
attack. In a letter to his parents, he wrote, 'Truthfully, it is
such a strange feeling to know I'll be in the first line of attack.
The mood in my regiment is grim, and none of us can stop
thinking about dying.'

At first, Gather had fervently hoped that 'the Danes would
withdraw from their position before they could attack, or that
an international peace conference would be set up, and the
attack called off'.

He realised, of course, that these were merely wishful thoughts. So, rather than long for the impossible, he set his hopes on being deployed as a rifleman. A rifleman would fire at the Danish defence line from a distance, and, as he later explained to his parents, therefore had the advantage of being able to seek cover from the dreaded case-shot that was sure to kill swathes of the men storming the Danish position.

He also tried to assuage his fears by noting to his parents that while many men would fall, there were always some who made it. There were always survivors, and why shouldn't he be one of them?

Gather was a well-trained soldier. Like most Prussian men, he had gone through three years of mandatory military service, completed in 1862. He had been called up for active duty when war threatened, and, much to his chagrin, had been forced to put on his uniform again. Despite all his military training, Gather did not feel like a soldier. In fact, from day one he absolutely hated the war, simply could not stomach the hardships and dangers on the front. He was a farmer at heart and longed for the peaceful life on the family farmstead in the village of Hohenburg in the Prussian Rhine Province. The family farm was situated on the slopes of the Rhine and had a grand view of the river. In letters to his parents, Gather lovingly and fittingly referred to his home region as 'Vater Rhein' (Father Rhine).

So far in the campaign, Gather had been lucky. He had been spared serious action and felt he had much to be thankful for when he attended the outdoor service in Nybøl on 17 April. Though the war had been going on since 1 February, the 3rd Army Corps to which his regiment belonged had not been involved in any major battles, unlike the allied forces' two other corps. Still, the months-long campaign against Denmark had been trying for Gather.

It had been freezing cold when they were based at the Dannevirke fortification forty kilometres south of Dybbøl, where the Danes had initially taken position. And no one doubted that the capture of the Dannevirke would inflict heavy casualties on the Prussian and Austrian troops. Gather therefore found himself in a state of extreme agitation when an order was given on 5 February to row across the Schlei Bay and conduct a flank attack on the Danish line. For days the sound of booming cannon had rung out along the thirty-kilometre front line. Both sides had suffered great losses and a palpable fear had gripped the men. To his great relief the attack was called off. In the dead of night and unbeknownst to the Austro-Prussian forces, the Danes had managed to evacuate their position.

In the weeks that followed, Gather's regiment was deployed to the east coast of mid-Jutland: first to the town of Kolding, just south of the Kongeåen River, and then to Fort Frederi-cia. The allied troops had besieged the fort and subjected it to several heavy artillery attacks during the month of March.

Gather got his first taste of battle in a minor skirmish near Kolding, where he witnessed a fellow soldier being shot through the chest. Gather was not so much as scratched, but his luck was about to change. By the end of March his regi-ment was deployed to Dybbøl, now under siege by Prussian troops. The trenches here were cold and wet and the men were miserable. Provisions were miserly, and Gather complained about the meagre rations in letters to his parents. Sometimes, he wrote with much scorn, they did not even get their ration of tobacco. Making matters even worse were the ludicrously low wages of a Prussian conscript. It did not matter much, though: there was little of interest to buy from the stores in the North Schleswig villages or from the sutlers, those itinerant merchants-of-fortune who seemed to appear wherever nineteenth-century armies set camp. According to Gather, the quality of Danish beer and schnapps was terrible.

At the beginning of April, Gather's fear of combat rose again as plans of an attack on the island of Als were set in motion. Hundreds of rowing boats were to carry large units, including Gather's regiment, across the widest part of the sound to Als. The thought of sitting exposed in a rowing boat in open water was terrifying to him. If discovered by the Danish warships circling these waters, the regiment would have a minimal chance of survival, and to boot most of the men could not swim. Bad weather, however, set in and the dangerous crossing was cancelled. Gather felt a huge surge of relief when he heard the news, and admitted as much in a letter to his parents.

On 17 April, however, Gather understood he was running out of luck. Everything indicated that a grand assault was imminent. Nearby villages with foreign-sounding names such as Vester Sottrup, Avnbøl, Smøl, Stenderup, Skodsbøl and Bøffelkobbel bustled with the activity of military build-up. Soldiers were quartered in farmhouses and stables, and new camps were being built in the open; the biggest of these was near Nybøl, where sutlers had begun setting up trading tents and stalls. Clusters of soldiers could be seen in town squares, open spaces and among the trees in nearby woodlands. Both camps and villages filled up with carriages, carts and horses; lines of laundry hung wherever possible, rifle piles and fire-pits were scattered over the area. And at all hours of the day, orderlies could be seen tearing through the camps at full gallop.

Gather was one of 11,000 troops that were to take part in the first wave of attack. Another 30,000 reserves and cavalry had been moved forward, and a great number of mobile field batteries were being emplaced near the Dybbøl position.

Other sure signs of the impending assault were the long trains of ambulance carts lined with hay for the wounded on the main road, the double rations of meat – sardonically named 'last supper' by the men – and the great number of church services like the one Gather was attending.

The general staff, however, were not forthcoming with the actual date of the attack, so Gather and his fellow soldiers lived in great uncertainty over how long they could count on being alive.

After the service Gather went to his quarters, a stable assigned to his company in the village of Nybøl. Lying on his stomach, he penned a letter to his parents, using his knapsack as an impromptu table: 'I focus all of my energy on what a blessed day it will be when I will see you all again,' he wrote.

The battle plan

At exactly 12 p.m. an imposing figure with impeccable posture and striking looks arrived at Hvilhoj Inn near Nybøl. The man sported a well-groomed moustache, a red Prussian hussar's uniform with white braiding, white cross-belt, white armband and tall, shiny black boots. Already present at the inn were the Prussian generals Canstein, Raven, Schmidt and Goeben and the commanders of the assault troops, the artillery and the engineer troops. They all cordially greeted the newcomer, as well they should: he was none other than Prince Friedrich Karl of Prussia, supreme commander of the Prussian army at Dybbøl.

'Tomorrow, gentlemen,' he announced without preamble, 'I bestow upon you the honour of taking the [Danish] entrenchment. His Royal Highness has instructed me to relay to you his best wishes; he will pray for us and be with us in spirit.'

Throughout the campaign against Denmark, the prince, known as the 'Red Prince' for the colour of his hussar's uniform, had often appeared insecure and out of sorts. But on this day he emerged as a strong and decisive leader. In light of the upcoming peace conference on 20 April, the timing for an assault was perfect: 18 April would be the Day of Destiny.

Prince Friedrich Karl of Prussia, supreme commander of the Prussian Army at Dybbøl, known as the 'Red Prince' because of the colour of his hussar's uniform. Throughout the campaign he had often appeared insecure but emerged as a strong and decisive leader at the battle of Dybbøl.

The prince was no novice to warfare. In 1848, after two years at the University of Bonn, the twenty-year-old prince had joined General von Wrangel's military staff as a captain in the campaign against Denmark in the First Schleswig War, where he acted as adjutant. Awarded a medal for bravery and unerring judgement on the battlefield, and promoted to major, he had then participated in a military operation against insurgents in the Baden Revolution of 1849, where he was wounded. During these engagements, the prince had managed to earn not only his men's respect but also their loyalty and trust. Strict, caring and courageous, he was perceived to be the ideal Prussian officer – a model soldier to his men.

In 1856 he was promoted to lieutenant general, and in 1860 he was given charge of the 3rd Brandenburger Corps. In the campaign against Denmark in 1864, he initially headed the 1st Army Corps, but in March he was promoted to supreme commander of the allied forces of Austria and Prussia at Dybbøl. The well-being of his men was of the utmost importance to the prince – too important, according to some of the more senior generals, who now felt his consideration for the men's welfare rendered him weak and ineffectual.

There was some truth to these accusations, and the prince admitted as much after the war. He hated exposing his soldiers to undue danger. And when it happened, he was much affected by it. He had trouble sleeping on nights when Danish artillery batteries returned fire from Dybbøl.

The prince understood his battle-worn men; he, too, was weary of the campaign. Only a couple of months earlier, on 2 February, he had launched an attack with 10,000 men and an artillery battery consisting of sixty-six field pieces against an advanced Danish trench position at Mysunde near the Dannevirke. Despite his superior military strength – the Danes had only twenty cannon and 2,500 men on this section of their defence line – the prince had been forced to retreat.

It had been a miserably cold day and a heavy fog had made it nearly impossible to see more than a metre or so in any direction. The prince had felt wretched, knowing that his decisions alone would decide the fate of so many soldiers; he was sick with worry, and on top of that his bones had ached with cold.

The Prussian troops had been met with vigorous fire from the Danish artillery at Mysunde. The cannon had boomed, the ground shook, and thick plumes of gun smoke had mingled with the increasingly dense fog. Mysunde town was ablaze; within a few hours, nothing was left but a heap of smouldering ruins.

Prussian siege-artillery. The Prussians deployed batteries
along the entire Danish line. Night and day there was
a hissing and bursting of shells at Dybbøl.

As the prince charged, Danish artillery returned fire with ferocious willpower. Exploding shells burst through the air, striking the ground with loud hissing noises; a good many landed near the prince. Confused, he had looked to the Danish entrenchment, realising that despite his superior strength he would not be able to crush the determined Danish resistance. Reluctantly, he had ordered a retreat, knowing full well that his troops would sustain serious casualties. Case shot had torn through the retreating columns and many Prussian soldiers had fallen and been left behind on the frozen ground as quiet testament to the failed operation.

It all seemed hopeless. The first attack on Danish positions had been a failure, and the prince knew Berlin would take a stern view of the situation. His failure would give the war-sceptics grounds to withdraw their support from the Scandinavian campaign.

The prince had known a similar despair in late March,

following another failed operation. The weather had been miserable: overcast, rainy and cold. He was in poor health, and he had found it increasingly difficult to fall asleep at head-quarters on Gråsten Castle, which was dark and damp. 'It's as if there's no warmth at all in this part of the world,' he wrote.

With his chief of staff, Colonel Blumenthal, he had mas-terminded a grand battle plan to be carried out by the end of March. Referred to as Operation Ballebro, the plan was for a large force of Prussian troops to launch a surprise pincer attack on the Danish forces at Dybbøl from the island of Als. In the dead of night, they were to cross the sound to Als in rowing boats, encircle the unsuspecting Danish reserve troops there, completely disbanding and destroying them, and then proceed to attack Dybbøl from the rear. Based on the assump-tion that the Danes, who had naval superiority, would never suspect the Prussians capable of such a daring tactic, it was believed the manoeuvre would work.

The men selected for this operation, including Private Gather and his company, were visibly anxious; the prince, too, was filled with trepidation and uncertainty. On the one hand, he was excited by the prospect of a quick victory and the military glory this would bestow on him and his men. On the other hand, he was worried that he was taking too much of a risk. Was he gambling with the lives of his men? According to the plan, they were to cross at the widest part of the sound, where there was the least likelihood of encountering Danish resistance. However, if they were discovered, Danish warships could quickly be summoned and not only thwart their sur-prise attack but completely destroy them.

The prince was sick with the pale cast of indecision. The counsel of several of his generals and advisers to abort the plan did little, of course, to boost his resolve. Days passed, and still the prince could not make up his mind. One hundred and sixty rowing boats were moored at Ballebro; heavy, rifled field artillery had been dug in and was ready to open fire on Danish warships; 10,000 troops had been deployed; a diversionary frontal assault on Dybbøl was ready to be launched.

To attack, or not to attack? As the prince remained indecisive, his generals tore into a heated argument. The hot-headed and temperamental General Blumenthal was especially vociferous in his call to action. Though he was apprehensive about the attack, he had little patience with his superior commander's dawdling. At a meeting of the general staff, the other officers looked on open-mouthed as Blumenthal engaged in a shouting match with the prince, yelling at him to get his act together and issue the order to attack.

The prince, however, wavered, until on 1 April a massive storm broke out with howling winds and three-feet waves, preventing any attempt to cross the water. A relieved prince called off the operation; no doubt he saw the storm as a sign from God. It was, instead, unanimously decided to launch a real frontal attack on the Dybbøl position.

The defences at Dybbøl, however, were considered too strong to be taken in a quick decisive attack. The Prussian strategy, therefore, was to lay siege to the position and weaken it through continuous and heavy bombardments. However, time was of the essence as the Prussian generals were being strong-armed by Berlin, eager for a swift victory over the Norse.

By 17 April, the prince therefore felt compelled to push back the attack to the following day. He and his general staff had worked out an ingenious plan: a strategic masterpiece where absolutely nothing was left to chance. Detailed instructions on the execution of this battle plan were given to all attending officers at the Hvilhoj Inn meeting:

At 1.30 a.m. on 18 April the first attack columns were to move forward and, like shadows in the night, silently glide across no-man's-land through the communications trenches into the front-line trench (the so-called 'third parallel'). At 2 a.m. three more columns were to follow, quietly moving into position in the front-line trench. Once all 10,000 troops were in place, they were to lie down noiselessly and await the order to attack; meanwhile, the 102 Prussian cannon were to pound the Danish position. At exactly 10 a.m. the cannon were to cease fire and the attack commence.

The Prussian generals listened carefully. They were ready. For days now they had drilled their assault troops on Broager and Nybøl, where replicas of the Danish trenches had been built. All attack columns were deployed, all batteries dug in and the last front-line trench finished.

'Any questions, gentlemen?' asked the prince.

No one uttered a word until a voice from the back of the room cut through the silent acquiescence: 'If the first column of attack is brought to a halt, should the next fire at it to force it onward?'

All eyes fell on the speaker: General von Goeben, a tall, lean man with a pointy chin, an aquiline nose and wire-rim glasses. According to Adjutant von Geilsler, the question was put forth in a calm, business-like tone.

Nonplussed, the prince seemed momentarily at a loss for words, but he quickly recovered and assured Goeben that the situation would never arise. 'That won't happen,' he reiterated with a dismissive wave of his hand.

4

The butcher's block

As the meeting came to a close, and while Wilhelm Gather was penning a letter to his parents in Nybøl, the prince and his generals prepared to go for a ride along the main road of Sønderborg to the Dybbøl front. The party's first stop, one kilometre west of the Danish entrenchments, was Avnbjerg, the highest point in the area. Avnbjerg afforded the prince a formidable view of the theatre of war. 'I felt like King Poly-crates beholding the recently occupied Samos,' he later wrote of the experience.

The prince took in the coves, the hill ranges and the great Prussian batteries on Broager – the so-called 'Gammelmark batteries' – that continuously sent shells whirring across the Vemmingbund Bay and into the Danish defence works. These batteries were the Prussians' trump card. They comprised modern, rifled, breech-loading guns, which were effectively destroying the left flank of the Danish line. Until the begin-ning of April, the Danes had bravely accepted the challenge and engaged in a ferocious artillery duel with the Prussian batteries at Gammelmark. Redoubt II, on the highest point of the defensive line, had been particularly active in returning fire. Two cool-headed Danish gunners, Lieutenants Ancker and Castenskjold, were in charge here. They had earned the respect of the enemy and were seen as heroes by their men. The fighting between Broager and Redoubt II had been intense throughout March and the beginning of April. But the fortifications at Dybbøl had been built primarily to withstand frontal attacks, rather than flank attacks from Broager, and there were only a few fixed guns in place to return the Prussian fire. As April wore on, Prussian reinforcements arrived and the Danish guns grew quieter. By 17 April, all serious resistance had come to a halt.

The Gammelmark batteries constituted only a small part of the Prussian artillery. Along the length of the Danish line, the Prussians had dug in thirty-three batteries. In every direction the Red Prince looked from his vantage point in Avnbjerg, he could see Prussian cannon muzzles spewing fire like angry dragons at the crumbling Danish defence works. He heard the boom of their fire, felt the ground shake, and saw gun smoke rise in the air. Shells hissed across Vemmingbund Bay and over the Prussian zigzag trenches and parallels, hitting their targets with blind precision. To warn fellow soldiers of the direction of the shells, the Danish men had given them names that corresponded with the location they came from, calling out, 'In-coming Broagers' or 'Partridges' or 'Storks'.

The Prussian trench system was only a few hundred paces from the Danish line now. So close, in fact, that it seemed to the men in the redoubts that all the Prussians had to do was lean slightly forward in order to give them the kiss of death. The prince could follow the trajectories of each individual shell and see exactly where they hit the burnt-out Danish redoubts.

Dybbøl Hill had been turned into a wasteland, grey and scarred. The area's farms had been razed and the nearby villages of Dybbøl and Avnbjerg were by now nothing but heaps of debris. Large parts of Sønderborg and Als lay in ruins. There were no longer any trees left on the hill, only a few charred, skeletal shrubs on the barren ground. It had become a war-torn hell-scape: ugly, misshapen and twisted, as if in painful solidarity with the long-suffering troops.

Only a month ago a majestic white mill had stood on top of Dybbøl Hill. Virtually destroyed during a previous war, it had been painstakingly rebuilt to its former glory. Now, however, the upper portion was gone, the massive walls riddled with bullet-holes, the white plaster coming off in huge chunks. Half a kilometre west of the collapsed mill were the ten redoubts that made up the Danish fortification. In front of and behind the works was a maze of trenches connecting the redoubts, the ground everywhere punctured by shell-holes. The Danish front line was roughly two kilometres long, stretching along the crest of Dybbøl Hill from Vemmingbund to the Sound of Als.

It was a so-called 'flank position', established on the eastern tip of a blunt peninsula, bounded by Vemmingbund Bay to the south and the Sound of Als to the north. From this position, Danish military strategists had theorised that they would be able to dissuade attackers from coming from the south by leaving them vulnerable to a rear attack. The position also allowed for a retreat to Als, if necessary, with cover from the strong Danish fleet that controlled the surrounding waters. This at least was the strategic thinking that lay behind the construction of the Dybbøl fortification in 1861.

It was intended as an offensive position from which attacks could be launched, supported by artillery fire from the redoubts. But the Danish troops deployed at Dybbøl in 1864 had no offensive power: they were outnumbered and outgunned. Even at the beginning of the war, at which point the Prussians had fewer troops deployed than their opponent, the Danes had been on the defensive. Prussian weaponry comprised highly effective modern rifles and cannon and their troops were fit and well trained. Neither was true for the Danish side. Mounting an offensive, despite the relative strength of the position, was therefore out of the question. Instead the Danes had dug in, basically inviting a siege. Trenches were excavated between the redoubts, and fall-back positions were constructed behind the line. Observation posts, saps, traverses and various defensive structures had been erected in front of the line, but this ground was lost in mid March.

The Danes' defensive structures consisted of clever obstacles, strategically positioned to slow down charging attackers. There were chevaux de frise, spiked monstrosities that could impale infantry crossing the battlefield; likewise fences of pointed stakes driven into ramparts (known as 'fraises'), flesh-tearing entanglements of wire and sharp-toothed harrows able to cause severe injuries to soldiers, who might fall on them during a heated charge. Attackers also risked falling into fox-holes or stepping on the dreaded caltrops, jagged iron devices that could pierce straight through a man's foot.

In mid February, the first time the prince had seen the fortification, he had grown utterly dejected, and written to his uncle, King Wilhelm I: 'Dybbøl is another Sevastopol. Even a superior enemy would hesitate attacking a position of this strength.'

The mere mention of 'Sevastopol' sent chills down the spines of most European army commanders at the time. In 1855, during the Crimean War with Russia, British and

French troops had, after a protracted year-long siege of the city of Sevastopol, suffered severe casualties storming the strongly fortified seaport. The French and the British were superior in number and military strength, and yet the storm had turned into a bloodbath, the loss of life unprecedented. No officer, including the prince, now relished the thought of subjecting his troops to a similar fate.

However, while the prince did not favour a long siege, Dybbøl was – like Sevastopol – too strong a fortification to be captured quickly. During the siege of Sevastopol, British and French troops had pounded the fortress with bombs and shells for months without being able to destroy it. Every night the Russian defenders managed to repair the damage caused by the day's bombardments. The Danish line of defence at Dybbøl was also well designed and strong. Ironically, though, only the Prussians seemed aware of this; the Danish defenders did not have much faith in the works. Nor has history been kind to Dybbøl, no doubt coloured by the devastating defeat Denmark ultimately suffered.

Dybbøl was situated on high ground, which gave the Danes several advantages: a commanding view of the terrain and oncoming attackers, the ease of directing fire at an enemy coming at them in the open, and finally excellent cover from enemy fire. Seven out of the ten redoubts were enclosed, that is, dug-out field works surrounded by deep moats and solid palisade walls. Once the bridge was pulled in and the gate closed, the redoubt turned into a classic fort with banquettes – infantry firing steps – cannon positions, blockhouses (bomb shelters, which, as it turned out, could not withstand fierce shelling), solid concrete powder magazines and traverses.

Three of the redoubts – Redoubts III, V and VII – were lunettes, that is, structures that were open to the rear. While these works were also equipped with deep moats, palisade walls, and banquettes for the infantry, they were primarily designed for the emplacement of heavy artillery.

Based on the lessons learned at Sevastopol, military strategists understood you could not conquer by a war of attrition alone; you had to systematically destroy the enemy's artillery, silence their cannon one by one, all the while wearing down the enemy's morale.

The Danes had eighty cannon at Dybbøl. Loaded with case-shot, they could tear through attack columns and inflict serious damage. Case-shot was the period's most effective means of crushing attack columns, its impact almost more deadly than that of modern-day machine guns. One blast of well-directed case-shot could take out an entire unit.

By 2 April the Prussians had deployed batteries along the entire Danish line, including its flank positions. The position received intense bombardments, the Prussians intent on destroying as many of the Danish cannon as possible. According to foreign observers, the Prussian shelling far surpassed the bombardments at Sevastopol – not just in intensity, but also in its persistent and methodical destructiveness. There was a mechanical element to the process that was reminiscent of industry, the cannon firing with the repetitive precision of pistons. Night after night, day after day, there was a hissing and bursting of shells. Sometimes there was a lull in the bombardment, but as soon as the cannon had cooled, the firing started up again.

For weeks the Danes persevered. Nightly, they pushed to repair the trenches damaged by the day's bombing. But as

April wore on it became increasingly dangerous to carry out repairs. The day came when the defence works on the left flank collapsed. A few attempts to patch up the parapets were made, but the works were never fully restored.

Despite the devastation and destruction, there was a bustling hive of life behind both lines. On the Danish side, thousands of non-combatants such as drivers, depot managers, workmen, musicians, kitchen staff, carpenters, tool-makers, blacksmiths, engineers, army chaplains, nurses, ambulance personnel and doctors worked to serve the troops. And, of course, there were a great number of animals, primarily horses. Danish troops had 10,000 horses at Dybbøl.

Poor sanitary conditions plagued both sides, with the Danish sector suffering especially, resulting in an onslaught of infectious diseases such as typhoid fever. Soldiers in the most advanced front-line sectors endured the worst conditions. Approximately 5,000 men were on duty here. The latrines constructed closest to the entrenchments had been bombed to smithereens, and those that remained intact were too exposed; no soldier in his right mind would risk his life by venturing out into the open simply to go to the toilet. So they all did what they needed to do, right where they stood.

Human waste became mixed in with dung from the animals, kitchen waste and the decomposing body parts that lay scattered everywhere, creating an unspeakably filthy sludge. In the words of the Danish poet Holger Drachmann, Dybbøl Hill had been turned into a dunghill.

The Prussian troops did not fare much better. The men in the third parallel, closest to the Danish redoubts, had to crawl or elbow their way through a muddy soup that quickly became as filthy as the brew in the Danish trenches. The

Prussian soldiers in this parallel had very little mobility, certainly unable to rise to a standing position, as this would get them instantly killed. For 24-hour stretches the Prussian soldiers would lay pressed to the ground in their own filth.

Fortunately, it would not be long before at least the lucky ones could escape the filthy confines of these parallels; the prince felt sure victory was imminent. Notwithstanding, there was one component of the Danish defence that rattled the prince's confidence. Not visible from Avnbjerg, but seemingly always lurking about in the surrounding waters, was nothing less than a giant, fire-spewing sea monster: *Rolf Krake*.

5

The ironclad warship

Perhaps it was not the best idea to name a warship after a legendary warrior king who, despite many victories on the battlefield, came to an unfortunate end. Nonetheless, Denmark's first ironclad warship was named *Rolf Krake*, its namesake's unfortunate fate chronicled in the nine-volume history of Denmark written by Saxo Grammaticus around year 1200.

According to legend, Rolf Krake's scheming and power-hungry sister, Skuld, concocted a devious plan with her husband, Hjarvad, to overthrow her brother at a grand feast in Lejre on Zealand, to which they had been invited. They arrived by boat, bringing, or so they claimed, a large cargo of gifts for Krake. As the party wore on, Krake and his men, all heavy drinkers, fell into a drunken stupor. Skuld and Hjarvad chose this moment to unload their ship. As it turned out, the cargo consisted not of presents but of warriors, who proceeded to storm the castle, killing Krake and all his men, who were too inebriated to put up effective resistance.

The story of Rolf Krake serves as an excellent parable of the war of 1864, as it is known in the Danish vernacular – though the Danish navy was undoubtedly not thinking along these lines when it christened Denmark's very first ironclad warship, designed by pioneering British naval architect

Captain Cowper Phipps Coles and built by Napier & Sons in Glasgow.

Ironclads were top of the line, the most powerful seagoing warships at the time. The Prussians' fear of *Rolf Krake* was therefore well founded: she was a sea monster to be reckoned with, and there was certainly nothing 'gnarled' or 'weathered' (the literal meaning of 'Krake') about her.

Since the Royal Danish Navy had acquired its first steamer in 1824, the design of warships had undergone remarkable changes. And despite the howling wind of objections that blew in from the conservative Danish naval establishment, steamers proved far superior to their wind-powered cousins. They were more manoeuvrable and not dependent on weather, and by the 1820s even the most obdurate of conservative naval officers conceded that these new technological wonders were the future.

The last purely sail-driven warship in the Danish navy was the *Dannebrog*, a 5,000-ton, 65-metre ship of the line, armed with 70 cannon. She was launched in 1850, but dry-docked after a mere eight years at sea for conversion into an ironclad, fitted with a steam engine and a screw propeller for locomotion.

Invented by Swedish naval captain John Ericsson, the screw propeller replaced the slower paddle wheel, the latter being best known to readers for gracing the boats of Mark Twain's Mississippi. Far into the eighteenth century, however, most converted wooden vessels retained their masts and could be powered by both wind and steam.

In 1864 the Danish fleet comprised fifteen warships; the biggest was screw ship-of-the-line *Skjold* and the screw frigates *Jylland*, *Sjælland* and *Niel Juel* – not by any standards an impressive fleet. Denmark had not been a naval power since

The Danish ironclad *Rolf Krake* was a powerful, top of the
line warship dreaded by the Prussians. *Rolf Krake* served as
a significant psychological deterrent for the Danes.

1807, when it was forced to surrender its fleet to the British
in the Second Battle of Copenhagen. In this battle, the Royal
Danish Navy lost thirty powerful ships of the line and its status
as a significant sea power. Despite this, Denmark's fleet, with
its first-class screw steam battleships, was more than adequate
to do battle with its neighbours to the south. Though Prussia
was in the process of building a larger fleet, it had only four
minor screw corvettes and a small fleet of screw gunboats for
coastal defence. And while far superior to Denmark's fleet,
the Austrian navy was deployed in the Adriatic and posed no
threat to Denmark.

Because Denmark had to rebuild its fleet from scratch after
1807, the Danish Royal Navy was open to innovation and welcomed the idea of armoured vessels. Other navies were experi-
menting with armoured vessels as well, a development that
was pushed forward by the innovation of modern rifled guns,
against which wooden vessels were devastatingly vulnerable.

During the American Civil War (1861–5) ironclads as well as iron-hulled (that is, all-steel built) turreted battleships had been widely employed. On a turreted battleship, the cannon are placed in rotating towers – turrets – rather than broadside. French and British armies had also deployed ironclads, popularly called 'floating iron batteries' during the Crimean War. In appearance alone, they were intimidating. Heavy clouds of steam always hovered above these black, menacing and seemingly invincible ships, spreading terror wherever they steamed in. The first naval engagement of ironclads took place in 1862 during the American Civil War. The Union's USS *Monitor* and the Confederacy's CSS *Virginia* clashed at Hampton Roads, Virginia, in an encounter that lasted several hours; despite many direct hits and a serious pounding of shells from both vessels, little damage was inflicted.

The Danish navy followed the developments in America closely, and as soon as the 'Schleswig issue' arose, they purchased a state-of-the-art turreted ironclad warship: a proud 56-metre-long ship with an 11.6-metre-wide beam, a draught of 3.2 metres, a tonnage of 1235, two cannon turrets, four heavy 64-pound cannon and 12-centimetre-thick black hull armour.

To prevent the dreaded *Rolf Krake* from moving in too close to shore, the Prussians had laid out fishing nets in Vemmingbund. Such measures, however, would hardly hinder the warship from supporting Danish land-based troops during a Prussian storm. But gauging how much of a threat *Rolf Krake* actually posed was difficult for the Prussian army commanders. As an element of surprise, the warship could potentially become a decisive factor, they reasoned. The battleship thus functioned as a significant psychological deterrent – a good thing for Denmark, which needed all the help it could get, being in almost all other aspects the underdog.

By April, Denmark had 52,000 men under arms. Almost every able-bodied man fit for combat had been mobilised. Prussia and Austria initially sent 56,000 men, but these were merely expeditionary forces. As the war progressed, they deployed another 50,000 men. Fully mobilised, the Prussian and Austrian forces would number 1 million men.

Tough odds for Denmark, as Danish troops, to exacerbate matters, were poorly trained. The average Danish soldier typically had one year of military training, while most Prussian soldiers had three. Also, while conscription was universal in Denmark, exemptions were allowed if you could afford to pay for a substitute to take your place. As a result, most men from the upper echelon of society opted out of military service, with unskilled day labourers, farmhands and other persons of limited means mostly filling the lower ranks of the Danish army. The Prussians had the great advantage of being able to choose their officers from a roster of highly trained men and were able to deploy the very best of these to the Danish front. It is well known that a strong army is dependent upon a skilful and plentiful number of officers, and while Denmark did have militarily skilled officers, they were far too few in number. Consequently poorly trained reserve officers were being called up, and even within this group the pickings were slim.

In terms of armament, however, the Danish army was not as poorly equipped as has commonly been suggested. The dark blue Danish uniform, including boots and cap, were of high quality and excited the envy of their opponents. Danish weaponry resembled that of the average European army. Danish

Danish soldiers were armed with muzzle-loading, rifled muskets.
The Prussian, on the other hand, had adopted the next generation of
firearms, the breech loader, which proved to be a far superior weapon.

soldiers were armed with muzzle-loading, rifled muskets
with an effective range of 400 metres. The long-range accuracy of these rifles had made them a favourite among most
armies in the world, including the mass armies of the American Civil War. Only the Prussians – not the Austrians – had
adopted the next generation of firearms, the breech-loader, or
'needle gun' as it is commonly called.

The Prussians, as it turned out, were fortunate to have
visionary commanders who saw the potential in the new
weapon's technology and understood that these weapons
heralded the dawn of a new era of warfare. During the
Napoleonic Wars armies charged in column formations,
first firing volleys into each other's lines and finally engaging in bayonet combat. Danish and Austrian commanders
favoured such tactics, but the Prussian military strategist
Chief of Staff Helmuth von Moltke recognised that needle
guns allowed for a different – and less costly – attack strategy. Needle guns were more than twice as fast to reload as
muzzle-loaders, which made it possible to charge in swarms
rather than in columns. Swarms were faster and less densely

packed than columns, and incurred fewer casualties than the former, where the soldiers marched slowly, shoulder to shoulder, straight into enemy fire. Moltke's swarms had overwhelming firepower, compared with their Danish counterparts. According to the Prussian military service manual, a needle gun could fire four to five shots a minute and reload while the soldier was lying down or on the move. According to the Danish military manual, an experienced rifleman could fire only two shots a minute with a muzzle-loader and had to stand in an upright position while reloading. The muzzle-loader had a more effective accuracy at long range than the first generations of breech-loaders, but the speed of the breech-loader far outweighed their relatively ineffective accuracy, as was soon apparent to Danish soldiers. In letters home, they complained that they could not keep up with the enemy's 'fast fire'.

The Danish army also came up short on artillery. Initially, they had as many guns as their opponent, and Danish gunners, the best trained among the troops, were on par with their Prussian counterparts. Danish ordnance, however, was comprised mostly of smoothbore cannon, which had a shorter precision range than the rifled cannon that made up most of the Prussian artillery; the latter could therefore be deployed out of range of the Danish cannon, and the Prussians were able to shell the Danish position with impunity. For Prussia, superior military technology and strategy was half the battle won.

Still, in the eyes of the rest of the world, the formidable *Rolf Krake* was seen as the war's biggest technological star – the first of its kind to come into action in Europe. Consequently, the great number of foreign correspondents on assignment in

Denmark – some from as far away as Japan – wrote extensively about this iron-armoured, fire-spewing water beast.

Sea monsters make great copy.

6

The war correspondent

One of the best contemporary war reporters covering the war on the Danish side was British journalist Edward Dicey. A painting of Dicey from the period shows him as a strikingly handsome young man. It is painted in the highly idealised, romantic style typical of the time, such as that of famous portraits of Lord Byron, Beethoven or Napoleon. In romantic portraiture, male subjects all seem to be based on the same model – full whiskers; thick wavy hair; rouged, full cheeks; and a faraway, dreamy expression in their eyes – the backdrop often an Olympian-type landscape. By today's ideals, Dicey may appear like a bit of a milksop, but on closer inspection you sense that he has a strong character and is a man of action. In the painting he is dressed in a double-breasted dark jacket, elegant yet understated, with a cascade of ruffled frills pouring from a crisp, standing white collar.

On the afternoon of 17 April, however, there was nothing dreamy or crisply laundered about the 32-year-old war correspondent, making his way through the bombed-out town of Sønderborg. For the past couple of weeks, none of the amenities of normal civilised life had been available to him. Decent meals had been infrequent, and he had had no means of washing either himself or his clothes.

Until the Prussian bombardment of Sønderborg during the first days of April, he had taken lodgings in a small house in Sønderborg, where he had worked and sent his war dispatches to the *Daily Telegraph*. Though young, Dicey was a seasoned war reporter and had recently covered the American Civil War. He therefore seemed an obvious choice for the *Daily Telegraph* to hire as war correspondent for the Schleswig War. Dicey's keen instinct for hunting down the action and the drama of war enabled him to find and report on the sporadic skirmishes and encounters along the front even before the war was in full flow.

In the early hours of 2 April, though, the war found Dicey and the 2,000 other residents of Sønderborg. A fierce bombardment hit the town that night, and several neighbourhoods were completely destroyed. Many civilians were killed and the conflagration kindled by the bombardment had, within hours, left almost the entire town in ruins.

Dicey managed to save himself but lost most of his personal belongings, including his clothes. Shelling pulverised his lodgings, and, like so many of the town's residents, he became homeless. He fled inland from the burning town by small bumpy roads, and in his dispatch that day, he wrote:

The people were flying from the town, as the inhabitants of Sodom and Gomorrah may have fled from the accursed cities. There was little time to take anything with them in their flight. Women with scared pale faces, dragging little toddling children by the hand, were hastening away, God knows whither. Old men, bowed with age, were groping their way timidly up the long winding street. Some of the wayfarers had got bundles of bedding in their hands;

For almost three weeks the town of Sønderborg, situated
behind the Danish lines, was bombarded by the Prussians and
many civilians were among the killed and maimed.

others had articles of household furniture; long processions
of carts, laden with every object that could be gathered
together hastily, were rattling away as fast as the terrified horses could drag them; and the whole current of
the population, which at this hour on ordinary evenings
is coming homewards, was streaming out of the city. The
wounded soldiers in the Carolina Amelia hospital, which
stands, or used to stand, close to the church, had been torn
from their beds, and were passing in a file of carts up to
Augustenburg.

And then, mixed up with the citizens and the soldiers,
came in the wounded men from the front. No estimate can
be formed yet of the loss beneath this afternoon's deadly
fire, but it must have been a heavy one. Dead bodies,
half covered with the blood-stained straw in which they
lay, were carried by in a dismal progress. File after file of
soldiers moved on, bearing their wounded comrades on

stretchers through the streets, and the moans of some of these poor wretches could be heard for hundreds of yards away; others lay senseless, and, to all appearance, lifeless, with their wounds half bandaged, and with dark streaks of blood marking their heads and breasts. I have no wish to describe to you the horrors that I saw; men with their legs blown off, their bodies ripped open with shells, and their faces battered into a mass of shapeless flesh, are sights not pleasant to see, or to think of when seen.

Dicey suffered the same pitiful plight as the hundreds of Danish refugees fleeing the Prussian shelling. Exhausted, unwashed and hungry, he roamed about Als for days until he finally found new lodgings on a farm near Ulkebøl.

The bombardment of Sønderborg fully opened his eyes to the devastation and destruction of war. The suffering and discomforts he experienced did not resonate at all with the prevailing glorified ideas of war. With the destruction of the area's main city, most grocery stores had disappeared and there was little food to be had. Dicey sometimes ate with the soldiers and officers on the farm where he stayed, but decent meals were few and far between. He rarely got a full night's sleep, and the sleep deprivation was perhaps the worst of it for Dicey. The sound of bursting shells seemed even more fear-provoking at night, and he slept in fits and starts, waking up in a fright every time a shell struck, believing it to be near his dwelling even though it had hit miles away.

Dicey noticed how worn out the Danish troops looked: their faces were gaunt, drawn and weary, their eyes cold and detached. Patrol units now moved to the front in silence. The previously upbeat sound of voices singing 'The Brave Foot

Soldier' – a favourite Danish marching song from the victorious First Schleswig War – had stilled.

Being surrounded by so much death and destruction was taking its toll on Dicey as well. Images of dead soldiers kept haunting him. One evening at dusk, he had witnessed a train of carts laden with dead soldiers, driving through Sønderborg towards the town's churchyard. It would be more accurate, he later noted, to describe the carts' terrible cargo as bloody body parts. A head torn from the body of a soldier rolled about in one cart: 'The features were utterly indistinguishable; the skin was that of a mummy, thousands of years old, smeared over with blood; and yet, in spite of the disfigurement of the face, there was upon it an expression, so it seemed to me, of unutterable terror …'

Dicey felt wretched and barely human. He had no soap and was as filthy as a rag. His living conditions were squalid. He had turned and returned his collar, but both the collar and his one shirt were now so dirty it no longer mattered, he told his readers. All in all there was little resemblance between the war-weary, increasingly dispirited Dicey and the handsome youth of his portrait. The weather, however, offered some consolation. It had been rainy and cold for weeks, but now finally the sun had come out. In his dispatch from 17 April, Dicey noted that although 'the wind is fearfully cold and cutting … in sheltered spots, out of the wind's way, the air was so hot that an overcoat was almost unbearable'. If you stretched your imagination, you could for a few moments pretend there was no war and simply enjoy the spring sunshine. There was a lull in the bombardment of Als, and Dicey felt comparatively safe and comfortable walking through the bombed-out and deserted town.

The northern part of the town was relatively unscathed as it had been out of range of the Prussian Broager battery. Conversely, the southern part was a heap of ruins. Dicey wrote that there was 'something ominous in the silence that reigned for a considerable portion of the day'. And as he was making his way through the bomb-torn town, he thought to himself that this would likely be his last visit to Sønderborg. Everyone was expecting a Prussian assault on Als and Dybbøl, perhaps even as early as the next day.

Dicey passed the open square in front of the battered castle, a massive structure, which although it had been hit repeatedly was still intact. Here there was lots of activity. Army carpenters were manufacturing coffins: one detail was sawing and hammering, another painting. Fittingly, the colour was a dull, deep black.

'[D]emand [would] exceed supply, and stock in hand [was] very low,' Dicey wrote. The implication was clear: the number of casualties would far exceed the number of coffins. What awaited most of the men who did not survive were crude mass graves dug in the ground.

With a sinking feeling, Dicey also understood how demoralising the sight of these coffins – row upon row of them – must have appeared to the soldiers marching past them on their way to the front.

7

The ailing general

By 17 April, the Danish army was bleeding to death. Morale among the men was low, and at headquarters, in the vicarage of Ulkebøl, the situation was deemed critical. An aide-de-camp was therefore sent to the mailboat at Hørup Harbour with a desperate plea to the Ministry of War in Copenhagen. The commander-in-chief, Lieutenant General G. D. Gerlach, wrote:

> The position is too weak to hold. The troops are exhausted – any day now their strength will give out – and I will be forced to make a decision: either I have to risk a terrible defeat or counter the cabinet's orders to hold the position at all costs. I would ask that the cabinet give me full authority to decide at which point it will be prudent to withdraw, so that I may secure an honourable retreat to Als.

General Gerlach usually cut an imposing figure, though he was neither particularly well built nor handsome: he had a broad, fleshy face, bushy eyebrows, a heavy chin with billy-goat whiskers, and a barrel-shaped torso. Yet under normal circumstances he carried himself with such dignity that he fully looked the part of a high-ranking officer. On 17 April, however, Gerlach exuded none of his usual poise. A riding accident, in which he had injured his leg, had confined him to bed, and he was exhausted, physically as well as mentally.

Gerlach was promoted to commander-in-chief in mid February, following the controversial dismissal of the competent but supposedly too high-handed General Christian de Meza. It was de Meza who, on his own counsel, had evacuated the Dannevirke position. Gerlach, however, turned out to be a poor choice for the job. The responsibilities of being commander-in-chief wore him down. He found it impossible to keep his cool while losing so many men. It further made him ill at ease to realise that he would not be able to hold the position. This had become only too clear to him on the night of 14 April, when the Prussians had managed to take the Danish ground immediately in front of their defence works. By 17 April, all Danish officers on the front knew the position was untenable, and a withdrawal the one wise choice left open to them. This was the very point Gerlach was trying to get across in his plea, which, alas, arrived in Copenhagen on 19 April.

Why Gerlach chose to send a letter by mail rather than transmit his message by telegraph is a mystery. Perhaps he thought the ministry would be more attentive if they received a message from him personally and in black and white. Thus far, the ministry had indeed turned down all telegraphed requests from the front. In the past week alone, several messages had been dispatched by telegraph, requesting permission to evacuate Dybbøl. A direct and sobering telegram from the front had arrived in Copenhagen as early as 9 April, making it clear that the troops at Dybbøl would not be able to hold out against the increasing strength of the enemy. More Prussian cannon had been deployed, and every time the Danish

Georg Daniel Gerlach (above), the Danish commander-in-chief at Dybbøl. The siege exhausted him physically and mentally. He knew the Danish army stood to lose the coming battle but he lacked the resolve to oppose orders from the Minister of War, C. C. Lundbye (below), who demanded they held the position at any cost.

batteries opened fire, their cannon were immediately brought to silence by concentrated volleys from the Prussian batteries, the telegram explained.

Gerlach had emphasised that the position would not be tenable for long and that the time had come to start thinking about pulling the troops back. He therefore respectfully requested new orders from the ministry and the Danish cabinet. On 11 April, Gerlach received the following brief order in response: 'Defend Dybbøl at all costs!'

On the morning of 14 April, Gerlach dispatched yet another telegram, this time calling for immediate orders to prepare a retreat. 'We can no longer hold the position,' the telegram stressed.

Upon receiving this telegram, Carl Christian Lundbye, the Danish minister of war, finally seemed amenable to listen. He requested a telegraphic conversation with General Gerlach, who, however, was laid up with his bad leg and unable to ride to the telegraph station in Augustenborg; instead, his chief-of-staff, Stiernholm, took the call for him. An animated exchange followed:

'Is the bombing still heavy?' came Lundbye's question across the wires.

'Yes, over the batteries on Als, less so over Dybbøl,' tapped out Stiernholm's telegraph operator in reply.

'Have you initiated the withdrawal?'

'No.'

'Are you expecting an assault, and do you think you would be able to withstand it? Are the troops exhausted?' probed Lundbye.

'An assault is likely and must be withstood as preparations to secure Als must be further along before a retreat.

The troops are not exhausted yet, but the heavy enemy fire is affecting them.'

'How long will it take to prepare a retreat?'

'A couple of days.'

'Do you have anything to add?'

'It is of vital importance that headquarters is permitted to exercise its own authority to make decisions now.'

There was a moment's pause over the wires. 'Granted! The cabinet trusts that the Supreme Command will make the best possible and militarily sound decisions.'

Throughout the war, Minister Lundbye had tried to control events from his office in Copenhagen. Like most classic armchair generals, he had meddled in all decisions, big and small – often based on little or no understanding of the actual situation on the front. Now, though, having served in the First Schleswig War as an artillery field officer, he had enough soldierly sense to grasp that the situation on the front was so serious it outweighed any political considerations.

Unfortunately for Denmark, the minister was of a weak disposition and only held on to his clear-sightedness for six hours. By 6.30 p.m., he had performed an about-turn, and in Augustenborg the telegraph rang out with the message: 'The Danish cabinet maintains its original standpoint to hold the position even if it means sustaining heavy casualties.'

What changed Lundbye's mind was a meeting with the rhetorically gifted and imperiously vain prime minister of Denmark, D. G. Monrad. Monrad had easily swayed Lundbye with his fiery patriotism: 'If we succeed in sustaining a Prussian assault,' he said, buoyed by the memory of past glories, 'we could rekindle the victorious spirit of 1848,' adding, 'Denmark will win international respect and secure its interests at the upcoming peace conference in London.'

Monrad's outlining of such a magnificent scenario would come to have serious consequences, as it prompted weak incompetents in positions of responsibility to make a series of weak and incompetent, yet crucial, decisions. Years later, Monrad, from his self-imposed exile in New Zealand, would admit that he had misread the situation and wholeheartedly regretted his decision. Lundbye, rather than try to correct Monrad's error of judgement, immediately sent the fateful telegram to Gerlach, ordering the Danish troops to hold the position at all costs. Everyone at headquarters, including Gerlach, knew that following this order was tantamount to a bloody defeat, possibly a complete annihilation of the Danish army. Gerlach, however, did not have the courage of his convictions either. All the faint-hearted commander-in-chief could muster up was enough strength to send the desperate letter of 17 April in the hope that it would change Monrad's mind.

8

The Red Cross delegate

In nineteenth-century wars, the death toll was often exceptionally high. In the Battle of Austerlitz in 1805, the French army lost approximately 9,000 dead and wounded, the Russian-Austrian opponent 26,000. In the Battle of Borodino in Moscow, 1812, the French lost 28,000 and the Russians 40,000. In the Battle of Waterloo in 1815, Napoleon lost 23,000 and the Prussian and British opponents 15,000 and 7,000 respectively. In the American Civil War the number of casualties reached a staggering 620,000.

Dying on the battlefield was not, however, necessarily the worst fate that could befall a soldier. Field surgery was still in its infancy, and the techniques available then were often barbaric. Most field surgeons were, in fact, barbers – *Feltskærer* ('field cutters'), in Danish military parlance – with no medical training. And while anaesthetics in the form of ether and chloroform were widely used in the United States and throughout Europe, Danish army doctors believed anaesthetics could be harmful, impeding healing in patients who had undergone major amputations.

Contrary to this piece of unfortunate misinformation, it was widely accepted that good hygienic practices vastly increased surgical patients' chances of survival, though, at the time, no one knew why. Bacteriology was still in the future. Hygienic conditions in field or tent hospitals close to the battle line were, of course, often horrendous. When a battle was in full flow there was simply not enough time to clean surgical instruments between amputations. The same knife was used over and over and only perfunctorily dried off with an apron, soiled by dirt, blood and other bodily fluids.

Amputations were performed daily on the front. Some surgeons of the day claimed with great pride that they could perform one every minute. The survival statistics for their patients were less impressive, however. Post-op infections proved a more nefarious enemy than the one the soldiers encountered on the battlefield. So-called 'surgical fevers' took the life of one in two amputees in nineteenth-century wars: not great odds by any standards, but given contemporary surgical practices it is actually remarkable that anyone made it out of battlefield tent hospitals alive.

At Dybbøl, the Danish wounded were especially hard hit. The Prussian shells tore terrible wounds on impact. The injured soldiers were often so badly mauled that it was impossible to stitch them back together.

Into this world of mutilated, bleeding bodies and raging surgical fevers walked a well-dressed man of forty-six armed not with a rifle, but with a mission. From 16 April he had visited tent hospitals near the battle line on the Danish side. He was an anxious man with a poor constitution who felt squeamish at the sight of blood, not to mention at eviscerated intestines, and had stressed this point many times in letters. Still, he had arrived in Denmark with the express purpose of reviewing conditions at Danish tent hospitals. His name was Charles William Meredith van de Velde, and he was known as

Captain van de Velde. He was Dutch, lived in Geneva, and was one of a two-member delegation from the recently formed, as yet unknown, Red Cross. With his fellow delegate, he was the first to turn up on a battlefield with the now famous Red Cross armband. Captain van de Velde was to observe conditions on the Danish side, while his colleague, Louis Appia, was on the Prussian side.

Both van de Velde and Appia were close friends with the founder of the Red Cross, Jean Henri Dunant, and were prominent citizens in Geneva, known to the upper middle class as outstanding humanitarians and philanthropists.

Van de Velde was a devout Christian with gentle eyes and impeccable manners, who dressed conservatively and had an air of respectability. As a captain in the Dutch navy he had travelled extensively, though his heart lay with the arts. During his training at the Dutch Naval Academy, he had met the famous marine painter Petrus Johannes Schotel, with whom he subsequently studied to become a draughtsman and surveyor. He went on to serve as a cartographer in the navy and was commissioned to draw maps in Syria, Palestine and Indonesia. Some of the best mid-nineteenth-century maps of Jerusalem were drawn up by van de Velde.

On 17 April, however, he was in the far north, penning a letter to the chairman of the Red Cross in the room he shared with army chaplain Erik Høyer Møller in the wheeler's house in the village of Ulkebøl. The house was situated near the Danish headquarters, where General Gerlach was phrasing his letter to Copenhagen. Van de Velde wrote:

At nine this evening, we arrived at one of the few intact buildings in Sønderborg. [It now served as an infirmary.]

It was, however, not protected against the many shells and shell fragments flying through the air. What a night!! Though there had been a lull in the bombing, the infirmary received 30 wounded from the Dybbøl fortifications. About half were lightly wounded, and of the rest, three died, and three were so badly wounded they had to have an arm or a leg amputated. All wounds were caused by shrapnel, and these wounds are much worse than those caused by bullets. Limbs and meat are torn from the body in the most horrible way imaginable. They require strong nerves just to look at.

Van de Velde readily admitted that he did not seem to have the nerves for it: 'I just could not stomach the sight of a shattered arm being amputated. It affected me so deeply, I was ill all night.' With sardonic self-awareness, he noted, 'I will probably never be a good nurse if I do not learn to handle such situations better.'

But at least he had not fainted on this occasion. During an earlier visit to a field hospital, he had swooned. It was his room-mate, the army chaplain Erik Høyer Møller, who had procured access to the hospital and vouched for him.

The first patient they had seen was badly wounded by shrapnel: 'One entire side of his body was shredded, and his intestines were hanging from a huge gash in his gut.' Witnessing such horror, conceded Møller, who, as a veteran from the First Schleswig War, had seen a lot, could 'leave one slightly overwhelmed'.

Møller had left van de Velde alone with the doctor on duty at this point, but van de Velde did not get along well with the doctor, in large part because the sight of the shredded soldier

There was a shortage of Danish doctors and for weeks on end Norwegian volunteer Dr T. D. Reymert was constantly at the operation table.

had caused him to faint. Møller later received 'a note from the surgeon commander in which he declined more spectators of his sort'.

In the early hours of 17 April, van de Velde had nonetheless gathered the courage to visit the new infirmary in Sønderborg. Here he met one of the best surgeons in the Danish army, the Norwegian volunteer doctor T. D. Reymert.

Reymert, born in Kristiansand, Norway, is of interest to our story because of his meticulous, if sparing, recordings of events from the front. Reymert was forty-nine years old in 1864 and a doctor in the Norwegian army's medical corps. A few years earlier in 1857, while still a student, he had been on a tour of Denmark and fallen in love with the country, so when the war broke out, volunteering seemed like the right thing to do. Reymert arrived at Dybbøl by the end of February, at which time there was relatively little action on the front, and he was given a hearty welcome by the otherwise brusque corps chief surgeon, Professor John Rørbye. Rørbye was so pleased to have a competent doctor on board, he dispensed with the gruff manners. When, by 13 March, the number of casualties began rising, Reymert was promoted to chief surgeon of the Danish army's Second Division. He oversaw a field hospital called the Second Ambulance, established in the former poorhouse in Sønderborg. Reymert was promoted mostly for his qualifications but also simply because there was a shortage of Danish doctors. From then on, as his diary shows, Reymert was constantly at the operating table:

24 March: Heavy bombardment, 250 shells from [Prussian batteries at] Broager hit Redoubt II ... five wounded arrived here; I performed seven amputations.

28 March: Heavy shelling from 3 to 10 a.m., fifty-seven wounded, I performed five minor and major amputations on four men. Similar operations were carried out in other field hospitals. Heavy incendiary shelling resulted in fire in Sønderborg. Shells struck near the hospital and one man was wounded.

3 April, 10 p.m.: The sky is ablaze from the fire. Twenty-six wounded from a shell that burst in the midst of a regiment, marching towards city hall. Three died. One of them, Schmidt, a student and reserve officer and son of a vicar from Næstved, got both his legs crushed. They were amputated during the night ... we were operating at four tables.

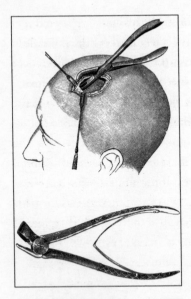

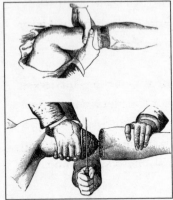

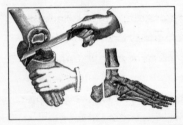

Drawings from Friedrich von Esmarch's *Handbook for War Surgery* which was widely used by medics until World War One. An acclaimed German surgeon, Esmarch worked in the Prussian field hospitals in 1864 where he conducted some of his studies for this book.

4 April: Last night at 3 a.m. the Prussians attempted a storm of the entrenchment. A lively cannonade and rifle fire took place. The sky was crimson from the flames. A lawyer from Copenhagen was brought in; he declined transport to the hospital in Augustenborg for fear that the trip would kill him. [After three days of fever he died.]

5 April: The shells cause the most terrifying lesions. Limbs are crushed and torn to pieces. Intestines are ripped from the body and brains spattered in the faces of the unfortunate men standing close by. Many areas of Sønderborg are nothing but smouldering ruins. Incendiary shells fly like dragons from Broager into the unfortunate town. On Sundeved farms are ablaze; black smoke is enveloping the area.

8 April: Approximately sixty wounded every day. Heavy bombing. The situation is critical.

10 April: Five wounded arrived at the hospital yesterday. Two amputations, an arm and a leg at the thigh.

11 April: Continuous heavy bombing. Sixty to seventy wounded were brought to Sønderborg. Possibly ten amputations.

12–13 April: This night continuous cannonade. Impossible to count the number of shots, sounds like volleys from a battalion. Ninety-eight wounded came in from Sundeved.

14–15 April: I was at the operating table until 1.30 in the morning. Many wounded.

17 April: Heavy cannonade, especially during the night.

In a report on the war which Reymert later wrote for the Norwegian military authorities, he goes into much more detail and his descriptions are gut-wrenching. One soldier, he notes, had his entire face shot off. 'His jaw was crushed and all soft tissue gone, including his tongue. At every breath, blood gushed from his throat. Shreds of torn facial tissue hung in the elastic skin down his chest.'

It was in order to ease the pain and suffering of such men that Dunant had wanted to establish an international humanitarian organisation. To fully appreciate Dunant's vision, it is constructive to look at the life experiences that led him to pursue the creation of the Red Cross.

The year was 1859. Jean Henri Dunant, then a businessman, was in financial trouble: land investments in Algeria had collapsed due to drought-induced crop failure. But he had an idea for a large-scale water-supply project in Africa and was hoping to convince the emperor to provide the funding. North Africa held great potential as France's future breadbasket, Dunant was sure of it, but the emperor was not an easy man to pin down for a meeting.

France was at war with Austria, and Napoleon was on the battlefield with his troops. France had formed an alliance with Italian separatists from Sardinia, who fought for secession from Austrian hegemony and a unified Italy.

And so it came to pass that the civilian businessman Jean Henri Dunant, dressed in a white suit, trailed the French troops through Italy and on 24 June became witness to one of the bloodiest battles in human history thus far. Two armies (200,000 troops) clashed that day at Solferino. Dunant later wrote about the battle in *A Memory of Solferino* (1862).

It had been an unseasonably hot month and 24 June was a real scorcher; the men were suffocating in their woollen uniforms. There was no clean drinking water, so all they had to drink in the sweltering heat was schnapps. As they had been on the move for days without much food, they were famished as well as parched and worn out. The two opposing armies had not expected, much less prepared for, a battle that day. Failed reconnaissance on both sides meant the two armies almost literally bumped into each other. Intense fighting erupted suddenly and spontaneously. The men fought in blind rage. Both sides, the Franco-Sardinians and the Austrians, had marched towards Solferino, intending to occupy the hilly area surrounding the city, but neither adversary had apparently been aware of their opponent's movements. The battle lasted fifteen maddening hours.

In the middle of all this sound and fury was Jean Henri Dunant, whose sensibilities, like van de Velde's, were severely affected by the sight of suffering in others. Dunant wrote in his memoirs:

> Compact columns of men throw themselves upon each other with the impetuosity of a destructive torrent that carries everything before it; French regiments, in skirmishing order, fling themselves upon the Austrian masses, which are constantly reinforced, and become more and more solid and menacing, resisting attack with the strength of steel walls. Whole divisions throw off their knapsacks in order to be able to charge the enemy more freely with fixed bayonets. As one battalion is repulsed, another immediately replaces it. Every mound, every hill, every rocky crag,

is the scene of a fight to the death; bodies lie in heaps on the hills and in the valleys.

Dunant spent three days on the battlefield among the dead, dying and severely wounded.

When the sun came up on the twenty-fifth, it disclosed the most dreadful sights imaginable. Bodies of men and horses covered the battlefield; corpses were strewn over roads, ditches, ravines, thickets and fields; the approaches of Solferino were thick with dead [...] The poor wounded men that were being picked up all day long were ghastly pale and exhausted. Some, who had been the most badly hurt, had a stupefied look as though they could not grasp what was said to them; they stared at one another out of haggard eyes, but their apparent prostration did not prevent them from feeling their pain.

There was almost no drinking water and a desperate shortage of doctors and nurses; the medical corps had been dissolved during the fighting, and there seemed no end in sight to the men's suffering. Dunant tried to help out as best he could, comforting the dying, holding them until they drew their last breath. Dunant also organised relief assistance among the local population and convinced the Franco-Sardinian victors to release Austrian prisoners of war with medical training, so they could treat the wounded. Still, the help was inadequate. One ray of comfort darting across the gloom, however, was the compassion shown by local volunteers – among them many women – who tended to the wounded regardless of their national affiliation. 'Tutti fratelli,' they said, by way of explanation: 'We are all brothers.'

Dunant remained deeply moved by what he had seen on the battlefield, and a few years later, in 1862, he decided to record his experiences. The result was *A Memory of Solferino*, which he published at his own expense. At first he gave it only to friends and family, but he soon began travelling around Europe, handing out his book to leaders and princes in the hope that he could stir up enough sympathy for the military wounded to get support for a neutral, international relief organisation of doctors and nurses. It was crucial, Dunant felt, that such medical personnel were granted a neutral status, so that they could work safely and freely in all war zones.

Readers were shocked by Dunant's book, and he quickly garnered support for his project. Dunant, however, was not the first to advocate for better medical care of the wounded on the battlefield. His most famous predecessor is inarguably the legendary British nurse Florence Nightingale, who came from a rich family and dedicated her life to reforming health care. Florence Nightingale served in the British medical corps in the Crimean War and was, like Dunant, appalled by the horrific conditions the wounded had to endure.

Dunant was very much inspired by her work as well as by the progressive, humanitarian and ruthlessly realistic writer Harriet Beecher Stowe. What set Dunant apart from Nightingale was his ambition to form a supranational organisation.

On 17 February 1863, Dunant met with four influential Genevans, and later that same year delegates from fourteen countries, including Prussia, but not Denmark, met to discuss the creation of such an international organisation. It was decided that delegates in the war zones would wear a white armband with a red cross (an inversion of the Swiss flag, in honour of Dunant) as an emblem of neutrality.

The Red Cross was formed. The next step was to ensure the support from the international community. To this end, delegates were sent out to inform political and military leaders as well as gather knowledge of contemporary warfare and the conditions of the wounded in war zones.

And so it was in this context that van de Velde arrived in Denmark with the dual purpose of convincing the Danes to support the new relief organisation and studying the battle-field; the latter also involved tending the wounded should the opportunity arise.

Van de Velde, however, soon felt discouraged, not merely by the atrocities he witnessed in the field tents, but by the almost uniformly cold shoulder the Red Cross received in Denmark. Van de Velde, who spoke four languages – French, German, English and Dutch, but not Danish – was met with scepticism. 'What good could an international organisation possibly do in Denmark?' was the objection most Danes raised. As a people, the Danes were 'insular, narrow-minded, and provincial', he noted in letters, and became fond of telling others that the Danes were in fact 'islanders'. In a letter of 11 April to the chairman of the Red Cross, van de Velde wrote, 'Danes keep to themselves and are stubbornly unreceptive to new ideas … They clearly resent and fear all things foreign to their own culture, which makes my job here very difficult.'

In addition, Danes lived in the most godforsaken area of the world, according to van de Velde. To get to Denmark, he had travelled by train from Paris through Cologne, Hamburg and Lübeck, from there with a steamer to Malmö, and then on to Copenhagen. The 'journey was exhausting, freezing cold and left me drained'.

To impress upon his readers how cold it was on the train,

van de Velde noted that 'despite the heat emanating from six fat Germans, a thick layer of ice covered the windows'. The temperature aboard the steamer to Denmark had been even lower. The passage had taken eighteen hours, and throughout a beastly northerly wind had blown, icing up all cordage. 'In general,' he wrote, 'the climate in these parts is terrible. Not until today did the wind let up, but then a heavy fog set in, much like the fog we know in February in Geneva.'

The mood in Copenhagen was as gloomy and depressing as the weather. The latest bulletins from the front showed 5,136 wounded and sick. They were to be hospitalised throughout the country, with the majority in Copenhagen 'where there are too few infirmaries to accommodate them all'. Van de Velde noticed that all of Copenhagen seemed engrossed in the war:

> Brothers, fathers, and friends [...] gather on street corners to read the latest about the bombardments at Dybbøl – new reports from the war are constantly being posted. I empathise with these anguished people, whom I meet everywhere I go. I listen attentively to the stories they tell me about their loved ones, who are exposed to enemy fire day and night. These people try to balance their love of country with their fear for loved ones on the front.

In Copenhagen, van de Velde met international war correspondents who had fled from Dybbøl because they 'had found it impossible to stay. Sønderborg was completely destroyed. In Augustenborg typhoid fever had raged, [devastating] the troops and civilians. Food and lodging came at exorbitantly high prices ...'

Van de Velde spent several days in Copenhagen trying

to win support for the Red Cross. He was met with some sympathy by Prime Minister Monrad and Minister of War Lundbye as well as the queen dowager. But in general the Danes responded in large measure with scepticism and to a degree that made the otherwise polite and well-mannered van de Velde seethe with prejudice: Danes are 'slow on the uptake' and 'incapable of showing enthusiasm', he quipped.

The army chief surgeon Michael Djørup was especially exasperating, according to van de Velde, who later described him as obstinate and 'blinded by pride' as he had refused to let women take on the job of caring for the wounded in the combat zone, a concept close to van de Velde's heart. Based on experiences gained at Solferino, he knew female nurses were more than capable of withstanding the hardships of the battlefield. Djørup, however, told van de Velde during a meeting that nursing was a male profession for which women had neither the aptitude nor the strength of nerve. To his amazement van de Velde discovered that the Danish army medical staff had refused female volunteer nurses from Sweden simply because of their gender.

Though van de Velde found his stay in Copenhagen to be somewhat unsuccessful, he was dragging his feet on going to the front, fearing the battle zone. He wrote that he hoped God would spare his life as 'danger surely awaited at the front [Sønderborg and Dybbøl], where constant shelling pounded'.

On 16 April he finally arrived at Dybbøl.

In his letter of 17 April he noted that the opposition to an international relief organisation he had met in Copenhagen was nothing compared to what he encountered at the front. Chief surgeon John Rørbye had in no uncertain terms told van de Velde that there was no need for an international organisation such as the one van de Velde represented. Each country was well served with its own charity organisations. The Danish army, Rørbye claimed, did not need more men to 'assist with medical care. And certainly not foreign doctors. The language barrier would impede our efficiency.'

'I offered to arrange for Dutch doctors to be sent to the Danish front, which he flatly declined. Then I suggested help from Geneva, but at this he baulked completely. I also made some suggestions as to how they could improve their stretchers, but Rørbye responded by saying, "No, no, no – this really isn't a good time to start with such newfangled notions."' 'Imagine,' van de Velde wrote to the chairman of the Red Cross, 'that such an old, hidebound man is in charge of the military medical corps.'

Louis Appia, van de Velde's fellow delegate on the front, had considerably more luck expounding the value of a neutral, international relief organisation to the Prussian commanders. King Wilhelm I had offered enthusiastic support when Dunant spoke with him in 1863, and Appia was immediately granted an interview with the Prussian generals at Dybbøl – and was even invited to dine with Field Marshal von Wrangel. He was also given unlimited access to all areas of the front. Prussian medicine was far more advanced than the Danish, which may in part explain why the idea of an international relief organisation was so well received. No doubt it was also to Appia's advantage that some of the German Confederation's best physicians, such as Friedrich von Esmarch (widely recognised as the father of modern military surgery, due in part to his many inventions, among them the Esmarch bandage), had been sent to the front. In addition, the Prussians had seen the advantage of procuring the assistance of volunteer medics, so other charity organisations, such as the Order of Malta, and several deaconesses – especially Lutheran – were already involved.

As a consequence there were more caring hands available in the Prussian tent hospitals, resulting in a relatively high standard of hygiene. It is remarkable that the Danish–German war therefore became the first war in history where at least one side lost more men to bullets than to disease – a milestone of sorts in the history of humanitarian work.

9

On the front

Johan Peter Larssen, gunner no. 68 of the 4th Support Regiment, bent over a badly wounded comrade. A firebomb had just hit Redoubt IV, 'filling the air with suffocating, thick, sulphurous fumes. I completely lost my bearing and had taken a hard blow to my leg. It hurt terribly, but I was relieved to find that I could move it.'

The man by his side had not been so lucky. He screamed, 'I'm burning! I'm burning!' while intermittently asking Larssen, 'My legs, how bad are they?' The man was mortally wounded.

His right leg had been shot off just under the knee, and the severed limb – attached only by an inch or so of skin – lay crushed beneath his body; his left kneecap was completely shattered, the bones exposed, and there was no bleeding. Above the knee was a large gaping wound stretching almost to his hip. It looked as if his flesh had been shredded, and worst of all there were pieces of flaming trouser-leg embedded in the wound. While calling for help, I tried to put the fire out with my hands. When finally a kind-hearted soul brought me some water, I doused the fire, and was able to examine the man more closely: his upper left arm was clearly broken, blood was pouring into his mouth and his entire face was smeared with blood as well.

The soldier rushed off as soon as he had handed me the pail of water, and no one else offered help.

Larssen continued to call for medical assistance, his desperation increasing. But no one came. What should he do? He looked at the wounded man, who was begging him to stay. 'Please, I beg you, in the name of our Saviour Jesus Christ, don't leave me.' Their eyes locked. 'I will probably never forget that moment,' Larssen later noted:

> I have since wondered much about the strange power of the human gaze, as it was the expression in his eyes that kept me from leaving him to run for help, and it affected me much more than the sight of his mutilated body and his pleading words. It spoke more loudly of his fears, suffering and hopes than anything else could have. He lay with his left leg bent under him, and several times asked me to stretch it out, but this only caused him more pain. Every time we heard a shot ring out, he trembled with fear and squeezed my hand tightly.

It is easy to imagine that at this moment Larssen sorely regretted his decision to volunteer for active duty. Signing up, he had envisioned heroic actions, wave after wave of assaults, lively artillery fire, lightning manoeuvres ... bravery and glory. But this? This was hell.

By 17 April Larssen had been on the front less than two weeks. He was a tall and sinewy man with a full, dark beard. At forty-two, he was the oldest soldier of private rank in the Danish army. When he had enlisted, there had been a shortage of standard army regulation uniforms, so he wore a civilian jacket over his uniform trousers. He did, however, have an army greatcoat and a gunner's cap.

When the war broke out he had been out at sea, working as a skipper on a lightship deployed in the Læsø Channel. It was a lonely job for the former navy lieutenant, who had commanded a gunboat during the First Schleswig War. It was not until 2 February 1864, when a schooner sailed by his station, that Larssen learned of the war and the Danish victory at Mysunde. Larssen, who was by nature a restless and adventurous man, found it increasingly hard to carry out his monotonous and humdrum job in the knowledge that war raged to the south. An experienced soldier, he worried about whether Denmark was strong enough to beat the allied armies. For ten days he had no news. Then the mailboat from the town of Sæby on the mainland came by and he learned that the Dannevirke had been evacuated.

These ancient defensive earthworks –popularly known as Thyra's Fortress after the wife of Denmark's first king, Gorm the Old – had become one of the most evocative symbols of Danish national pride. Larssen was so upset by the news of their fall that he immediately wrote to the Ministry of Naval Affairs, offering to serve his country. Larssen took it for granted that he would be accepted with gratitude, and so was disappointed to learn they had turned him down. 'During these troubling times', the ministry wrote, they preferred he 'stay in his current job, which he did so well'.

Larssen, however, was not the kind of man who took no for an answer. An experienced gunner – he had even commanded three artillery batteries armed with coastal defence guns at the Fredericia fortifications – he firmly believed he could once again be of value to the Danish army. He wrote to his brother, who was a combat engineer at Dybbøl, and also

At forty-two Johan Peter Larssen was one of the oldest soldiers of
private rank in the Danish army. Signing up as a volunteer he had
envisioned heroic actions, bravery and glory. Instead he experienced
hell while serving as a gunner in the Danish redoubts.

to one of his friends, Gerhard Hagerup, who served as a field
artillery captain, asking, 'Don't you think a man with gun
practice could be accepted into service at Dybbøl?'

He avoided mentioning that 'this man' was in fact Johan
Peter Larssen. A reply came saying that 'this man' was
welcome, Larssen quit his job, and he set out for the front.
When he showed up at his friend Captain Hagerup's quarters,
the officer was stunned and by way of greeting exclaimed,
'What the devil are you doing here? Are you mad?'

But Larssen had come to fight, and since he so adamantly

refused to back down, Hagerup arranged an interview for him with the well-liked artillery commander Major Jonquires. Larssen must have made a good impression on the major: within a few days Larssen had his written recommendation and had been enlisted as a gunner with the 4th Support Regiment. The captain of the regiment issued him with a knapsack and a sword but no tunic. 'You'll have to wait for a tunic until we lose another gunner,' the captain explained in a brash tone. As it happened, a gunner was killed during the interview, but he had been so badly wounded his tunic was in shreds. 'I guess you'll have to wait for a head wound,' the captain quipped.

Larssen was on duty for the first time in Redoubt VI on the evening of 8 April. As he climbed Dybbøl Hill, entering a world of exploding shells that hit near and far, Larssen was shocked by the state of the redoubts. While on a visit the summer before, 'they had been so neat and clean and welcoming he had felt like putting on slippers for fear of dirtying them, just as he had heard visitors to quaint Dutch cities say'. There was, however, nothing quaint or clean about Redoubt VI on 8 April. 'The fine embankments were torn by shelling and haphazardly repaired with sandbags, and completely unrecognisable ... the entrance to the redoubt was no longer welcoming. The breastwork and traverses were so shot up that the cannon had to be lodged between gabion baskets and sandbags.

Though it was tough-going, Larssen had tried to be optimistic and encouraging during his first few days on duty. He had organised a work detail to right the toppled guns, only to see them destroyed at once by Prussian shelling.

In the early hours of 11 April a massive hailstorm of bullets swept laterally through the redoubt. The Prussian soldiers were so close, the men could hear them shouting at each other in the front-line trench. The Danes felt sure that the long-awaited Prussian assault was about to begin. In a flurry of adrenalin-infused excitement, Larssen and his fellow gunners rushed to ready the few operational cannon for battle. But this day was to end no differently from all the others which had preceded it.

On 12 April the bombardment of the entrenchment was 'so heavy', Larssen wrote, 'that the ground shook from the explosions; sandbags, backpacks, tools and God knows what else flew through the air'.

Several of the soldiers were killed and wounded that day; one man who sustained a serious head injury began, according to Larssen 'wildly flailing about. He must have gone mad.' The rest were cast into despair, and Larssen heard some of them comment that 'it is obvious that we are only here to be butchered'. Larssen's own resolve and optimism also began to fade. With gloom all-pervading, 'I did not believe we [could] hold our position much longer.'

In the following days many of his new comrades fell, and by 17 April the once gung-ho, middle-aged soldier – now bending over the mortally wounded comrade – had become hardened and disillusioned. The dying soldier squeezed his hand again, clearly in great pain; Larssen shouted at the top of his lungs, 'Somebody, please get this man some help!' Finally a Swedish volunteer showed up with a stretcher.

All along the Danish front similar incidents were taking place. Four thousand, two hundred and twenty-two shells hit the entrenchments on 17 April, though the Danish casualties were neither particularly heavy nor light. It was about average: seventy-seven dead or wounded.

10

The last letter

'My darling Friede, if I should fall in battle, I hope by the grace of God that we will meet in the afterlife.' These words were written in haste by Major Ernst Schau to his wife on 2 February 1864, moments before Prince Friedrich Karl ordered the assault on Mysunde. Major Schau had been posted at a different sector of the front that day, so he did not see any combat. Still, he appeared sad and pensive to his fellow officers. They had noticed that the otherwise kind and cheerful man had been unusually quiet and withdrawn of late. Schau sensed it too, and knew he had lost some of his customary drive and energy. He suffered from indigestion, he felt weak, and he looked pale.

Still, as always he had found time to write a few reassuring lines to his family. Schau was not forthcoming about his own ailments, but he wrote honestly about the war. The major understood how critical the situation was for Denmark, and had been aware of this from the beginning. The enemy was overwhelming, and he knew casualties would be heavy among all ranks. In his letters, though, he always made an effort to assure his family that while the situation was grim, he himself was doing very well.

On 17 April he was posted at the ferryman's house close to

the Danish bridgehead near the two pontoon bridges crossing the sound to Als. The bridgehead, situated a few kilometres behind the entrenchments, was Denmark's last line of defence on mainland Schleswig. If it were necessary to evacuate the Danish troops to Als, the bridgehead position could provide cover and delay a Prussian advance. From a window in the house, Schau looked out across the pontoon bridges towards the town of Sønderborg, where war correspondent Edward Dicey was just at that moment strolling past the crew of carpenters building coffins in the Castle Square. Schau looked down at his letter to Friede and wrote, 'God willing I will be back on Als tomorrow.'

God had not been very forgiving to the Schau family so far, however, especially not to Ernst's mother, Dorothea. She had married Hans Schau, an officer known for his great stamina and excellent leadership skills. They had had eight children: one daughter, who died at the age of two, and seven sons. Hans died in 1842, leaving his wife to take care of the large family on his meagre pension. But Dorothea was a resourceful woman and managed to keep the family afloat until her seven sons were old enough to take care of themselves. Dorothea was exceedingly proud of all of them – with good reason. They grew into fine young men, talented, full of life. All chose military careers and became accomplished officers, serving with distinction in the Danish army. Their futures were so bright, and their downfall so total, that it seems like something from a Hans Christian Andersen fairy tale, perhaps called 'A Mother and her Seven Sons'. In the imaginary fairy-tale version of the story, an evil spell, which could never be broken, was cast upon Dorothea and her seven sons in the mid 1840s.

Her second son, Edward, a lieutenant in the Dragoons in

Vordingborg, died of typhoid fever in 1845. In 1850 her sec-
ond-youngest son, Gustav, studying at the military academy in
Copenhagen, also succumbed to typhoid. The First Schleswig
War, in which all of her surviving sons fought, robbed her of
two more. Her eldest son, Field Artillery Officer Boe Schau,
fell in the Battle of Mysunde on 12 September 1850. A year
later, her fourth son Harald died of complications arising
from wounds sustained at the Battle of Fredericia in 1849.
The youngest son, Valdemar, a first lieutenant in the artillery,
died of typhoid in 1859.

At the outbreak of the Second Schleswig War, Dorothea
was left with only two living sons: Ernst and his younger
brother Emil Victor, a lieutenant and commander of the 16th
Regiment, 8th Company. Both were deployed to Dybbøl
immediately following the withdrawal from Dannevirke.

Ernst and Emil had both attended Odense Middle School
on the island of Funen. At the age of fifteen Ernst was
accepted to the military academy (Landkadetakademiet) in
Copenhagen, from which he later graduated with honours.
As a lieutenant in the Rangers at Kiel, he fought in the First
Schleswig War and saw combat in the war's very first battle,
at Rinkenæs, where the soldier next to him, Sejer Steffensen
Botterup, was shot almost immediately, becoming the war's
first casualty.

Ernst's younger brother Emil had also received his military
training at the military academy in Copenhagen. He graduated at the top of his class and, like his brother, fought in the
First Schleswig War. Emil had a commanding presence and
was respected by both his men and his superiors, who readily
praised him for his courage and military leadership qualities.
He was commended for his brave actions in the Battle of Isted,

The Danish Major Ernst Schau and his wife Friede. 'My darling Friede, if I should fall in battle, I hope by the grace of God that we will meet in the afterlife,' he writes to her in this letter from the front.

in which he was wounded twice, and in 1858 he was made a knight of the Order of Dannebrog, a great honour for him and the Schau family.

Ernst himself was involved in a number of minor skirmishes and some larger battles during the First Schleswig War: in the Battle of Fredericia his horse was shot from under him, but he managed to pull himself out of the fray; his participation in the later Battle of Isted earned him a distinction for gallantry under fire. Ernst Schau remained in the army after the war and rose steadily through the ranks until finally becoming a captain on the general staff.

In the early 1850s, Captain Ernst Schau was a dashing, debonair young man who, according to a minor biography, was 'completely smitten by the graceful twenty-year-old Miss Frederikke Louise' – Friede – the daughter of an army major and toll collector. Both her parents had died young, so she was raised by her aunt and uncle. As her uncle was the chamberlain to the Lord of Juelsberg, the couple were given a fairy-tale wedding at Juelsberg Castle in 1856.

Friede and Ernst had two sons and a daughter. The girl, Magda, was born in 1862, the same year her father was promoted to chief of staff in de Meza's army. The family relocated to Flensburg, bringing with them Ernst's mother. Two happy years followed. Then came the war.

Ernst Schau was astounded by the Danish cabinet's lack of sound judgement on the creation of the November Constitution. In fact, he thought it downright stupid to uphold a constitution that violated international law and was therefore sure to result in hostilities with Prussia and Austria. He had no doubt that Denmark would stand alone in this, and without international support would have little chance of winning the war – especially since the Danish army was outdated, disorganised and completely unprepared for action.

Like hundreds of Danish women and children living in Schleswig, Friede, Dorothea and the children fled Flensburg soon after the Danish army's evacuation of the Dannevirke.

While Ernst remained in Schleswig, the family settled in Copenhagen, and husband and wife began an intense exchange of letters. The separation was clearly made more painful and difficult by the dangerous situation. Yet the war itself never takes centre stage in their letters, which mostly focus on minor as well as major issues concerning the children's welfare and, of course, on their love for each other: 'How delighted I will be to see your lovely face,' Ernst wrote on 22 January 1863. At this time the Danish army was still deployed at the Dannevirke, and the Schau family still lived in Flensburg. When Friede visited her husband at the Dannevirke on 23 and 24 January, neither had the slightest premonition that they would never see each other again.

On 25 January an elated Ernst wrote to his wife:

With this morning greeting, I want to let you know that my heart is full of gratitude – your visit yesterday brought me such joy. Only what a shame our time together flew by so quickly and that you cannot stay with me, as I do not know when I'll see you again. But we must go about our work filled with joy by the memories of the time we passed together and cheered on by the hope that the ominous clouds now gathering on the horizon will soon break and not inflict upon us more than a few months of separation.

Dorothea wrote to her two sons often. Her last letter of 13

April to Ernst has been preserved. Dorothea had lost so many of her loved ones, and from the tone of her letter we sense how terrified she is of losing her two remaining children, Emil and Ernst, who at this time were both deployed to the most dangerous sections of the front.

> You know it is difficult for me to write to you, my wonderful, precious son. My strong longing to have you near is awakened with renewed force by writing, and it brings tears to my old eyes … I cannot tell you often enough how dear you are to me, more than anything else in this world, and I cannot imagine a life without you. Even if I should turn eighty, I would follow you wherever you go. The bullets cannot hurt you, they will respect your wife's and your old mother's love for you. And I put my faith in God that we will see each other again, smiling and happy and ready to give thanks to our Maker for protecting the life and limbs of you and your brother. Still, this moment is difficult to endure, and if I did not have the company of your lovely wife and your blessed children I do not think I could bear the agony. You will so spoil your lovely daughter when this is over; she is at that age when everything dangerous is appealing, and she is adorable to look at – I have never seen a prettier girl – and she loves you much, the four months of absence have not changed that; when her eyes fall upon your picture she still yells 'Pappa' and smacks her lips.

The little girl, Magda, was on Ernst's mind on 16 April when he wrote what would be his last letter to his wife. In a previous letter she had told him she was having Magda's portrait taken and would send it to the front. Ernst responded,

'How I look forward to receiving it … I really cannot picture how much my little sweetheart has changed since I left Flensburg four months ago.' He closed his letter with these words:

> I must conclude my letter to you now and am sending you my fondest farewell and a thousand kisses to the children and my little old mother. Stay well, my love. God willing it will not be long before we shall see each other again.

11

The changing of the guards

As the sun was setting over the bomb-torn front on 17 April, the 2nd and 22nd Regiments had just marched passed the coffins lined up on the square in front of Sønderborg Castle. They were on their way to the front to relieve the 2nd Brigade. The city's mayor had just begun a letter to his wife, Olufa, who had fled to Copenhagen with their children. Mayor Hilmer Finsen wrote from Als:

> The situation for our troops on Dybbøl Hill is desperate. How many of our brave troops will be alive by nightfall tomorrow? The blow may come at any time now. It is hard to fathom that the enemy – taking cover in their trenches, some of which are only 150 metres from our entrenchments – still has not attempted to overrun our position. I doubt it would be difficult for them since at such a short distance our cannon would not, I believe, be able to fire more than a few shots. When you read these lines, the newspapers will undoubtedly have reported that we have lost Dybbøl, but I have faith that the enemy will not be able to cross Als Sound. It is wide enough to stall the advancing enemy and allow us to hold Als for another couple of weeks. But how much blood will it cost, I wonder, when the bridges are to

be demolished to stop the enemy? All today we have had the usual thunder of cannon, but now as the sun is setting it seems to increase in vigour.

Every night on the front, the puzzle of where to station the relief regiments had to be solved. The relief took place at nightfall, allowing the men to move into the open under the relative cover of darkness. Still, the manoeuvre was fraught with danger and, in order to minimise the risks, the Danish soldiers had developed an intricate dance in which they moved forward in rapid spurts, one small unit at a time rather than in entire regiments or battalions. Like fluttering black swans the men darted across no-man's-land in complete silence, towards their designated positions.

The most dangerous section of the front for the Danish soldiers was the stretch running from Redoubt I to Redoubt VI on the position's left flank. The right flank (Redoubts VIII–X) was less vulnerable and, though it had been subject to much shelling, was relatively intact. The redoubts on the left flank, though, had taken heavy damage, as they received both frontal and flank fire. They were also the most exposed, and as a consequence only a handful of gunners and a few infantrymen manned them.

In reality, however, none of the redoubts was really safe at this time. It was practically suicidal for Danish soldiers to move about inside any of them, and the men tried to avoid this as much as possible. In order to survive, most of the gunners took cover from the nightly shelling in the damp, dark and cramped powder magazines, and the infantrymen, in turn, sought cover behind the redoubts in foxholes, support trenches and interconnecting passages, though these were in as bad shape as the redoubts. In case of an assault, the soldiers taking cover in the trenches would have to sprint in order to make it into the redoubts before the enemy.

The 2nd and 22nd Regiments, which formed the Danish army's 1st Brigade, were to relieve the 3rd and 18th Regiments, that is, the 2nd Brigade. The entire 2nd Brigade was to be redeployed to the bridgehead for a two-day duty shift. Redeploying so many men was a complex process. From the right flank, the 8th Brigade, comprising the 9th and 20th Regiments, moved down the hill towards the barracks, situated midway between the entrenchments and the bridgehead. Meanwhile, the 3rd Brigade, comprising the 16th and 17th Regiments, moved in to relieve them. The 4th Brigade, comprising the 4th and 6th Regiments, had been on duty since 13 April, and was to march to Als, where a few days of well-earned leave awaited the men.

The soldiers who came on duty on the evening of 17 April were all combat veterans. The most hard-boiled were the men of the 18th Regiment, composed of soldiers from the mid-regions of Zealand. The Prussians had learned to respect the men of this regiment, who were easily recognisable as they were the only soldiers in the Danish army who wore the tall shako caps. They had won special recognition for their actions in the Battle of Mysunde, in which they formed the core force responsible for beating back Prince Friedrich Karl's army. Since then, they had participated in a skirmish on 22 February and a major engagement on 17 March. The regiment had also fought vigorously in a number of nightly outpost skirmishes.

Unfortunately for Denmark, this regiment of fierce veteran soldiers would be on duty at the position's bridgehead on 17 and 18 April rather than at the entrenchments, which would bear the brunt of the assault. The 2nd and 22nd Regiments posted on the left flank, however, were no novices. Both regiments had participated in the victorious battle against the Prussians in the early hours of 28 March. They had also spent endless days and nights on the front being subjected to Prussian shelling, so they knew what to expect when they began their march to Dybbøl across the pontoon bridges.

One of the best descriptions of the march that lay ahead of them can be found in author and combat veteran Peter Frederik Rist's fictionalised memoir *A Recruit from 1864*, published in 1889. Though written as a novel, the fictional recruit's experiences at Dybbøl are widely held to be an accurate description of actual events. Literary critic Oluf Friis has said that the book gives 'a human side of the war'.

The author, who was in the 8th Brigade deployed to Dybbøl on 14 April, describes a company's march from Als to Dybbøl:

The soldiers hurried along as fast as their legs could carry them. You could hear their resounding footsteps tromping across the bobbing pontoon bridge. When they reached the halfway point, a shell exploded. Everyone looked up, and the men in the lead instinctively began running forward, screaming wildly in the confusion. The rear stayed back and a gap in the column arose in the middle of the bridge. But the fragments from the shell fell into the water near the other bridge.

Once on the other side, the men would have had to sprint to take cover behind the cliffs on the beach, where they could

Danish troop positions at
bøl, 18 April, 1864

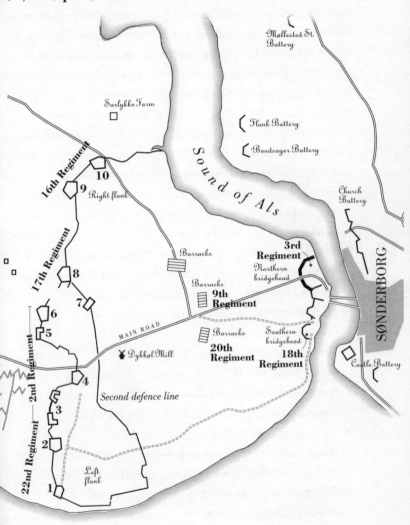

Møllested St.
Battery

Surlykke Farm

Flank Battery

Baadsager Battery

S o u n d   o f   A l s

16th Regiment

10

9   Right flank

17th Regiment

8

7

6

5

2nd Regiment

Barracks

Barracks

9th
Regiment

Barracks

20th
Regiment

MAIN ROAD

Dybbøl Mill

4

Second defence line

3

2

22nd Regiment

1   Left
flank

3rd
Regiment

Northern
bridgehead

Southern
bridgehead

18th
Regiment

Church
Battery

SØNDERBORG

Castle Battery

0   1 km   2 km

ready themselves for the dreaded march across the open ground to Dybbøl Hill. This next part of the march was much feared, as there was nothing to offer them cover in the barren fields leading up to the entrenchments. Halfway up they would reach the large barracks, which were badly shot up but still considered a stronghold. Nonetheless, there would be nothing to take cover behind here either.

The sun had dropped behind the hill, and the ground was growing dim in the deepening twilight. Every now and then, the dull thud of a cannon rang out from the other side of the hill, which loomed like a mountain in the dark night. Then they heard a hissing sound of a shell cutting through the air and saw the tail of light in its wake. Just like fireworks. All eyes followed it, faces turning slowly to follow its trajectory until it hit the ground somewhere in the distance with a grating, whizzing sound.

The men sat on the ground, one detachment behind the other, clutching their guns. No one made a sound. A bit further down the hill in the direction of the water, they could make out the dark shapes of the other companies lying on the hillside like large motionless bodies ... every sound seemed to be accentuated in the vast stillness.

They passed a cart, rattling along at a snail's pace. Was it carrying wounded? Or was it laden with dead soldiers? They had little time to speculate. 'There was a loud report, louder than before, and then a seething, boiling projectile came flying over the hilltop, passing straight over their heads.' The soldiers hurried on across the fields until they reached the main road leading to the barracks:

The wooden walls [of the barracks] shone white in the
night. The scream of [another] shell could be heard, there
was a deafening crash, and then a flash lit up the sky. Everyone fell flat on the ground or to his knees, while rocks, dirt,
wood splinters and shrapnel hailed down upon them.

The company crossed the last stretch of ground to the
entrenchments, running wildly 'in the dark across the uneven
field, stumbling into pits, crawling up embankments and then
forward on flat ground' until they finally made it to their designated sector of the front line, where they were subjected to
more shelling. 'A shell struck immediately after we arrived,'
Rist's recruit writes, 'hitting the earthworks with a crushing
blow. The men shrieked as rocks and lumps of dirt rolled into
the trenches with a loud noise.'

The 2,400 or so non-fictional men of the 2nd and 22nd
Regiments, who were to occupy the Danish left flank, had
a similarly dangerous march ahead of them on the evening
of 17 April. The 'Black Regiment', as the 2nd Regiment was
called because of its black regimental flags, consisted of some
1,200 men (and two doctors). They were to occupy Redoubts
IV–VII.

The 22nd Regiment, made up of men from all parts of
Denmark, took up their position in Redoubts I–III on the
south side near the beach. The 22nd had originally been made
up of men from Holstein, but as the majority of them had
refused to show when called up for active duty, the ranks had
been filled with a hotchpotch of men from all over, who were
now destined to defend the famous Redoubt II.

12

The doomed

On 1 December 1863, Niels Larsen from Hellum near Hjør-ring in northern Jutland received notice of his call-up to the Danish army, as did tens of thousands of Danish men. Larsen was to report to his old battalion, which became part of the 22nd Regiment.

At less than three months from his thirtieth birthday, Niels Larsen was relatively old for active duty, as were many of the reservists, who had been called up in great haste when the war broke out.

Niels was born on 25 February 1834. His parents were poor and Niels had worked from an early age as a farmhand on various farms in the villages of Bjergby, Mygdal and Astrup in northern Jutland, before being called up for military service at the age of twenty-four. After concluding his military service in 1859, he had taken a position as a foreman on a mill in Hellum, where he met and fell in love with dairymaid Inger Marie Christiansen. The two soon married, and as Niels had proved adept at running the mill, he took over the entire oper-ation when the old miller fell ill. The newly-weds oversaw two mills, a dairy farm and a staff of ten. A lot of work, to be sure, but the future looked bright for Inger Marie and Niels Larsen. Shortly after their wedding, Inger Marie gave birth to the couple's first child, a boy christened Christian. When news of Niels's call-up arrived, Inger Marie was pregnant with their second child and close to her delivery date.

Private Niels Larsen and Major Ernst Schau, though of different rank, were in many ways similar. Like Schau, Larsen was a loving husband who wrote to his wife often. He was also a devout, God-fearing man who, like Schau, put his faith in the Lord. In his letters home, he repeatedly told his wife as much, and that he hoped God would spare him so he could meet his new little daughter, whom Inger Marie gave birth to on 19 January, only a few weeks after he had left for the front.

Like Schau, he too had a vague and worrying premonition that despite all his prayers he was destined never to return home to his wife and children. After a couple of days of particularly relentless shelling in April, he wrote to Inger Marie, 'We must have faith in God, as He is the only one in whom we can trust,' sombrely adding, 'Our reunion [may not, however, occur] until … we are in the place where there is no more pain and sorrow.'

Niels Larsen had travelled to Copenhagen to enlist, arriving on 12 December. The mobilisation was chaotic: there were not enough uniforms and not enough beds, so most soldiers had to find their own lodgings and even pay their own travel expenses. Some soldiers were forced to sleep in the street, but Niels was lucky. He found decent lodgings, and so a bed to sleep in. His first letter home concluded with these words: 'My greatest desire is to return home soon, so that I may again embrace my never-to-be-forgotten wife and beloved son.'

On 31 December, Niels's company boarded a steamboat for Flensburg. After a couple of days in Flensburg, the company advanced to the Dannevirke. The march was the the hardest

Lieutenant Gustav Herman Knorring, a Swedish volunteer
rushing to the frontlines eager to meet his maker.

Niels had ever experienced: 'marching thirty kilometres with
full equipment … many of the men became so exhausted they
gave up or collapsed on the road'. Niels also told his wife about
the two soldiers who had died from the exertion.

In his next letters, he spoke of the intolerably cold temperatures at the Dannevirke: 'Our daily three-hour training is
bad,' he wrote, 'neither head nor hands are covered, and our
fingers almost freeze to our rifles, it is horrific, and, on top
of that, we are constantly yelled at.' Like Schau, however, he
focused mostly on the situation at home. He wondered about
grain prices, whether the hired hands on the farm and the
mills were doing a good job. He expressed concern for his

wife's well-being, a repeated theme in his letters. In response to the happy news of his daughter's birth, he wrote, 'I have been so worried that something would happen to you and that I would be left alone with the two little ones. I will give thanks tonight to God for watching over you in your hour of pain, and ask that He will keep you and our children safe.'

Niels Larsen did not see combat in the campaign's first encounters, as he had injured his foot and was hospitalised in Odense on the island of Funen. He was in the hospital on the night of 5 February, so he escaped the exhausting withdrawal from the Dannevirke. He was discharged in late February and returned to the front, where he immediately partook in several outpost skirmishes. 'I have heard the bullets whizzing past my ear twice, but God spared me even though the fighting was brisk and our regiment was the core force and suffered many casualties. Almost every day there are minor skirmishes. But on that particular day, the enemy was so close to Dybbøl, the cannon were put into action.' However, Niels's focus quickly shifts to the home front:

> You ask what I think we should call her, and whether to baptise her before my return. I think you should have her baptised, as I don't think I will be returning any time soon. And I think you should call her Marie or Ane Marie. But I'll leave this decision up to you as you may have another name in mind, and we will have no opportunity to talk about it.

Their daughter was named Marie.

Like everyone else on the front, Niels Larsen was aware that the situation was growing increasingly critical for the Danish army. In the first major battle, on 17 March, the

Danish army had suffered heavy casualties, and even though Niels's regiment did not participate, the outcome affected him greatly; in fact it had sent shock waves through all the Danish troops. The bombardment of the Danish fortifications had grown heavier and more constant towards the end of March. 'We have several times felt marked for the enemy's bullets and shells; daily they shoot hundreds of rounds at us, but surprisingly without causing much damage. Still, when they strike on target, one single shell can slay twenty men. So God must indeed be protecting us.'

At the beginning of April, however, God seemed to be less benevolent to those seeking His favour on the Danish side. The tone in Niels's letters became noticeably darker:

You cannot know how much I long to hear on the word of God at Easter, but this will not be. I have not heard anything but the boom of cannon and the whizzing of bullets for so long, which, of course, reminds me that in my hours of peril all I have to comfort me is the Lord. I would so have preferred to hear His words and sung a psalm with you at home though. But I pray God will have mercy on me, so we can all meet again either here or in heaven.

A couple of days later, he wrote that:

outpost duty has become very dangerous, because we are right in the thick of it, shells flying overhead, and every day a man gets wounded ... more than a thousand rounds are shot every day ... I'm on outpost duty tonight and only God knows if I'll get through it unharmed. I have as much of a chance as the next man.

Before Niels and his company moved out to the trenches for the last time on 17 April, he found time to write a letter to his friends at home:

Forever memorable friends!

I think about you every day and wanted to let you know what my life is like out here [on the front]. It is anything but comfortable … we can barely return fire, when we fire one shot, they return two, and many of our cannon are unfit for use. Consider yourselves lucky that you do not have to hear and see the horrors of this place: houses and farms are burned to the ground, or otherwise destroyed. God has so far spared my life, but many of my comrades have wetted the ground with their blood. At Dybbøl, death may come calling at any time and take any one of us.

However, although Niels Larsen hated life on the front and longed for his peaceful home life, this wasn't true for all of his comrades.

On 17 April, a small, dark blond officer in Swedish uniform moved briskly across the pontoon bridge from Als to the mainland on what would be both his first and last march to the entrenchments. Lieutenant Gustav Herman Knorring was a handsome young man with the lithe body of a dancer, wavy hair and a bold moustache. A Swedish volunteer, Knorring seemed positively eager to meet his maker on the battlefield. He had enlisted in Copenhagen, but had been in such a hurry to get to Dybbøl that he had waived his right to a proper Danish officer's uniform.

Knorring was one of the 650 Scandinavian volunteers who had come to support their Nordic neighbour, but their numbers were a far cry from what Denmark had expected in late 1863 when war began to look likely. Both the Danish cabinet and the Danish population had put their faith in Sweden, hoping it would send a large relief force. King Carl XV of Sweden, who was capricious and impulsive, had promised the Danish cabinet as much. The Danish newspaper *Fatherland Times*, a mouthpiece of the Danish National Liberal party, had further fuelled Denmark's convictions by reporting shortly before the outbreak of the war that Sweden would send 22,000 troops commanded by the king himself. The Swedish cabinet and the majority of the Swedish population, however, did not see why Sweden should form an alliance with Denmark against two major powers like Prussia and Austria in a territorial conflict over the relatively obscure Duchy of Schleswig. The Swedish king proved easily cajoled, and no forces were sent to Denmark.

Instead the Danish army had to make do with a few hundred volunteers. Nonetheless, since many of them were officers, this small transfusion was of considerable help. Some volunteers came to gain military experience and further their career. Others were a kind of 'Scandi-cowboy', out seeking adventure, while some were there because they were genuinely outraged by the situation.

Knorring, son of a captain in the Swedish army, was by no means outraged. He was one of the adventurers, driven by dreams of glory on the battlefield. Knorring veritably jumped for joy when on 7 April his Swedish superior notified him that he could enlist in the Danish army. The young officer was in such a hurry that he did not even wait for the paperwork to go through. He left for Copenhagen immediately and, as noted, did not stay there long either. He took a steamer from Copenhagen and arrived at Hørup Hav Harbour on the evening of

13 April. The Danish army was in desperate need of officers, and Knorring was at once deployed to the 22nd Regiment and given command of a half-company.

Knorring wrote to his parents on 15 April that Sønderborg 'looks a fright. The church and northern parts are somewhat intact, but the rest has been completely razed and the ruins are still smouldering. The town seems completely deserted; there are no people in the streets or houses.'

When Knorring joined up, the 22nd Regiment was posted at the barracks near the bridgehead on the Dybbøl side of the sound. 'You could not really sleep in the barracks,' Knorring wrote, 'because they were within range of the Prussian cannon. So the soldiers were camped about a hundred feet behind the barracks in two-feet-deep dugouts behind quickly thrown-up earthworks and seemed quite safe.' The regiment had been sleeping in that way under open skies for nine days now. But soon, Knorring wrote, they would enjoy a few days in proper quarters on Als, before taking up position in the entrenchments again on 17 April.

Knorring's adventure lasted exactly five days. Knorring and Private Niels Larsen would share a final resting place in a mass grave atop Dybbøl Hill. These men were later commemorated by the German victors, who erected a monument over the grave with the inscription: *Hier ruhen 209 tapfere Dänen* – 'Here lie 209 brave Danes'.

Rasmus Schmidt Nellemann, a 34-year-old estate manager, was one of the older reservists who had been called up for duty. He had completed his military service as far back as 1853 and had the Danish army not been so desperate for men, he would have been spared because of his age.

Corporal Nellemann, deployed with Gustav Knorring and

Niels Larsen to the 22nd Regiment, was, like Larsen, a family man. He lived with his French wife and their two-year-old daughter on Allingskov Estate, which he managed for his father. He also oversaw Frijsenborg Estate in Hammel, near Viborg, in central Jutland. His skills as a farmer and manager were widely recognised and both estates thrived under his administration. Nellemann enjoyed farming and had deliberately chosen not to pursue a military career. His track record from ten years earlier, however, was enough for the desperate Danish army to promote him to the position of non-commissioned officer. For Nellemann the war was a terrible inconvenience: all he wanted was for it to be over as soon as possible so he could get back home and tend his large and demanding estates. His last letter home reads:

> I cannot tell you how much I wish I had something joyous to report, but unfortunately life is so bleak on the front. Living in Copenhagen, you simply cannot imagine how horrible outpost duty is – it is almost unbearable to be out there now … we lie flat on the bare ground, with not even straw for comfort, and during our six-day shifts we are subjected to terrible shelling. I cannot blame the men for losing heart, as we cannot return fire. All we can do is lie in our trenches, passively awaiting death by the shells from hell. On Easter Monday, our company had 600 shells fly overhead, yet strangely enough we only lost one man. He was standing right next to me, talking quietly, as a shell struck with cruel suddenness, his head blown off in an instant. It was awful to watch, but these are the kinds of hardships soldiers have to endure.

He concluded his letter with these words: 'It is not with great joy that I march tomorrow for outpost duty, but I will put my fate in God's hands and trust that He knows what is best for us.'

While Nellemann was penning his last letter home, the eccentric and highly strung poet Hans Christian Andersen, loved the world over for his fairy tales, was pacing the floor of his bedroom. The poet was devastated by the war. Bad news from the front put serious strain on his already overwrought nerves. He suffered a particularly anxiety-ridden night on 17 April. Though he was more than 300 kilometres from Dybbøl, he was plagued by ominous premonitions and slept fretfully, as if engaged in a battle of his own right there in his bedroom in Copenhagen. The following morning, on 18 April, he awoke groggy and out of sorts:

What a tortured night, suffused with strange notions; in a moment of madness I saw myself at the bottom of a ship, thrown into a dark brig, battered and miserable – I'm making a spectacle of myself by writing of this; I was in such a sweat and did not sleep until the break of dawn. I confided in Jette Colin, who, upon seeing me, immediately noticed my state of exhaustion. But she made jest of me and called me 'mad'. Later that morning, we received the news that the assault on Dybbøl had begun …

Part Two

THE ROAD TO DYBBØL

Christian Julius de Meza, the seventy-two-year-old eccentric but highly competent Danish commander-in-chief as he looked at the outbreak of the war. He had a peculiar phobia of cold air but was cool under fire. The drawing was done by one of the Prussian officers who handed the general the declaration of war on the morning of 31 January, 1864.

13

Les jeux sont faits

The war began on 1 February 1864. At the end of January the Danish army was deployed in Schleswig at the Dannevirke, and the allied armies only twenty kilometres to the south, by the Eider River, which formed the natural border to Holstein.

After a few days of thaw the temperature had suddenly dropped again to ten degrees below freezing. The biting winter cold, combined with fierce winds, made for miserable conditions for the troops on both sides. In the early morning of 31 January two Prussian general staff officers ventured out in an open horse-drawn carriage. Leaving the small town of Rendsborg by the Eider River, they drove across the frostbitten landscape into enemy territory.

The two men wore long fur-collared winter capes, from the folds of which peeked brass-hilted swords. Underneath they wore tight-fitting jackets with gold buttons, gold stripes on their high red collars. White armbands on their left arm signalled their affiliation with the allied forces of Austria and Prussia. Their dark grey woollen trousers with red piping were tucked into tall, shiny black boots. Completing their finery were golden-spiked helmets adorned at the front with proud golden eagles.

These were Major von Stiehle and Captain von Gottberg,

the former being among a select few who had managed to earn the trust of Prussian commander Field Marshal Friedrich von Wrangel. Stiehle had therefore been a natural choice for what was an important and potentially perilous mission: to carry a letter to the Danish commander from Field Marshal von Wrangel, who was headquartered in Hamburg. As the troops had been transported by train from Prussia and Austria to Hamburg, it had been possible to reach the Danish position within a few days. It was the first time in German military history that the railway was used to transport troops.

Little is known about Stiehle and Gottberg, their military careers or life stories, but the letter they carried has been preserved:

I, the undersigned Royal Prussian field marshal and commander-in-chief of the allied Prussian–Austrian forces Baron von Wrangel, am honoured to deliver to the commander-in-chief for the Danish Royal troops in the Duchy of Schleswig His Excellency Lieutenant General de Meza the following message [...] I, the undersigned, have been given orders to occupy the Duchy of Schleswig with the allied Prussian and Austrian troops under my command and to set up a provisional cabinet for the area [...]

As I, the undersigned, respectfully beg to inform His Excellency Lieutenant General de Meza of these orders, it is also my humble duty to acquaint His Excellency with the command to vacate the Duchy of Schleswig and to pull his troops out of this area.

Allow me further to express my high regard for His Excellency.

Your most obedient servant,
Commander-in-chief of the Allied Forces, v. Wrangel.

As Wrangel was well aware that de Meza had orders to hold the Duchy of Schleswig at all costs, this letter was in point of fact a declaration of war on Denmark. The Duchy of Schleswig was under the Danish Crown, so the Danish army had orders to put up a fierce resistance if the allied forces attempted to cross the Eider. For several weeks now, Danish engineer details had worked on enlarging and improving the redoubts and earthworks of the almost seventy-kilometre-long Dannevirke, stretching from the Baltic in the east to the mudflats of the Wadden Sea at the foot of the Jutland peninsula in the west. One hundred and seventy-two cannon had been deployed in the redoubts and now stood with their muzzles pointing south. In addition, the artillery park comprised endless columns of guns, ammunition and wagons. Denmark had called up all active-duty soldiers as well as a large percentage of reservists, and deployed the vast majority of them at the Dannevirke to receive the enemy troops, which consisted of three corps: two Prussian and one Austrian, under orders to wipe out Danish resistance. Until the war had actually been declared, however, neither side could fire so much as a single shot.

The task of delivering the declaration was by no means a small one. Gottberg and Stiehle had to travel a good distance through heavily militarised Danish territory and were no doubt aware that their mission was fraught with risk.

The main road on which they drove took them through myriad villages with strange Danish names, such as Duvensted, Oxlev, Boglund and Lottorp. These were the Danish army's command posts. On the morning of 31 January, approximately 9,000 Danish soldiers were deployed in the open in this area, which served as a buffer zone against attacks from the south. The ubiquitous presence of Danish soldiers must have been unsettling to the Prussian officers. That dark winter morning, however, none of the Danish soldiers seemed concerned by the carriage and its spike-helmeted passengers. Gottberg and Stiehle therefore drove unencumbered deeper and deeper into enemy territory. By daybreak they had reached the Dannevirke's most advanced defence works: Greater Dannevirke and Bustrup Outwork, both built to withstand massive frontal attacks. Bustrup Outwork boasted ramparts almost ten metres high, as well as newly constructed steep-sided redoubts, deep moats and treacherously sharp-pointed palisades. The Danish soldiers jokingly referred to this section of their defensive line as Denmark's 'Gibraltar'.

Just north of the fortification, in the town of Schleswig, where the Danish general staff was headquartered, a meeting between the Danish king, Christian IV, Prime Minister Monrad and the Danish army commanders was scheduled to take place within the next twenty-four hours.

Gottberg and Stiehle passed by the Outwork, crossed the Eider River, and as dawn's first light broke through the winter morning's fine frost mist, they rode through the village of Frederiksberg, which was little more than a cluster of houses. Shortly thereafter they reached the town of Schleswig, the county seat, which had a population of 10,000. Plumes of grey-white smoke ascended from the many chimneys, and everywhere they looked there were Danish soldiers. More than 15,000 Danish troops were based there.

Captain Christian A. Hoffmann, a Danish officer stationed

in Schleswig at the time, has given a vivid description of the scene that met the two officers:

> There was a bustle of activity, especially around Gottorp Castle and on the road through Fredericksberg to Bustrup Outwork and nearby sections of Dannevirke.
>
> Large numbers of troops had gathered in and around the town of Schleswig and the castle, crowds of soldiers of all weapons milled about, and from morning to night long columns of cannon and ammunitions' wagons were en route to Dannevirke, and engineer details constantly marched to and from the position. When you crossed the southern bridge to the castle and walked through its court-yards, you were surrounded by colossal piles of cannonballs, ranging in size from 6- to 84-pounders. Heavy reinforcement of regiments and battalions was clearly taking place.

It is easy to imagine Gottberg and Stiehle discussing how to explain their presence in the area to inquisitive and potentially hostile Danish soldiers. After all, they could easily have been accused of spying. Everything was in plain sight, and they had ample opportunity to appraise the military might of their opponent: counting the number of ordnance and units as well as sizing up the depth of their defences, for instance the height of redoubts and position of embrasures. But thus far no one had seemed to pay them much heed, and they made their way unhindered to the Prinzenpalais (the Prince's Palace) near Gottorp Castle, where the Danish command was headquartered.

According to the commander's diary entry of that day, the two officers arrived at exactly 7.30 a.m. The Danish soldiers on guard saluted them, as military protocol demanded; they were not, however (as protocol also required), immediately taken to see a high-ranking Danish officer. The Danish chief of staff, Colonel Kauffmann, and all his officers were out inspecting the defensive works along the Schlei River. So they were instead introduced to an elderly gentleman dressed in a housecoat and a Turkish fez. As it turned out, this bizarre-looking man was the commander-in-chief of the Danish army, Christian Julius Frederik de Meza.

Denmark has produced its fair share of colourful eccentrics – notably Søren Kierkegaard and Hans Christian Andersen – and that phrase certainly also fits de Meza. Colonel Kauffmann described him as a 'slender man with delicate features, blue eyes and lots of dark curly hair'. De Meza was seventy-two years old when Kauffmann gave this description. Contemporary photos of de Meza confirm that he did indeed have a full head of dark hair, which, coupled with his peculiar style of dress, gave him an oddly youthful appearance very much unlike the usual image of a general.

Nonetheless, de Meza was all soldier and had been his entire adult life. He had participated in every single major Danish campaign he'd lived through, which is to say the wars against Great Britain, including those known in Denmark as the English Wars (1807–14), and the First Schleswig War (1848–51). His father was a medical doctor, and no one really knows why de Meza, born in 1792, chose a military career rather than follow in the footsteps of Dr Jacob Theophilus de Meza. But at the age of thirteen, de Meza was enrolled in an artillery apprenticeship programme, and a few years later he was an officer cadet. During the British siege of Copenhagen in 1807, then-Sergeant and Master Bombardier de Meza was responsible for a piece of ordnance on the fortified city walls. This siege culminated in a massive bombardment of Copenhagen, with considerable loss of both civilian and military life.

The crushing defeat and subsequent forced surrender of the Danish fleet to the British victors made it all too easy for Denmark to choose sides in the Napoleonic Wars. Seven hard years of conflict followed. De Meza was promoted to second lieutenant. Two years later, he graduated from the military academy and was assigned a teaching position at the Copenhagen School of Artillery. While holding this job, he also trained for a position on the general staff. By all standards, he seemed destined for a stellar military career. However, after Napoleon's defeat in 1815, de Meza saw his career grind to a halt.

Denmark's participation in the Napoleonic Wars on the French side had been a costly affair. The country went bankrupt in 1813, and in 1814 Norway, hitherto under direct rule from Copenhagen, was ceded to Sweden. Therefore, while the monarchy survived, it had been vastly truncated and faced a serious financial crisis. Military spending was cut and the number of staff officers reduced. De Meza became a casualty of the cost-cutting and found himself demoted to his former teaching position. Rather than become discouraged, however, he seized the opportunity to indulge his passion for languages. He used his position as a teacher to gain fluency in French, German, Italian, English and Dutch – languages he had already mastered to varying degrees. He travelled extensively and for extended periods of time. During a long stay in Paris, he made it his mission to produce and publish a phonetic French dictionary. For de Meza, proper pronunciation was of the utmost importance; in fact he appears to have been almost obsessed by it. Unfortunately, he never managed to secure sufficient funds for the publication, which may explain why he was so strict with the hapless students who inadvertently mispronounced or garbled their words in his classes.

Though de Meza was generally perceived as a kind man, most of his students disliked him. 'He would taunt and tease us; for instance, he liked covering our school uniform jackets with chalk marks as punishment for poor performance,' one student remembered.

A peculiar phobia of cold air was another of de Meza's eccentricities. De Meza was convinced that breathing in cold air was dangerous, and he did everything in his power to avoid it. According to a short biography written by the military historian K. C. Rockstroh, de Meza would, after entering his classroom on chilly winter mornings, head straight for the hot stove – not to stoke it, but to crouch down behind it to warm his curly hair.

Another episode recorded in the biography tells of a time just before exam season when de Meza had written to a colleague that if it proved 'absolutely necessary to clean the classrooms before the tests to please warn the cleaning people to use as little effluvium as possible … so that tomorrow, we may not find ourselves in a position of being forced to mop the floors with our breath'.

No doubt de Meza's eccentric behaviour, together with his idiosyncratic, somewhat effeminate style of dress, hurt his career. Though promoted to major in 1842, de Meza did not make lieutenant colonel two years later as was the custom; it must have been an affront to him that younger officers were being promoted over his head.

At the outbreak of the First Schleswig War in 1848, Major

de Meza was fifty-six – under normal circumstances far too old to have any real hope of a second chance in the army. But as the diminished Danish army desperately needed qualified officers, de Meza was called up for active duty. And during the next three years of war he got a chance to prove his mettle – giving credence to the old adage that it is never too late.

Though he remained hysterically fearful of cold air and refused to change his style of dress during the campaign, Field Officer de Meza exhibited great courage under fire. According to one of many anecdotes about him, a cannonball burst through the walls of his office as he was dictating a letter; reportedly he had barely blinked, quickly resuming his dictation. Later, however, he did lament the hole in the wall, saying that it would surely cause an awful draught.

During the war in which Schleswig-Holstein rebels fought for independence from Denmark, de Meza advanced quickly through the ranks, as much to his own as to others' surprise. By 1849 he was a major general and, moreover, a national war hero. The latter status was first bestowed on him after he successfully beat back entrenched Schleswig-Holstein rebels on 6 July 1849. He led this attack from the besieged city of Fredericia. De Meza also played a decisive role in the Battle of Isted, though he had been wounded and was barely out of surgery when it began. Divisional General F. A. Schleppegrell, however, fell early on, so de Meza was forced to take over his command, successfully defending Isted and thereby crushing the insurgency. His actions on the battlefield solidified his status with the Danish population as a war hero.

In the years after the war, de Meza enjoyed great popularity in Copenhagen society, not only because he was a war hero, but also because he was an accomplished musician, composer and singer. De Meza would often entertain at parties, singing and accompanying himself on the piano.

His increasing obsession with cold air did not seem to bother the Copenhagen elite. Visitors to his office had to negotiate an obstacle course of chairs set up between his desk and the door. De Meza believed that slowing the pace of his callers reduced his chance of catching 'cold air'.

Despite his advancing age, de Meza was chosen as commander-in-chief of the Danish forces in 1864. Stories of his heroic actions during the First Schleswig War still flourished, and to the men he appeared larger than life. De Meza was perhaps the most respected officer in the Danish army at the time. His issues with cold air, however, were to become a problem during the war, which much to Denmark's consternation began in the middle of winter. De Meza rarely left his quarters at the Dannevirke, and he may well have greeted Stiehle and Gottberg with a worried, 'Have you brought in cold air?' Probably not what they had expected when they entered his office on the last day of January 1864. Cold air, however, turned out to be the lesser of two evils, de Meza discovered as he read Wrangel's letter.

Sure that a look of shock was registering on his face, de Meza made a failed attempt to hide behind the letter. Stiehle saw it at once, though, and later noted that 'the withered old man's face sustained a look of surprise'.

De Meza's hands shook slightly when he crumbled up the letter. He had not expected a war so soon and was confounded. The Danish Command had anticipated a spring campaign – an error of judgement, which was owed in part to Denmark's grave misreading of the international political climate and Otto von Bismarck's intentions, and in part to pure wishful thinking. Denmark was far from ready to go to war. Still, de Meza managed to collect himself and, after thinking the matter through for a few minutes, told the Prussian officers that 'if the Marshal wanted to expedite matters, I will be ready for him'.

The two officers allowed de Meza six hours to pen a written reply. They waited at a nearby hotel, where Gottberg amused himself by drawing a caricature of de Meza. De Meza, though, was a quick thinker and enjoyed making rash decisions without consulting his staff. Within two hours, and despite a minor glitch in the transcription, the response was prepared. Chief of Staff Kauffmann, who had immediately been sent for, never made it back to headquarters in time to influence the content of the response.

It was a Lieutenant le Maire who had made the fair copy of the letter, but he had used the Latin alphabet, which outraged Stiehle and Gottberg. Field Marshal von Wrangel expected Gothic letters, they said. So the letter was restyled in Gothic script. By 3.30 p.m. the two officers were ready to depart. This time, however, no one saluted them as they left the Danish headquarters.

De Meza's reply – devoid of ceremonious courtesy phrases – simply read:

Undersigned cannot accept Prussian and Austrian forces occupying any part of Denmark as is the intent expressed in your letter of 30 January. This is contrary to the Danish cabinet's instruction, thus we will be prepared to meet any act of violence with armed response.

Field Marshal von Wrangel, too impatient to await the return of Stiehle and Gottberg, had journeyed north with his staff to meet them halfway. By the time they met up, it was evening. Wrangel tore open de Meza's letter and seemed to not even notice the rude lack of formality. He had the message he wanted and could now, at long last, give the signal to start the war: '*In Gottes Namen drauf!*' – 'In God's name, let us fight!'

14

The Baltic powder keg

Most armed conflicts, even the First World War – the confused origins of which have always been the subject of much discussion – have a defining moment, a proverbial 'shot in Sarajevo', that signals the inevitable slide towards war. The catalyst that set in motion the string of events leading to the war of 1864 was the signing into law of the November Constitution of 1863.

From a Danish perspective the new constitution solved an increasingly burdensome problem of cabinet involving the two duchies of Schleswig and Holstein. Hitherto the two duchies had been under the rule of the Danish king, but had not been subject to the Danish constitution, a situation that often impeded Danish policy-making, particularly because Holstein's interests were typically at odds with Denmark's. The new constitution stipulated the incorporation of Schleswig into the kingdom, subjecting it to the Danish constitution, and the secession of Holstein. Schleswig was historically Danish territory, while Holstein was not only historically German territory but also a member of the German Confederation, so the division made perfect sense to the members of the Danish cabinet.

There was, however, one major snag: the new constitution

violated an international agreement, the 1852 London Protocol, signed by Great Britain, Russia, France and Prussia, as well as Denmark and Sweden. In accordance with the protocol, Denmark was to remain a unitary state made up of four autonomous parts: the Kingdom of Denmark, and the duchies of Schleswig, Holstein and Lauenborg. The duchies of Schleswig and Holstein were subject to the authority of the Danish king, albeit in his capacity as the Duke of Schleswig-Holstein rather than as the monarch of Denmark. The duchies had an absolutist system of cabinet with advisory estate-assemblies drawn from the most powerful and affluent members of society. Conversely, the Kingdom of Denmark was a constitutional monarchy with voting rights for men, protected by the constitution of 1849.

The new constitution not only violated the London Protocol, it also breached an even older agreement still on the books: the Ribe Treaty of 1460, in accordance with which the two duchies were to remain always in indissoluble union – *'up ewig ungedeelt'* ('forever undivided'). While this contractual 'marriage' held great meaning for the inhabitants of the two duchies, it was immaterial to the Danish rulers and the architects of the new constitution.

Seen through a twentieth-century lens, the new Danish constitution was decidedly discriminatory against the German majority in Schleswig, whose natural affiliation was with Holstein and the German Confederation rather than with Denmark and the Danes, with whom they felt little kinship.

The National Liberal Party in power at the time, however, did not concern themselves with cultural and ethnic issues. Rather they were informed by the wave of nationalism that had swept across Europe since the late 1840s, when political upheaval led to a string of revolts against European monarchies, starting in Sicily and spreading to Paris, Vienna and Berlin. The ideology of nationalism soon became infused with a strong romanticism. And it was romantic nationalistic sentiment that moved the Danish parliament in the beginning of the 1860s to focus blindly on the fabled tales of Schleswig having been ruled by Danish kings and queens since ancient times. In their view, then, Schleswig was Danish.

Another contributory factor explaining the Danish parliament's, in hindsight reckless, decision to take steps to incorporate Schleswig and secede Holstein without securing international approval was their victory in what today is known as the First Schleswig War, fifteen years earlier. The smouldering dissatisfaction which led to revolts elsewhere in Europe in the late 1840s also took hold in the duchy of Schleswig, where a majority of the population wished to break its ties with the Danish monarchy in favour of forming closer ties to Holstein and by extension the German Confederation. In March 1848, separatists declared Schleswig and Holstein independence from Denmark.

Its declaration of independence was in many respects a godsend for the Danish king, who was also facing political unrest at home. King Frederik VII only narrowly escaped a hostile revolt in Denmark proper by readily acquiescing to the people's demand for more influence. The sudden emergence of a common enemy in the form of the Schleswig rebels – as they were known in Denmark – made the Danes rally behind their king.

Denmark won a narrow victory against Schleswig (supported by Holstein) and only because Russia and Great Britain pressured Prussia to withdraw from the conflict. Prussia had come to the aid of the duchies with 30,000 troops in the first phase of the war. Russia and Great Britain intervened on behalf of Denmark to preserve the territorial status quo of the two duchies, as they thought it vital to the maintenance of the delicate power balance in Europe.

By 1850 Denmark was therefore able to beat back rebel resistance in hard-fought battles at Isted, Mysunde and Frederiksstad in Schleswig. The Battle of Isted is to date the largest battle ever fought on Scandinavian ground. The Danes were jubilant. The brave soldiers were hailed as heroes, the Danish flag waved its red and white everywhere, and the National Liberal party began to dream of restoring Denmark to its former military glory. Denmark, once a considerable sea power, had been reduced to nothing more than a tinpot military power in the wake of the Napoleonic Wars, in which she was forced to surrender her entire fleet to Great Britain after a devastating assault on Copenhagen in 1807.

In the exhilaration of victory, everyone seemed eager to embrace the idea that Denmark had now risen as a military phoenix from the ashes of defeat. The Danes also felt confident that Russia and Britain would be willing to intervene on her behalf should the Schleswig issue ever arise again.

However, when Denmark ushered in the November Constitution in 1863, she seemed oddly oblivious to a number of critical differences between the current situation and the First Schleswig War. First, the new constitution dissolved the very structure Russia and Great Britain had intervened to protect in the first conflict. Second, by signing it into law, consciously violating the London Protocol, Denmark was perceived by the European community as the aggressor rather than, as in the first conflict, the victim of aggression. Consequently, no one rushed to Denmark's aid when the Federal Diet in Frankfurt demanded the repeal of the constitution, if necessary by military force.

Still, it takes two to tango, and while Denmark may have taken the initiative by ratifying the November Constitution, Prussia was not slow to follow. In fact, the Prussian minister-president Otto von Bismarck practically leapt out on to the dance floor. For years he had been looking for an opportunity to trigger a war with Denmark, but he had never imagined that she would take the lead herself with such reckless aplomb.

While Denmark and Prussia were preparing the ground for their dangerous dance around the Schleswig Question, the Great Powers of Europe remained impassive but alert, keeping a watchful eye on events in southern Denmark. The European balance of power that had been negotiated during the Congress of Vienna (1815) following the Napoleonic Wars had begun to sway dangerously in the wake of the Crimean War (1854–6). Even a minor conflict like the one brewing between Prussia–Austria and Denmark could set off the European powder keg at this time, potentially resulting in a Continental conflict.

France and Great Britain were concerned that if the old rivals Austria and Prussia, who now united against Denmark, remained allies after the war they would dominate the European continent. Great Britain was furthermore anxious that a strengthened Prussia with access to the Baltic Sea could become a serious threat to British naval supremacy. France and Great Britain thus had a vested interest in formulating a joint policy towards the Danish–German war, but this proved inordinately difficult. To safeguard its political interest in Italy against its arch-enemy Austria, France needed to be on good terms with Berlin and was therefore not interested in pursuing too tough a course of action against Prussia. In Great Britain the conflict led to a clash of wills between Queen Victoria and Prime Minister Palmerston. The prime minister, influenced as much by a Danish-friendly population as by the larger political issues, was at the outset more kindly disposed towards tiny Denmark than towards Prussia, and so immediately set to work on brokering a peace. In fact, Palmerston offered to mediate a peace settlement as early as February 1864.

The British press was in general pro-Denmark, and stories about the little country's brave battle against the mighty Prussian–Austrian forces sold like hot cakes. In Parliament several influential politicians advocated supporting a military intervention. Though not unfavourably disposed towards Denmark, Queen Victoria remained staunchly opposed to any military involvement. The queen's natural sympathies lay with the German Confederation, in large part due to her German family ties. Her beloved Albert had been prince of the German state Saxe-Coburg-Gotha, and her son-in-law, Crown Prince Friedrich of Prussia, was married to the princess royal, Victoria. Queen Victoria, however, also had a Danish daughter-in-law, Princess Alexandra, who was married to her eldest son, Edward, the Prince of Wales, and because of this relationship as well as other political considerations, she did not wish for Denmark to be crushed in the war, nor too harshly punished in a peace agreement.

Russia, for her part, while still considered one of the five great European powers, had withdrawn somewhat from European power politics after losing the Crimean War to Great Britain, France and their allies in 1856. Russia was on excellent terms with Austria and was at this time attempting a rapprochement with Prussia, to whom it was indebted for the suppression of a Polish uprising in 1863–4, and with whom it would be prudent to form an alliance against Russia's old enemies from the Crimean War. Muddying the situation for Russia, however, was an anxiety regarding its own influence in the Baltic, which might be negatively impacted if Denmark lost the war and emerged from the conflict severely weakened. Nightmare aftermath scenarios for Russia included a Danish alliance with pro-British Sweden, which would leave Russia encircled; or a Prussian occupation of Denmark, which would give Prussia access to the Baltic Sea.

Despite their different interests and anxieties regarding the Danish–German conflict over the duchies, the great European powers had one thing in common: they all hoped for a speedy resolution.

15

The Iron Chancellor

Otto Eduard Leopold von Bismarck-Schönhausen was a shrewd political tactician who almost always played his hand to great effect. In November 1863 he pulled a particularly cunning bluff by letting it be known that Prussia would not intervene if Denmark annulled the London Protocol. He conveyed this message through Denmark's diplomatic representative in Berlin, as well as through other diplomatic channels. Thus there seemed no need for Denmark to be anxious about a Prussian intervention on behalf of Schleswig-Holstein.

As it turned out, however, Bismarck's overtures were a devious ploy. The day before King Christian IX was to sign the November Constitution, Bismarck performed a shocking about-turn. He informed Denmark that the new constitution would 'deepen the crisis' of the duchies. The subtext was clear: Prussia was threatening reprisals if Denmark signed the constitution into law. The Prussian envoy charged with delivering this message to the Danish king was so surprised by Bismarck's switching of position that he dispatched a telegram to Berlin to make sure Prussia was in fact now contesting the new constitution. The reply was swift and short: 'Yes!'

In later years, when Bismarck took stock of his political life, he would refer to his diplomatic manoeuvrings in the

Aged forty-nine, Otto von Bismarck was not yet the Iron Chancellor
but a very ambitious minister to the Prussian king, Wilhelm I. He
hoped the war against Denmark could bolster the power of the
king and strengthen Prussia within the German Federation.

run-up to the war of 1864 as his masterpiece. Bismarck's position in Berlin was fragile in the early 1860s. King Wilhelm I of Prussia, whose right-hand man Bismarck had become, was losing faith in his minister-president, and their opponents, the liberals, had recently won a great parliamentary victory and the majority of seats in the Landtag. Bismarck desperately needed some kind of crisis he could brilliantly manage in order to improve his standing with the king. He was, in his own words, 'closer to the gallows than to the throne'.

A so-called 'Junker', Bismarck was born into a landed, noble Prussian family. After graduating from the University of Göttingen, he carried on the family tradition for a few years by working on Kniephof, his family's estate in Pomerania. Yet, while he had an appreciation for the arts and enjoyed educating himself through reading, the quiet life of a country squire did not sit well with the restless Bismarck. In college he had been a heavy drinker, an incurable womaniser and a man who also enjoyed flirting with danger, reportedly participating in countless duels. Bismarck simply thrived on high-impact situations.

Politics, as it turned out, perfectly matched both his personality and his unique combination of talents. Bismarck was a brilliant orator and soon attracted the attention of influential figures in Berlin, where he literally and figuratively stood taller than most. His single-minded determination and unflinching confidence, coupled with his brilliant delivery and results-driven realpolitik, would within a few years make him one of Europe's most remarkable political powerhouses.

His political career began in 1851, when he was appointed as Prussia's representative in the German Diet in Frankfurt. Sharp political skills were needed to negotiate the interests of thirty-nine loosely associated states and his years in the Diet were formative. Here he also came to understand how deeply entrenched the nationalist German movement had become, and recognised that it was far too strong a cultural force to ignore politically. He also developed an intense antipathy towards Austria, seeing it as Prussia's main rival for dominance in the German Confederation.

In many German circles in Frankfurt a similarly intense antipathy had developed towards Denmark, and the lingering issue of Schleswig was frequently brought up for debate in the Diet. A majority viewed Schleswig-Holstein as German and argued that the Confederation should step into the breach for their brethren in the north against the terrible Danes.

In 1859 Bismarck accepted a position as Prussian envoy in St Petersburg and two years later was made ambassador in Paris. His years abroad gave him an international perspective and an understanding of European power politics that, combined with the political skills he had acquired in the German Diet, rendered him a good candidate for higher office. In 1862 Wilhelm I installed him as Minister-President of Prussia. Pushing for this nomination was the war minister at the time, Albrecht von Roon. Berlin was embroiled in a political quagmire over conscription, between the king and the arch-conservatives on the one side and the democratic and liberal-minded centre-left, who held the majority in Parliament, on the other. A full-blown crisis seemed increasingly likely, and Roon felt Bismarck was the only one made of the right stuff to prevent this outcome.

On the surface, the so-called 'military reform crisis' – igniting the political firestorm Bismarck was to extinguish – may seem somewhat banal and hard to take seriously. On balance, all they were squabbling about was whether or not to shorten military service from three to two years. However, while Prussia today is bound up in our awareness as a strong military power, it had at the time been left militarily weak by its engagements in the Napoleonic Wars and barely warranted being designated a great power. Prussia, which was founded in 1701, had had its heyday during the reign of the renowned King Frederick the Great, from 1740 to 1786. Frederick the Great created a bureaucratic state based on a strong, confident corps of civil servants and a large professional army, and his military genius helped him emerge among the victors of the Seven Years War, in which Prussia and Britain fought against France, Austria and Russia. By war's end in 1763, Prussia's series of victories had established it as a great European power.

A precarious status, as we have seen, since Prussia was almost overrun by French forces during the first phase of the Napoleonic Wars when it suffered two crushing defeats, at the battles of Jena and Auerstedt in 1806. Prussia lost 33,000 dead and wounded in these battles.

The Prussian army, which had inspired such pride in its domestic population, simply proved insufficient against the French troops. Napoleon's army was based on conscription, and French soldiers felt they played an important role in defending their country. The professional Prussian soldiers, on the other hand, felt no such loyalty and were basically treated like cattle by their officers.

A disbanding of the Prussian army due to mass desertion followed in the wake of the devastating defeats at Jena and Auerstedt. French troops occupied Prussia and Napoleon marched triumphantly through the Brandenburg Gate in Berlin a few weeks later – a smashing humiliation for the once so magnificent power.

Prussia, however, recovered some of its lost pride towards the end of the Napoleonic Wars when Prussian army corps helped defeat French troops at Leipzig in 1813 and in the decisive Battle of Waterloo in 1815. Thanks to Prussia's significant contribution in the final phase of the wars, its status as a great power was restored at the Congress of Vienna. Great Britain, its objective being a containment of France, helped strengthen Prussia's position in Europe by arranging for it to gain control of the rich Rheinland-Pfalz area. Nonetheless, Prussia emerged from the Napoleonic Wars broken in spirit and as a country divided against itself. The French occupation prompted a wave of civic nationalism directed as much at the autocratic Prussian cabinet as at the occupying forces. People wanted reforms and influence. With the establishment of the Landtag, the nobility and the monarchy's powers were reduced, and a series of reforms were implemented that came to impact all sectors of society, including the military. At the centre of the military reforms of 1815 was universal conscription (a basic three-year term of service, followed by two years in the reserve or Landwehr militia). The Prussian army would henceforth be based on military draft rather than on professional troops. Love of country was to be the prime motivator for Prussian soldiers, not fear of state, harsh punishments and generally inhuman treatment.

The modernisation of the Prussian military, however, did not sit well with the nobility. They saw the new modernised army as weak, undisciplined and comprising hopeless amateurs. Not surprisingly, they were enraged when, by mid-century, the increasingly liberal Landtag pushed for a shorter service term based on the conviction that Prussia's economic growth needed its young men in the workforce rather than in the army.

(Above) The forty-five-year-old Danish king Christian IX and his minister, fifty-two-year-old D. G. Monrad (below). The king distrusted Monrad whom he viewed as too liberal and erratic. Monrad was widely acclaimed as the main architect of the first democratic Danish constitution signed in 1849. However, he suffered from a bipolar disorder that severely clouded his judgment during the war of 1864.

Which brings us back to the key issue of the political crisis Bismarck found himself whirled into upon entering office as minister-president in 1862.

War Minister von Roon and King Wilhelm I were staunchly against a reduction of the service term; in fact, they wanted to increase the number of conscripts called up and preserve the active duty requirement of a minimum of three years. Roon and Wilhelm I were interested in strengthening the army and increasing its strike force, both of which would require a serious hike in military spending.

The Landtag agreed to raise the number of conscripts but baulked at the three-year service term. Hence the political deadlock. At the root of the conflict lay a much larger question, however: namely whether in the future Prussia was to be ruled by a military regime or a democratic cabinet.

When he arrived in Berlin, Bismarck initially tried to reach a compromise but his attempt to steer a middle course failed. Instead, he decided to take a hard-nosed, arch-conservative, loyalist position, becoming completely unwilling to compromise. His objective: a bigger and militarily stronger Prussia.

Bismarck outlined his political goals in the infamous 'Blood and Iron' speech, given to the Landtag in September 1862: 'Not through speeches and majority decisions will the great questions of the day be decided ... but by iron and blood,' he thundered, words that would later earn him the sobriquet the 'Iron Chancellor'.

The Landtag, however, was not swayed by Bismarck's rhetoric, and in October the liberals enjoyed a comfortable win in the Landtag election. The king was so distraught by the outcome he was on the verge of a nervous breakdown. Looking down on the Palace Square, he reportedly said to

Bismarck, 'Down there is where they will put up a guillotine for me.'

The king need not have worried about his head being severed from his body, though, as his new minister-president proved to be a crisis-management genius. In fact, Bismarck actively thrived under extreme pressure. In a wild gamble, he chose to ignore the liberals in the lower house of the Landtag and move ahead with plans for overhauling the army by securing funding from the more conservative members of the Landtag in the upper house. A loophole in the law made it possible for Bismarck to get away with this ingenious ruse.

Nonetheless, he knew that he was walking a tightrope and needed another crisis to divert attention from his unpopular political methods. So when, on 13 November 1863, Denmark passed its new constitution, Bismarck saw it as the perfect opportunity to start a little diversionary war. An armed conflict with Denmark, he reasoned, would not only get him out of his predicament, but also most likely garner support for increased military spending from the lower house. After all, the liberals would appear downright unpatriotic if they voted against increased funding and the three-year conscription in the midst of war.

Fortunately for Bismarck, no one in Copenhagen seemed aware of how precarious his situation actually was. Instead the city was consumed by a feverish and fateful lust for war – a desire that only intensified when Denmark suddenly, and unexpectedly, lost its beloved king on 15 November 1863.

16

The king is dead

In Denmark, Frederik VII is known as the People's King. Shortly after he took the throne in 1848, he renounced absolutism and signed into law a democratic constitution, becoming to all Danes a living symbol of democracy. Though politically inexperienced, he immediately revealed an innate talent for political survival. The smouldering popular discontent that led to so many bloody revolts throughout Europe in 1848 was quelled in Denmark by the new king's swift actions. Without striking a blow, and before the anger of the masses assembling in front of the royal palace burst into bloody rebellion, Frederik VII quietly acquiesced to the popular demand for democracy.

What further endeared him to the Danish people was Denmark's victory in the First Schleswig War. Frederik was seen as the king who restored the country to its former military might (if only in the eyes of the Danes). His easy, folksy demeanour and seemingly insatiable appetite for wine, women and food also ingratiated him to his subjects. Danes seemed especially to adore his appreciation for food and spirits.

Frederik VII went through two marriages before finally settling in a lasting relationship with a commoner named Louise Rasmussen. Owing to his great popularity, no one seemed to

Danish King Frederik VII and his wife, the commoner Louise
Rasmussen. The king was loathed by the old aristocracy but the
general populace adored his folksy style. He loved parties, food and
spirits. After his sudden death in November 1863, just before the
outbreak for the war, a sense of gloom descended on Copenhagen.

baulk at this breach of protocol. Louise was to become known as Countess Danner – a title bestowed upon her to paper over her humble origins.

To say that history and the Danish people have been extraordinarily kind to Frederik VII's reputation would not be pushing it. He was not a terribly bright man, and he spent most of his time travelling the country in a sedan chair carried by his servants. He would often bring bottles of punch, and enjoy drinking them while inspecting archaeological digs. On such trips he would typically end the day at some party, drinking heavily through the night. Reportedly he could consume fifteen glasses of punch or more during an evening of merriment, without, as his advisors said, 'it being noticeable'. It therefore caused quite a stir on the evening of 23 October 1863 when, while attending a civic ball in Flensburg, he became extremely intoxicated after drinking only three glasses of punch. The king started screaming and behaving like a raving madman. The scandal he caused did not seem to worry his advisors, who were used to his late-night, alcohol-infused ramblings. What did, however, frighten and concern them was the tiny amount of punch he had consumed. He had never before become so drunk from drinking so little.

As it turned out, those three glasses of punch would be his last. In the following days, the king felt 'sick as a dog' and was in fact very ill. A high fever made him too weak to travel back to Copenhagen and he was confined to a bed at Glücksburg Castle. At the beginning of November his doctor diagnosed him with necrotising fasciitis, but did not believe it to be serious. However, on 11 November the king's condition began deteriorating fast. Red rose-shaped blotches spread all over his body, and his face turned an intense crimson. By the next day he was delirious: his speech was garbled and his arms flailed wildly. To those present in his room, it was obvious that the king thought he was at Dannevirke leading his men into battle against the Germans.

'They're coming!' he was heard yelling. 'Attack!'

Thus, fighting imaginary Germans in his fever-induced phantasies – no doubt made worse by severe alcohol poisoning – Denmark's beloved king died on 15 November 1863, at 2.53 p.m.

The news of the king's death plunged the nation into deep mourning. Contemporary paintings depicting the event were done in muted tones, as if all colour had been drained out of the artists' palette. On 17 November, Hans Christian Andersen wrote in his diary, 'All day I have been languid, not accomplished anything; felt ill at ease, almost destroyed as if a light had gone out in me; the atmosphere in the city is dismal; wrote a poem about Frederik VII.'

With the death of their king, Denmark appeared to lose all sense of identity. The joy and optimism the king had fostered seemingly died with him. Certainly no one was able to appreciate the decidedly tragi-comic aspects of his demise.

The king's body was supposed to have been transported in a zinc-lined coffin, but as none could be found in the area, and it was agreed it would take too long to procure one from Hamburg, the body was wrapped in a waxed blanket and sealed in a lead coffin. This was then to be placed inside a wooden outer coffin before going on its journey to Copenhagen. However, the carpenter hired to build it had been so befuddled by the king's death that he had been unable to take accurate measurements and the finished outer coffin delivered on 16 November was far too big. With no time to make another, the giant wooden coffin was half filled with wood shavings before the lead coffin was lowered inside. The coffin was then kept in a very warm room, accelerating the decomposition of the royal corpse, and a foul smell of putrefaction filled the room. In an attempt to remove the offensive odour, large buckets of chlorine had been set out, but had little effect. Out of fear that the fumes would cause an explosion, it was decided to drill drain-holes in the coffin.

The body was finally shipped to Copenhagen on a warship with the fateful name *Schleswig* and escorted by the armoured schooner *Esbern Snare*. On their way to Copenhagen, they passed several transport ships carrying Danish soldiers south to the Dannevirke front. As they passed, the soldiers fell silent and stood quietly, taking in the sight of the squadron carrying the remains of their king. When, finally, on 16 December, the squadron docked in Copenhagen, the entire city seemed to be gathered on the wharf or in rowing boats in the harbour.

As the quiet, clear day declined, the flickering lights of hundreds of torches lit up the sky. In his diary, Hans Christian Andersen noted that:

> all ships were flying their flags at half mast, the air was red, the water clear, as tarred grommets were being lit on the royal dockyard and by Knippels Bridge on the other side. A crowd of people had gathered by 5.15 p.m. when the funeral procession arrived; it was magnificent with the music and all the lights. The grommets gleamed red and two blue stars were visible in the sky over Christianshavn.

The coffin was carried to Christiansborg Palace – the seat of the Danish cabinet – and placed in the procession hall to lie in state. Over the next several days, thousands of Danes came to say goodbye, Hans Christian Andersen among them. He arrived after the hall had been closed off to the public for the funeral preparations.

I walked up the narrow winding staircase into rooms where everything was veiled in black, and lights were dimmed; I then entered the equally darkened parade hall where a satin baldachin decorated the ceiling. There were candlesticks and chandeliers, walls were emblazoned with coats of arms, but the investiture stools with their orders and insignia had been removed. The coffin was being lifted from the catafalque upon which epigraphs were inscribed. The lid had been lifted from the coffin for decoration, the black wooden coffin itself was lined with lead, and I saw there were several wreaths from Glücksburg Castle in it. A foul smell of rot emanated from it, and I went to the open window.

Bizarrely, the decomposing, swollen corpse of the once so sprightly king is an excellent metaphor for the mental state Denmark found itself in during the winter of 1863–4. As the nation was mourning the loss of Frederik VII, a series of ill-advised political and diplomatic decisions were made, forging the unfortunate chain of events that led to war. With a little common sense and some diplomatic manoeuvring, Denmark could no doubt have avoided the war. In the words of Danish historian Niels Neergaard, Denmark set out to pursue a course they knew would lead to disaster.

The 45-year-old Prince of Glücksburg took the Danish throne on 16 November 1863, becoming Christian IX. The

Danes, however, jokingly referred to him as the 'protocol king' because his family's succession rights were, under Danish law, by no means clear-cut, and had been confirmed only as a result of a provision in the London Protocol. The new king had a composed and stately demeanour but cut a rather anonymous figure. Although he had grown up in Glücksburg Castle and participated on the Danish side in the First Schleswig War, he was more German than Danish. He spoke Danish with a heavy German accent and was in all respects very much a product of the old world order, which he knew and understood. He had enjoyed living in an ethnically diverse, integrated state and was a staunch proponent of the personal union between the Crown and the duchies as provisioned in the London Protocol. It is therefore quite ironic that one of his first acts as King of Denmark was to sign the November Constitution, whereby he dissolved the integrated state of Denmark.

The new king had initially tried to uphold the London Protocol, but he was very insecure and had stammered nervously whenever he tried to get his point across to the Danish National Liberals, who therefore paid him no heed. Christian IX, though a weak orator, had a strong sense of the workings of the German Confederation, and unlike the National Liberals he was keenly aware of the disaster course on which Denmark would set itself with the ratification of the November Constitution. Thus it was a somewhat dejected and despairing king who, on 18 November, found himself forced to sign the new constitution into law. Had he refused, he would most likely have faced either a deposition or a civil war.

At about the same time as Christian IX was putting his signature on a document that he suspected was setting Denmark on a course for war with the German Confederation, Otto von

Bismarck was lining up his diplomatic guns in Berlin. The time had come when he needed to act decisively if he were to control the course of events. Certainly, he did not want to miss out on the long-awaited opportunity to wage war against Denmark, and so he set to work on covering all his political bases.

In the Diet in Frankfurt tempers flared over Denmark's ratification of the November Constitution, and the delegates directed their anger at the newly crowned Danish king. The main argument against him was that he had violated the London Protocol and by extension his own rights to the throne. A majority of the minor and mid-sized states in the Confederation wanted instead to have the pro-German Prince of Augustenborg installed. Bismarck, however, staunchly opposed this suggestion. He was, as we have seen, not the least swayed by nationalism, and was therefore not interested in empowering delegates whom he knew to be of a nationalistic and democratic persuasion. On 7 December he successfully argued for upholding the sanctity of the London Protocol, and further persuaded the Diet that since Austria and Prussia had been signatories of said treaty, they alone should be the ones to conduct the campaign against Denmark. In this way he expertly managed to keep the question of German nation- alism out of the discussion *and* exclude all the other states of the Confederation from any involvement in the coming cam- paign. On the surface this was to be a war of retribution for Denmark's violation of the London Protocol.

Privately, however, Bismarck did not march to war for the sake of the duchies or the London Protocol. If Prussian blood was to be spilled, there had to be more at stake than a treaty regarding the Danish monarchy's rights of succession:

Bismarck wanted to annex the duchies following a victory over Denmark. Yet, while he readily confided his plans to close friends, he refrained from sharing them with Wilhelm I, as he believed the king would perceive them as far too radical.

Nonetheless, to ensure the most favourable conditions for his war, Bismarck still had some political manoeuvring ahead of him. He needed to isolate Denmark internationally. Prussian relations with Russia and France were good, and Bismarck felt reassured that neither would go against him in an armed conflict, but Great Britain was another matter. He knew there was a fair chance Britain would support Denmark if the country was attacked and the sovereignty of its borders threatened. However, if Denmark appeared to be the aggressor, they would most likely not get involved.

In his letter to the Danish cabinet, Bismarck explicitly stated that the new constitution was in violation of the London Protocol and demanded that Denmark revoke it. He presented the demand as an ultimatum, stressing that if Denmark did not comply there would be war. The letter, received on 20 December in Copenhagen, sparked a flurry of diplomatic activity. French, Russian and British envoys stationed in Copenhagen all requested an audience with the Danish prime minister, Carl Christian Hall, whom they practically begged to comply with the Prussian demand. The speech of British envoy Lord Wodehouse was especially strongly worded, taking pains to stress that if the ratification of the new constitution triggered a war, then Great Britain, as a signatory to the treaty which prohibited precisely the thing which the November Constitution made law, could not offer Denmark military support.

The message was unequivocal: if it came to war, Denmark was on its own. Still, Hall wavered. The king, however, made a last-minute attempt to salvage the situation. He called a meeting with his prime minister and begged him to do everything in his power to get the constitution revoked.

Hall refused. The king responded with a vote of no confidence, thereby obliging the Hall cabinet to resign. In the following days, the king frantically and unsuccessfully tried to form a new conservative cabinet that would invalidate the constitution. A new cabinet was finally sworn in on New Year's Eve. It was headed not by a conservative, as the king had so fervently hoped, but by the National Liberal bishop D. G. Monrad. Regardless of what the prime minister's political persuasion might have been, however, it was now too late to prevent the war. Monrad's temporary cabinet was something of a one-man show, as none of the established Danish politicians had volunteered to join him; instead, minor cabinet officials had to be persuaded to occupy the six other ministerial posts. Monrad's cabinet was jokingly referred to as the 'One Million' – that is, one politician was supported by six zeroes.

Monrad was known as a forceful and influential public figure. He was one of the founders of the Danish constitution of 1849 and was regarded as a hard-working and conscientious politician. A great orator and a consummate workaholic, he was seemingly able to make the impossible happen again and again. He could broker political deals where others failed, and build personal alliances across political lines. At the time of the cabinet breakdown he held the post of Minister of Cultural Affairs, but why he volunteered to take on the job of prime minister is unknown.

From a contemporary perspective, it is easy to imagine that he did it out of loyalty to king and country and based his decision on the assumption that he was the only man able to untangle the mess Denmark had got itself into.

As it turned out, however, Monrad did not prove to be the right man for the job. For one thing he was a National Liberal and did not intend to revoke the new constitution, nor to find a compromise in the Schleswig-Holstein Question. For another he was by now a mere shadow of his former self. He was unbalanced and suffered, according to medical historian Johan Schioldann-Nielsen, from bipolar affective disorder. Since stressful situations typically precipitate episodes of illness for people with this disorder, it is little wonder that the events of 1864 left Monrad feeling, in his own words, sometimes incapable of thinking clearly.

His symptoms manifested on 16 January, when Prussia and Austria demanded that Denmark revoke the new constitution within forty-eight hours. Like a deer caught in a bright light, Monrad was rendered paralysed by the demand. Not until 21 January did he regain his ability to think clearly and act. But by then, and despite a British attempt at mediation, it was too late. The machinery of war had been set in motion. According to Monrad's biographer, Peter Stavnstrup, within the next six months the mentally ailing prime minister would undergo great hardships and a seemingly endless series of tragic disappointments.

Thus, on the brink of war, Denmark had at its helm a bipolar prime minister, a king who was unpopular because of his German background, a war minister (Carl Christian Lundbye) in the early stages of another serious mental illness, and, in command of the army, an ageing and hypochondriacal general, Christian de Meza. Though de Meza would come to prove his mettle as commander-in-chief, it was all in all a rather sad gallery of leaders that led Denmark to war in 1864.

Bismarck, of course, had grounds to be overjoyed. The conditions for a campaign against Denmark seemed ideal, as a consequence of the country's weak leadership as well as its international isolation. Still, the question remained whether he would be able to secure the quick and decisive victory upon which both his and King Wilhelm's political life depended.

17

Thyra's Fortress

At first glance, Denmark would not have seemed quite so easy to overrun. Stretching across the neck of Jutland was the magnificent Dannevirke fortification. Thyra's Fortress, as it was popularly known, ran the entire length of the almost seventy-kilometre-long border between Schleswig and Holstein and was the largest defensive edifice in Scandinavia. The main line of redoubts and outer works was approximately fourteen kilometres long, extending from the town of Schleswig in the east to the village of Hollingsted in the west. It comprised cannon positions, ramparts, moats, walls and trenches. In total there were 27 earthworks and 175 guns, many of which were heavy siege cannon. For its time the fortress was quite impressive and would have seemed intimidating even to a strong army equipped with modern weaponry.

Thyra's Fortress, however, had one decisive weakness. Like General de Meza, she was hypersensitive to cold weather.

During warm seasons the two bodies of water flanking the position (the Schlei inlet on the left and the floodplains of the rivers Trene and Reide on the right), together with the fourteen-kilometre-fortification line, effectively blocked encroachment from the south. But in the dead of winter an enemy could easily march across the frozen bodies of water

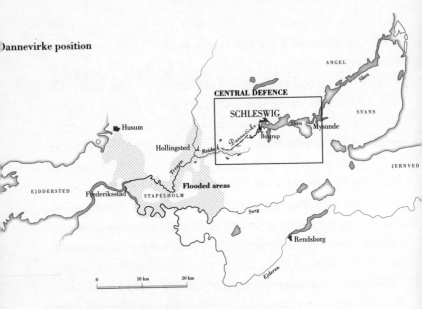

Dannevirke position

and in a rapid flank manoeuvre envelope and entrap the Danish troops holding the Dannevirke.

Unfortunately for Denmark, the winter of 1864 was one of the coldest in years. January saw temperatures plummeting and coming to a grinding, almost audible, halt well below freezing. Cutting sailing-channels through the frozen Schlei was therefore often the first order of business for new recruits arriving at the position.

Given the position's obvious weakness, it may seem puzzling that Denmark chose the Dannevirke as its main defensive line. However, as is often the case with human decision-making, it is as likely to be swayed by sentimentality as by rational thinking. To discover what motivated Danish leaders at the time, let us briefly dip into historic events preceding the war and into the mythical archives of Danish folklore. Denmark's founding legends are rich with stories of the country's first queen, Thyra Danebod, and her fabled role in the construction of a fortress that would allegedly safeguard Denmark for ever.

Thyra Danebod was married to Gorm the Old, Denmark's first historically recognised king. Upon her death, Gorm erected a memorial stone in her honour at Jellinge in southern Jutland, on which he calls her Denmark's 'jewel'. In the mid nineteenth century, the general assumption was that she had been heavily involved in the construction of the fortification bearing her name. It was believed to have been erected in the 900s to protect Denmark against German expansion – a misconception bolstered by a myriad of fantastic historical anecdotes.

In most accounts, Gorm the Old is portrayed as a lazy, good-for-nothing ruler who cared little about defending Denmark against its primary enemy. Conversely, Thyra is most often described as decisive, and heavily invested in the protection of her country. According to one tale, she mobilised all able-bodied men and women in Schleswig, equipped them with shovels and set them to work on the construction of her fortress, which supposedly took three years. In another version, godlike creatures came to her aid and within a single night built the several-metre-high walls of the Dannevirke.

According to one of the most fully drawn stories, however, Thyra is portrayed as a crafty and clever woman who manages to con the German emperor. The story goes that Denmark had fallen under German rule sometime in the 900s, and the Danes were obliged to pay taxes to the German emperor. The emperor, who loved beautiful women, had heard Thyra was the fairest of them all and decided he wanted to marry her. He set out to lure her away from Gorm, but the lustful emperor was instead lured into a trap by the crafty Danish queen. German envoys were sent to Schleswig to ask for her hand in marriage. She demanded time to think about it – three years to be exact – and requested that, during this time, the Danes be exempt from taxation. The emperor acquiesced, but insisted upon a number of hostages to use as leverage. Thyra used the tax credit to finance the building of the Dannevirke, and when, at the appointed time, the German emperor came to retrieve his bride, she received him with her army, heavily fortified behind the thick walls of the Dannevirke. When he discovered he had been duped, the enraged emperor killed the hostages in an act of revenge, a sacrifice Queen Thyra was apparently willing to pay for the freedom of her countrymen.

These tales had a wide appeal in the highly nationalistic Denmark of the 1860s. Archaeological data, however, tells an entirely different story. Since ancient times, several fortifications have apparently been built around the town of Schleswig, but there is no evidence of any construction taking place during Gorm and Thyra's reign. It therefore seems unlikely that the fabled first queen of the Danes was the master builder of the fortress bearing her name.

What we know today is that in the 800s a King Godfred used the Dannevirke to launch a successful offensive against the Franks. The fortification's first real glory days, however, were some 200 years after Thyra's death, under King Valdemar (1157–82) and his son King Knud VI (1182–1202), the latter credited with completing the construction of the fortress.

Father and son built the massive fortress with its four-kilometre-long defensive wall mostly to showcase Denmark's military might. The wall itself, made from approximately 20 million red bricks, fired in ovens on site, was staggering in scale, standing seven metres tall. Atop the wall, palisades were constructed, with deep moats in front. It took twenty years to finish the structure, but once completed it had already been rendered obsolete and was never, until 1864, that is, used to defend Denmark. One theory suggests that the edifice was intended to serve more as a psychological deterrent staving off attacks from potential enemies than as an actual fortification. A more likely explanation proffered by experts, however, is that the structure was abandoned upon completion in the late 1100s because it proved ineffective against attacks by heavy cavalry, which were the predominant strike force of armies at the time. With heavy cavalry, an army could easily outflank the position or penetrate the defensive wall in a frontal attack.

The ultimate irony here is that contemporary military strategists seemed oblivious to the very weakness that had rendered the Dannevirke useless as a defensive structure as early as the Middle Ages.

Several battles were fought in the area, near or on the old, collapsed earthworks during the First Schleswig War, but no measures were taken to restore the fortification or put it into operation as an actual defence work – the Schleswig-Holstein rebellion was crushed here simply because it erupted on the border between Schleswig and Holstein. However, as so many of the major battles took place here, the name became lodged in the Danish mindset as the country's first and foremost defensive work. Famous Danish poet and troubadour of Danish nationalism N. F. S. Grundtvig said that as a consequence the fort became part of 'the collective Danish imagination'. Journalist and editor Carl Ploug wrote in an editorial in his newspaper the *Fatherland*, chief organ for the National Liberal Party, that although the Prussians won one of the battles in 1848, it was a costly victory: 'Down Thyra's decaying walls ran the blood of our enemy the German. He paid a costly price for slaying our men.'

Thus in the wake of the First Schleswig War, the Dannevirke seemed imperceptibly to become synonymous with Denmark's new military glory, in turn prompting a revival of the old myths about Thyra and her fortress, which were readily accepted and promulgated by the vast majority of Danes, not excepting influential public figures from the political arena and academia.

Still, it would be ten years before Denmark began repairing and strengthening the old, decaying structure. Up until 1861, it was widely agreed that Denmark's defence was best carried out from its flank positions at Dybbøl and Fredericia, the latter located further to the north on the east coast of the Jutland peninsula. However, not much had been done in terms of modernising and strengthening these positions either. In 1861 appropriations were finally provided for such efforts. The Dannevirke was included and, against all sound military thinking, it received most of the funding. As a result the flank positions at Dybbøl and Fredericia were barely functional when the war broke out in the winter of 1864.

The myth of the Dannevirke as an invincible stronghold had become so entrenched in the Danish psyche that both politicians and the populace at large demanded Denmark be defended from this position. As previously noted, however, the Dannevirke was compromised in the winter when its flanks froze. In addition a defensive depth of at least 100,000 troops was required for a sufficient defence of the long line – a far cry from the number of men Denmark was able to mobilise at the time.

Curiously, while the National Liberals, who came into power in 1857, had adopted an aggressive foreign policy, they had done little to boost the shrunken army. Military spending had not been increased, nor had any measures been taken to train more officers and improve the military capabilities of the men already on active duty. Denmark's peacetime army comprised 12,000 men, but could, or so it was believed, be increased to 55,000 men in wartime. However, even after calling up older reservists, the Danish army comprised only 40,000 troops at the outbreak of war on 1 February. Apparently it had not occurred to anyone that a war could come on suddenly – not to mention in the midst of winter – leaving Denmark precious little time to expand and strengthen its forces. The Danish war cabinet was completely unprepared for a winter campaign, and when the threat of war loomed in the autumn of 1863, it was still believed they had several months to prepare. Why Denmark so stubbornly held on to the belief that the campaign would not begin until summer is an interesting question. Most likely they were influenced by the fact that the First Schleswig War had taken place at the height of summer. Several contemporary paintings depicting battle scenes from this war are not only rich in romantic and patriotic associations, but also suggest the fighting was like a summer picnic, Danish soldiers in crisp red-and-white uniforms easily crushing their enemy under clear sunny skies.

The fateful decision to rely on the Dannevirke as the main defensive line was thus heavily influenced by the previous conflict. By the time the Second Schleswig War broke out there were only enough barracks for 2,000 men at the Dannevirke, and thousands had to be quartered in farms and villages in the surrounding area. Another 10,000 men were forced to sleep in the open during one of the worst winters in the country's history. Troops expected to confront the two massive armies heading towards Denmark were thus, rather than strengthened and invigorated, weakened by poor accommodation. Incredibly, the poor planning at the root of the men's misery was all due to an unfortunate mix of fable, myth, past glory and misunderstanding of Prussian strategy.

18

The first days

Prussian military strategists, who had familiarised themselves with the strengths and weaknesses of the Dannevirke, were, unlike their opponent, ready for war; a detailed grand plan of attack on Denmark had been formulated as early as 1862. This plan later became the foundation of the famous Schlieffen Plan used by the Germans at the outbreak of the First World War. The main objective of the Schlieffen Plan was to ensure victory in a two-front-war against France and Russia. Accordingly, rather than attempt a first strike at Russia, German troops would push forward through Belgium and Holland, attacking the French flanks, then encircle, entrap and crush the French armies in one fast, crippling blow. The plan, which was masterminded by Count von Schlieffen in 1905 and finalised by Helmuth von Moltke in 1913–14, gave the Germans the advantage in the first phase of the First World War.

It was no mere coincidence that the job of finalising the plan fell to von Moltke: he had been the architect of the Prussian victories against Austria in 1866 and France in 1870–71, and the pincer movement practically ran in the Moltke family. Helmuth von Moltke was named after his uncle – now known as Helmuth von Moltke the Elder. Moltke the Elder was in his time one of Europe's leading military-strategic minds and it was he who had devised the pincer attack plan against Denmark which lay ready in a drawer when war broke out in 1864.

For Denmark, their bitter defeat was made even harder to swallow because Moltke had received his military training in Denmark, and so the Danes felt he owed his allegiance to their country, not to Prussia.

Moltke entered the military academy in Copenhagen at the tender age of twelve. By eighteen, he was a second lieutenant. The young lieutenant soon proved a military talent with ambitions to match, leading him to apply for permission to join the larger Prussian army, where, he felt, he could achieve a better and more professional military education. In his application letter to Frederik VII, he wrote, 'I hope I will some day be able to put the skills I acquire in the Prussian army to good use for his Highness and Denmark.'

Moltke, however, chose to stay in the Prussian army, where he trained under the legendary strategist Carl von Clausewitz. Nonetheless, despite his keen military instincts, Moltke's rise through the military ranks was not nearly as swift as the rapid pincer attacks he was later to develop; rather he rose slowly and steadily, becoming major general in 1856 and, the following year, chief of the Prussian general staff.

It was in his capacity as chief of staff that he masterminded the attack plan against Denmark. Moltke of course took advantage of his unique insights into Denmark's military strengths and weaknesses. Realising that Denmark was a strong sea power, he knew it would require a surprise attack to bring the country to its knees. The Danish fleet would allow the troops to remain entrenched in their flank positions (Fredericia and Dybbøl in Jutland), from where they could

Years before the war, Prussian chief of staff, Helmuth von Moltke
the Elder (left) had devised a pincer attack plan against Denmark.
However, eighty-year-old, slightly senile Prussian Field Marshall
Friedrich von Wrangel (right), was unable to act as swiftly as the
plan demanded and he failed to secure a quick German victory.

be shipped to the islands of Als and Fyn in case those original positions could not be held. Once the Danes were on Als and Fyn, Prussia had little, if any chance at all, of engaging them in further battle, as the Prussian fleet was still relatively weak.

Moltke therefore reasoned that Prussia's best chance of securing a quick victory would be through a rapid attack against Denmark at the Dannevirke during the winter, when the position's flanks were likely frozen over. Von Moltke was so convinced his plan would make short work of the inferior Danish army, he boldly announced that it would take no more than a day or two to beat the Danes – a boast that would come back to haunt him.

During the early stages of the war, however, everything played out as he had envisioned. It was winter and the flanks of the Dannevirke were indeed frozen over. Moltke had made one tactical error, though: he was directing the war efforts from his desk in Berlin, and had not taken into consideration that the geriatric commander, the eighty-year-old Field Marshal Friedrich von Wrangel, was too old for the kind of quick action his plan required. As a younger man, Wrangel had been, if not a military genius, then certainly a highly qualified leader. He began his combat career as an officer during the Napoleonic Wars. Later, as a major general, he had been responsible for crushing the 1848 uprising in Berlin. Wrangel had also been in command during the first campaign against Denmark in 1848–50. Fourteen years later, when war broke out against Denmark, Wrangel was the only one of a handful of senior officers in the Prussian army with actual combat experience and the only candidate Austria would accept as commander for the campaign. Wrangel, however, soon proved to be not just senior but long past his military expiration date. He had become senile and was, as it turned out, even more eccentric than de Meza. Once a relatively fair-minded soldier with an impeccably erect military bearing, by 1864 Wrangel had become a shrivelled, grumpy old man who took a dislike to people on sight, particularly his staff officers. In fact, according to the Prince of Hohenlohe-Ingelfingen, who participated in the war's first phase, Wrangel trusted no one but Major von Stiehle, who consequently became known as the only man who could talk to *der Alte* (the old man), as Wrangel was nicknamed. With everyone else he was curt and usually turned down all requests with a brusque 'no'. Hohenlohe-Ingelfingen writes in his memoirs:

> Wrangel had the strange notion that when in the field you should not use pen and paper. 'I write with my sword and will not tolerate pen and paper,' he declared. So the daily briefing was turned into a farce, where we all stood in a circle around the marshal, holding our sword in one hand and our headgear in the other. The marshal was the only one not holding a sword. He would be dressed in an open-necked tunic and pass from one officer to the next, expecting everyone to recite from memory what was happening in his area of responsibility. Then we were given orders, which we were supposed to memorise. Some, however, had hidden pen and paper and when the marshal was not looking quickly wrote down his orders; they were like little schoolboys cheating on a test.

Berlin, however, was not amused by Wrangel's eccentricities, nor thrilled by his inability to act quickly and decisively. Wrangel, perhaps because of his senility, could not muster the resolve to carry out Moltke's planned pincer attack plan on the Danish position within the first few days of the campaign. Instead, he was wracked with indecision and lost precious time, giving the Danish army room to manoeuvre; Moltke became anxious that a nightmarish protracted conflict would ensue.

The first day, however, went according to plan: during the dark morning hours of 1 February, massive columns of men, horses, artillery and transport wagons set off towards the Danish front, crossing the Eider River at three different points at 7 a.m. Prince Friedrich Karl's army corps moved towards the left flank of the Danish position. The Austrian army corps moved towards the centre, and close on its heels was the Prussian 3rd Army Corps with orders to move on the right flank.

In terms of actual combat, it was a relatively quiet day. The Danish outpost line had been given orders to pull back to the Dannevirke in step with the advancing enemy. There was a little skirmish action here and there, and a handful of Danish men were taken prisoner. A few were lightly wounded, and Prussian hussars pursued a small detail of Danish dragoons. A brief volley was also exchanged at the Eckernförde inlet between Prussian field batteries and the armoured schooner *Esben Snarre* and the screw corvette *Thor*. The two Danish ships, however, quickly steamed out of reach of the Prussian batteries, as they feared a repeat of the 1848 disaster, when the Danish ship-of-the-line *Christian VIII*, set ablaze by Prussian shelling, had exploded. Because the ship had sailed too deep into the Eckernförde inlet, it had run aground and been unable to escape enemy fire.

The following day saw more action. Prince Friedrich Karl received orders on 2 February to move forward to one of the

Dannevirke's outworks, at the village of Kokkendorf, with his corps of 10,000 men. Kokkendorf was located a few kilometres south of the Dannevirke, and the Prussians expected to meet resistance here and certainly some attempt to halt their further advance. But the Kokkendorf was not ready for combat, so the Danish command had decided to abandon it. Thus when Prince Friedrich Karl and his men reached the works, they found nothing but an empty, decaying defensive edifice. Prince Friedrich Karl immediately decided to push forward to test the depth of the Danish defence further to the north at Mysunde, a small ferry-town situated on the tip of a peninsula that extended far into the Schlei inlet, where the Danes had a bridgehead position comprising two redoubts. Capturing Mysunde would be a strategic windfall, as a crossing could easily be achieved on this bridge, which spanned the narrowest part of the inlet. The position therefore lent itself well for the planned flank attack. Prince Friedrich Karl believed it would be a simple manoeuvre to take the southern redoubts. Considering the size of his army corps and his battery of guns – sixty-four field cannon in total – the prince's reasoning was sound enough. The Danish 3rd and 18th Regiments occupying the redoubts numbered only about 2,500 men, and they had but twenty operable guns with which to engage the enemy.

Without further ado, the prince issued the order for a forced march from Kokkendorf to Mysunde. At 10 a.m. the Prussian advance troops made contact with the Danish outposts, three companies comprising 400 men posted less than a kilometre south of the Mysunde bridgehead position. There was an exchange of fire, during which the troops at the Danish outposts were driven back into the redoubts. The Prussian core force was then able to move forward and line up their artillery for attack.

Fortunately for the Danes a dense fog had come down, reducing visibility for the Prussian gunners, who could barely discern the outline of the Danish position. Most of their shells passed over the redoubts, exploding behind them and setting fire to the village situated there. Visibility was, of course, equally poor for the Danish gunners and many of their shells missed their targets as well. The fog, however, also provided great cover, allowing a handful of Prussian companies to creep up close to the redoubts. Once within thirty metres of the position, they crouched behind mounds of dirt from unfinished trenches and were able to fire directly into the redoubts. Four Danish gunners were killed within a few minutes near one gun platform.

The shelling continued and cannon fire roared across the battleground for several hours. In the early afternoon, Prince Friedrich Karl began forming up assault columns. The timing was right to attempt an assault.

Records provide us with a few snapshots of how nerve-wracking the fighting – even minor skirmishes – was for those involved, especially for the men who had never seen combat before.

The 26-year-old Danish lieutenant P. E. M. Ramsing gave the following account in a letter to his parents:

> The enemy had moved to within a 100 paces of the redoubts and proceeded to pick off our men one by one. For the first time in my life I got a sense of what it is like to be trapped in a hailstorm of bullets. They whizzed past me at close range, cannonballs tore through the air, shells exploded

everywhere, and flames burst from one house after another in the village behind our line. I will not deny that I felt rather anxious, especially as I was on horseback next to the general, thus an easy target, with no doubt that many of the bullets whizzing by were meant for me.

Ramsing was ordered to rally the battalion posted behind the redoubt and bring them into the fray:

Bullets ricocheted off the road I was riding on, and shells, apparently aimed at the houses here, exploded all around me, but my job was to assemble the scattered details of men. Most looked frightened and at a loss, being as they were quite without commanding officers. I seemed to have left the redoubts at the critical point when the enemy began amassing their assault troops and I needed to gather as many men as possible, so we could be ready to receive them.

While Ramsing was rallying the troops, Private Henriksen's detachment was ordered to move from Redoubt A to Redoubt B, which the Prussians were preparing to storm. Henriksen wrote in his memoirs:

I have to confess I was anything but brave – but we had to go: in wave-like movements we ran across the frozen ground, bullets spraying all around, two were lightly wounded and the second we passed through the palisade gate, a massive shell exploded nearby, perforating a sack of biscuits and showering us in a downpour of crumbs and shell fragments, but, as far as we know, no one was hurt. A barrel of schnapps had been hit a few minutes earlier, and the precious nectar ran freshly on to the ground … at the corner of the powder magazine, we saw a lieutenant with half a face, his brain spattered on the wall of the magazine and ground.

It was no less intense on the Prussian side. One Prussian private, J. Bubbe, described in a memoir the move towards Mysunde and his experience of being in a combat zone for the first time:

> When we climbed the hill [in front of the Danish position] at Mysunde, it seemed as if someone had pulled the veil of fog from our eyes. Two incredibly loud crashing sounds could be heard. A few seconds later, two massive shells flew overhead, exploding right behind us, fragments piercing the air. One fragment fell near the first rank, covering them in dirt. Unused to combat, we were completely unprepared for the sheer noise of battle, so we all ducked as if on cue when we heard the terrible piercing shrieks from the 84-pound cannon.

Encamped with his detachment behind one of the earthworks near the redoubts was another Prussian, Captain Carl Bunge. Bunge and his men anxiously followed the trajectory of each shell flying overhead, seeming to strike closer and closer. Bunge wrote in his diary:

> First a platoon leader was seriously wounded by an exploding shell, then one of the company's drummers was hit and immediately thereafter a massive shell struck a detachment

of hussars close by. It was terrible to witness. All the horses reared up on their hind legs. The smoke and snow stirred up by the shell formed a thick cloud and we could make out the shapes of men and horses running confusedly about, and hear their screaming. Three horses died, many were wounded. Two hussars were seriously wounded, one lightly while the other, a very young commanding officer, had been hit directly in the abdomen by the shell. One leg had been completely torn off; the other was still attached but only by a few threads of flesh. His intestines hung from his gut, his horse was on the ground with a broken back, and the officer soon drew his last breath.

The Prussian aide-de-camp Christopher von Tiedemann arrived shortly thereafter and saw the badly mangled body of the young officer as it was being carried away. Tiedemann had come to observe the fighting:

> The fog had lifted, but it was raining; it felt like a spray of cold needles and the visibility was still poor. Approximately a thousand paces from the village of Kossel I saw a dead gunner in the road. A stray shell had struck him. As I got closer to the battleground, I passed more dead on the ground and saw many wounded being carried off on stretchers. I spotted the body of a gunner, half of whose face had been shot off, saw the body of an officer from the Red Hussars' regiment, who had received a cannonball in his abdomen. I climbed a hill to get a better view, but because of the rain I could still only make out the contours of the Danish redoubts.

Tiedemann was not the only spectator here: a large group of people, mostly local residents, had gathered on the ridge of the hill to watch the Prussian attack on the Danish position. One onlooker later remembered:

We saw the infantry push forward towards the redoubts. We believe we heard the signal to attack and the men's cheering. With great anticipation and excitement we followed their movement. The Prussian guns suddenly ceased firing; meanwhile we saw several flashing lights from the Danish redoubts. The Prussian infantry pulled back and then moved forward again. The Danish cannon fired again and the infantry disappeared from sight.

After receiving many rounds of devastating case-shot as well as fierce volleys from the Danish riflemen, the Prussian infantry pulled back to regroup for another attack. However, as soon as this was in motion, they were pounded by cannon again, and rather than push forward the several thousand Prussians fell to the ground, trying to avoid being hit by the deadly shots. One private remembered the failed attack:

Our lieutenant colonel had just ordered 'right shoulder arms' and 'left face' when he was shot in the right cheek and fell off his horse. In his stead stepped our most senior captain, Captain Kawisnisky. We proceeded to move 200–300 paces forward towards the redoubts, some in skirmishing order, some in close columns. Once there we fell to the ground, and remained lying down on the frozen earth for three hours. Whenever the gun smoke and fog lifted, we were able to take out an enemy gunner. There was a constant hail of enemy bullets, some bouncing off the ground like rubber balls, some hitting targets and piercing flesh, our men falling left and right. For hours we were forced to listen to the wounded's screaming without being able to do anything, and the roar of our own and the enemy's cannon was deafening.

After an almost eight-hour-long battle, a disappointed and discouraged Prince Friedrich Karl decided that the Danish defence was too strong and that he would have to give up trying to take the position. Despite their superior strength, the Prussian batteries had been no match for the Danish guns, which continued their vigorous firing undaunted throughout the day. Finally, as the day waned, the prince gave the order to withdraw.

The first day of actual fighting had been a complete failure for Prussia. The news of the blunder was received with great dismay in the Prussian camp. In his diary, Crown Prince Friedrich (not to be confused with Prince Friedrich Karl), wrote that 'it would be wrong to blame Friedrich Karl as forward reconnaissance was important but underestimating the enemy is foolhardy. Furthermore, I think Berlin is making the same foolish mistake. The Danish defence is in fact substantial.'

In his memoirs Prince Hohenlohe-Ingelfingen provides a vivid description of how the news was received by the Prussian general staff: 'Field Marshal Wrangel appeared in person with a somewhat dejected expression ... for several minutes everyone seemed stunned and appalled.'

No doubt their dismay would have turned to horror had they actually witnessed the battleground after the fighting had stopped. Danish private Peder Madsen, moving with the 16th Regiment towards Mysunde just as the fighting petered out, described the scene in a letter to his wife, Hansine:

> I have never seen a bloody battlefield before and hope no Danish soldier will ever have to witness the kind of misery I have seen today. When we neared Mysunde, carts carrying wounded and dying men met us. Some were full of mutilated bodies. It sent chills down my back to think that by tomorrow this could be our fate. There were many Prussians among the dead. In most carts the bodies were piled so high that a rope had been tied around them to keep them from tumbling off. Still some of the overburdened carts tipped over, spilling their cargo in the ditch, and from all sides we heard the wailing of the wounded. The poor residents [of the local village] greeted us in tears. The sky was crimson above their cottages. Everything they owned was going up in smoke. In the morning I saw a man who stumbled about on the ground where his house used to be; moreover the poor man had to stand by while our dragoons butchered his four geese, which was all he had left in the world. As we were driven by great hunger, we ate the lot. I will not share more of our wretchedness with you as I hope it will be all over soon, so I can come home and tell you the rest in person.

The dead and wounded totalled 400; the number of casualties was about the same on each side. The war had begun in earnest.

The following day there were skirmishes near the villages of Jagel and Ober-Selk as well as a fierce battle over Kongshøj, a strategically important outpost. In these battles more than 900 men were wounded or killed, twice the number incurred at Mysunde.

On the third day of fighting – 3 February – the Austrian troops saw their first combat in the campaign. There was to be a constant rivalry between the two German allies regarding who had the most success on the battlefield. It had begun badly for the Prussians; and the Austrians, eager to prove their superiority, were all the more set on succeeding with their operation, which was to beat back the outposts in the centre of the Danes' main line. The redoubts constructed there, as at Bustrup a few kilometres south, were practically small forts in their own right. A frontal assault on these works would be too costly. Still, it was important that the allied forces consolidate their position here in order to be able to support the major assault with a diversionary attack and to repel a possible Danish sortie.

As darkness fell, the Austrians had achieved their objective and more. They had in fact managed to push the Danes back further than expected. Lively exchanges had taken place all day. In some villages it had come to farm-to-farm fighting and by day's end most villages were ablaze or razed to the ground. The Austrian forces, which were larger and better led than the Danes, had gathered momentum and, buoyed by their early success, they pressed on, finally engaging the Danes in a larger battle over the highest point on the Dybbøl front, Kongshøj, which, as previously noted, had strategic significance, providing not only an excellent overview of the redoubts, but a great position for the emplacement of artillery.

It had been a magnificent day for the Austrians and a significant positional gain had been made. Apart from Mysunde, the Danes were now driven back into their positions. And that evening the two opponents were so close they were able to see each other's campfires along the entire extended line of the front. The soldiers encamped close to Kongshøj could also hear the moaning of the wounded, who had been left in no-man's-land between the hill and the Danish redoubts. Many of the wounded were Hungarians. A considerable number of the wounded froze to death before a truce, under which they could be collected, was negotiated the next day.

By the evening of 3 February the Danes had won a battle at Mysunde, the Austrians another. Both had incurred considerable casualties and neither battle had been decisive. Despite the Austrian victory, there was no denying that the Danes proved equal in strength. What had also become clear was that the two armies were both very much of the old school, employing similar tactics: advances in column formation; fixed bayonets, officers first; loud cheers and death-defying action – a mode of warfare that resulted in relatively high casualty rates even in smaller skirmishes.

With the occupation of the ground in front of the centre of the line, the allied armies had secured a strategically strong position. Still, morale was high in the Danish army. They had put up a brave fight and felt prepared to conduct a large-scale offensive. The cold temperatures were, however, beginning to wear them down. A majority were bivouacking in the open. And the men put on standby were chilled to the bone. They were particularly miserable on the night of 3 February, as a freezing rain had begun pouring down, drenching the men and turning them into human icicles. Food rations were meagre and unreliable; some men were already close to starvation. Under these circumstances, it was questionable for how long the Danish troops, however spirited their determination, could hold. The Danish soldier Mathias Storck wrote to his parents:

> These days of battle are incredibly exhausting; none of us have been to bed, so to speak. We are worn out and can barely keep our eyes open. To be on sentry duty, standing up for twenty-four very wet hours straight, is taxing. All we want is one night of rest so we can recover our strength, which is beginning to fail.

On the fourth day, the Danish commander-in-chief General de Meza actually overcame his fear of cold temperatures, mounted a horse and rode out to the twelve redoubts closest to the town of Schleswig to inspect the condition of the works and the men. He was not at all pleased by what he saw.

The massive and extended defensive line was manned by far too few troops. The men were freezing and ill-fed. De Meza quickly realised that their relatively good cheer would probably not be able to stand up to the harsh challenges awaiting them. He noted that the supply lines were not working properly, that there were no reserves available and that there was a severe shortage of horses – the commander of the cavalry, Hegermann-Lindencrone, needed 2,000 more.

De Meza understood what the enemy was planning and had a clear idea of how it would unfold. With large forces the Prussians would attack on the left flank by the Schlei, where, except for the redoubts at Mysunde, the Danes had no real defence. He envisioned the strike tearing the Danish defence asunder, the Prussians moving north and cutting off any possibility of retreat, leaving the Danish forces at the Dannevirke encircled with only two options open to them: surrender or a fight to the finish. Either way the war would be lost.

However, when on the evening of 3 February a general staff meeting had been held in the Prussian camp, Field Marshal von Wrangel had in fact presented this plan of attack: Prince Friedrich Karl was to cross the Schlei with his army corps, not at Mysunde, as originally planned, but further to the east where they would cross to the villages of Cappeln and Arnis on the northern bank. The water here, though, was not frozen over, so boats had to be procured. The plan was for Prince Friedrich Karl to occupy the north bank of the Schlei, and from there launch a major attack. To mislead and distract the Danes from the death blow they were about to receive, the plan was for the allied troops to conduct a diversionary attack on the centre position of the line, where the Danish defence was strongest.

Prince Friedrich Karl was, however, like his commander, not one to forge ahead at great speed. His defeat at Mysunde had seriously shaken his resolve, and like many of his officers he was anxious about crossing the Schlei in open boats. If the Danes caught on to their plan, his men would be target-practice for the enemy. He therefore requested more time to meticulously plan the attack. His request was granted and the attack was postponed from the 4th to the 6th.

As it turned out, this was a tactical error. The Danes used the delay to prepare a daring escape that completely derailed Moltke's brilliantly devised flank attack. De Meza and his chief of staff, Colonel H. A. Kauffmann, were in agreement: abandoning the Dannevirke was the only way to save the Danish army from complete annihilation. The plan was that the Danish troops – comprising 40,000 men, 10,000 horses, hundreds of munitions and transport wagons, 121 field guns and 33 of the 175 heavier fixed cannon – should withdraw from the Dannevirke under cover of darkness, without alerting the enemy stationed only a few hundred paces away.

On the evening of 5 February, the Prussians began preparing for the crossing of the Schlei, which was to take place on 6 February at 4 a.m. Prince Friedrich Karl was to lead the advance, and it had been decided that the area east of Mysunde was so sparsely filled by Danish troops, artillery and defensive works that a successful crossing was almost guaranteed. But planning it in theory, based on military maps, was one thing; another was carrying it out in the dead of night – and a very cold one at that. First the troops had to move soundlessly down narrow and icy country roads in unfamiliar terrain to the crossing point, where they had to wait for the appointed time in the freezing cold without being able to build fires, as that would alert the enemy. Further, as the supply wagons were too heavy to make it across the icy roads, the men also had to go without food. The most dangerous leg of the journey would of course be the actual crossing in the open rowing boats. If discovered by the Danish gunners on the opposite bank, the men would be sitting ducks; diving into the icy water for cover was not an option for the many who could not swim.

Prussian accounts of the first hours of this operation reveal how terrified most of the men were. In his memoirs, J. Bubbe, who participated in the Mysunde attack, delivers a vivid description of the mood among the men at this time:

There is a tendency to discredit the trials and tribulations of the men participating in the campaign against Denmark. It has been said that since circumstances were ideal, that is, the area of operations was relatively small, the provisions excellent, and our numbers superior, success was inevitable. Be that as it may, I think if the armchair generals slugging beer in the comfort of cosy restaurants had been exposed to the actual conditions during those first days of February, they would have taken a less disdainful position. We were never given a chance to rest. [Waiting to cross the Shlei] those who still had energy left paced back and forth in the hard snow to keep warm; others rested in the shrubbery, lying close together. Others were munching on whatever scraps of food they had left in their knapsacks and some were talking quietly, mostly in whispers. Spirits were low all round. Our captain noticed and gathered some of his men in a circle around him and reminded us of Frederick the Great's advice to his officers, namely to cheer them up with encouraging stories before a battle.

According to Bubbe, the captain proceeded to tell the story of the Prussian crossing of the Rhine on 14 January 1814, during the Napoleonic Wars. 'Your fathers,' the captain began, 'were only dressed in canvas trousers. They had no coats and yet they were able to accomplish great things. We are warmly dressed and are well cared for in terms of provisions. So, think of your fathers and their great deeds at this difficult time. What they did, you can do too. Cheer up!'

However, it was not just the men who feared the crossing. One of the most experienced Prussian officers in the army, 41-year-old Gottberg von Jena, shuddered at the thought of what might befall them in the tiny rowing boats out on open water, which, if the Danes opened fire on them, would splinter like kindling wood. Thus, though an experienced and

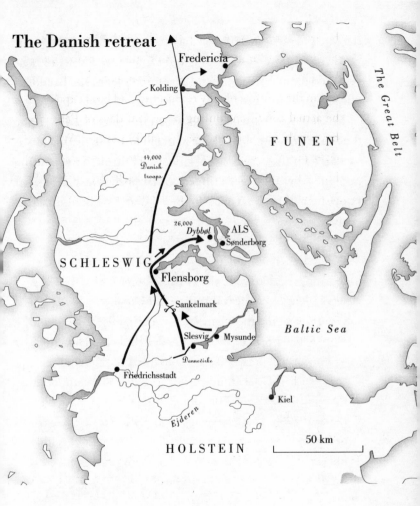

The Danish retreat

accomplished soldier, Gottberg had grave misgivings about the operation. He had trained as an officer in Potsdam and Berlin, but at twenty-five he had joined the Austrian army and participated in Austrian campaigns in Italy in 1848–9 and in 1859 during the French–Italian war. In the first campaign he was seriously wounded during an assault, hit by a bullet in the hip. He recuperated well and distinguished himself in the Battle of Solferino as a strong and capable leader. In 1861 he returned to the Prussian army as commander of the Brandenburg Regiment.

In a letter to his wife he described the hours leading up to the Schlei crossing. He relates in detail how exhausting it was to march for the better part of 5 February through the pouring rain and how they had camped in the open. He also lets her know he had been selected to lead the first wave of attack at Arnis:

> We marched as quietly as we could. At three in the morning we arrived at the crossing point where the boats were waiting ... all was quiet on the opposite shore, but I had to assume the enemy was waiting to receive us and would open fire once we had boarded the boats. Honestly, I had no wish to drown like a rat out there. So, I left my overcoat and my viklers [military leggings] on shore, thinking that since I was a good swimmer, I could make it back once the boat got hit. I was freezing, had not eaten anything for hours and was anything but thrilled. Still, I acted calmly like a man expecting the worst, yet hoping against all odds to survive. The men got in the boats ...

Just as they were about to push out from shore, an orderly came running down the shoreline shouting, 'The Danes have retreated!'

19

The funeral procession

As news of the impending retreat was communicated first to the Danish field officers and then to the men, tears of despair and anger welled up in their eyes. No one had expected this turn of events; rather, everyone had expected orders to prepare for a major enemy assault. Now, instead, they found themselves faced with the daunting task of an all-out evacuation. Everyone from the highest to the lowest rank dejectedly set to work on the enormous task of readying the army for the night-time withdrawal. Chief of Staff Kauffmann was seen with tears running down his cheeks, and Adjutant H. Holbøll of the 8th Brigade wrote to his parents that it was 'a dark moment when the order to withdraw had come. I saw officers as well as non-commissioned officers cry as we left the fortifications in which we had put so much faith.'

At first most of the men doubted the validity of the order. Withdraw? Why? Had they lost some major battle at another section of the front that no one had told them about? Or had they been surrounded? There had to be a good reason. Perhaps the enemy had received vast reinforcements? Some critical event, they felt sure, had to be behind this sudden decision to flee like cowards in the dead of night.

There was much confusion and the air was thick with

unanswered questions, the men becoming increasingly anxious about their situation. But as the officers were equally ignorant and uncertain as to what had prompted the change of plans, they were unable to provide satisfying answers; all anybody knew was that the retreat was to be launched as quickly as possible.

The decision to evacuate had been made the previous night during a war council at the Prinzenpalais – the Prince's Palace, just outside the town of Schleswig. Following orders from de Meza, Chief of Staff Kauffmann had summoned all generals with the exception of Lieutenant General Gerlach, as he was out on an inspection tour of the works. At about 6 p.m., eleven high-ranking officers were seated around a large table in the Danish headquarters. These proud and combat-seasoned soldiers were, like tragic Shakespearean heroes, tasked with answering a fateful question: to stay or leave? In effect: should they remain and fight to the end or save the Danish army?

They did not have long to languish in doubt. Time was of the essence, and they had but a few precious hours in which to make their decision. Throughout the meeting, de Meza remained steadfast in his belief that an evacuation was their only option. The Danish army, woefully inadequate as it was, could not defend the long defensive line of the Dannevirke against a major attack launched by their far superior enemy, de Meza argued, and so the only way to keep the Danish army intact, which was a key part of his brief, was to immediately abandon the position.

While the allied forces of Austria and Prussia had gone to war with a detailed plan of attack, Denmark had prepared none. And the Danish War Ministry's instructions to the Danish commander-in-chief were anything but clear. In fact they were fraught with ambiguities. While de Meza had been given full authority to make the necessary judgement calls in the field, he had at the same time been given two irreconcilable objectives: first, keep the army and its strike force intact, if necessary by retreating to the flank positions further north at the expense of position guns and other materiel; second, defend the Dannevirke against a major enemy attack.

The confusion regarding what was expected of the Danish army increased further following a visit to the front by the Danish king, Christian IX, and Prime Minister Monrad. While on an inspection tour of the Dannevirke line, Monrad, looking every bit the civilian he was, dressed in leggings and carrying an umbrella to protect his impressive bulk from the rain, shuffled along behind the king and the officers. His apparent lack of military acumen had not prevented him from meddling in the decision-making, however. In an odd conversation with Chief of Staff Kauffmann on the night of 3 February, he had expounded that Denmark would gain international support at upcoming peace talks if they received a large-scale attack at the Dannevirke. According to Kauffmann's memoirs, Monrad had rather callously opined that they could afford to lose a third of the army before retreating to the flank positions.

Kauffmann had tried to explain to the prime minister that losing a third of the men would effectively dissolve the Danish army, but to no avail.

De Meza was aware of Monrad's absurd pronouncement, but during the war council he chose to ignore it and keep to his first instruction of keeping the army intact. In other words, de Meza decided to follow his instincts as a soldier rather than the orders of his militarily ignorant prime minister. 'To prevent the total annihilation of our army and a quick decisive victory for our enemy, we must withdraw,' he contended.

However, as he did not want to make such a momentous decision on his own, he had called the meeting to allow everyone a say in the matter. One by one the assembled officers were asked to weigh in. Most of them – older, grey-haired and sporting impressive bushy moustaches – were prototypes of the archetypal soldier, instilled with values such as duty, honour and a strong sense of patriotism. They were also no-nonsense realists with keen military instincts, like their commander. All had combat experience and a majority had participated in the First Schleswig War fifteen years earlier. It would be by no means easy for any of these proud soldiers to support a decision which to the world, or at least to oblivious Danish civilians, would appear lily-livered and almost certainly provoke outrage.

These were the men who, as Danish historian Johannes Nielsen writes in his seminal *1864 and the Collapse of the European Order*, were fated with 'making one of the most important military decisions in recent history. [A decision that has] left its mark on [Danish] politics and culture for the past 120 years.'

The first to speak was the most senior division general, Hegermann-Lindencrone. He declared himself in support of de Meza's proposition, pointing out that they were in danger of being outflanked. He did, however, advocate a sortie to beat back the most advanced enemy forces before evacuating the line.

An argument ensued. Kauffmann was against a sortie, as it would most likely alert the enemy to their plans and cause them to lose their advantage. After several heated exchanges on this point, though, they reached an agreement: an immediate withdrawal had to be ordered. Only one man was staunchly against the retreat, and that was the artillery chief, General Lüttichau, who stood to lose most of his position guns, as they could not be dismounted and carried away.

In the end, all except Lüttichau signed a protocol committing the Danish army to 'a voluntary, regular retreat to be set in motion the following day, leaving all materiel behind'. The decision was made, the protocol stressed, on the grounds that the position had been deemed impossible to hold.

It had been an emotionally taxing evening for everyone present. Though the generals felt sure they were doing the right thing, most of them hated letting the position go, as Thyra's Fortress was Denmark's pride, her stronghold. It seemed like treason to leave her undefended.

After the other officers had left, Kauffmann and Rosen remained behind to prepare the retreat, an enormous and logistically demanding task. Once alone, the ramifications of their decision struck home and the two men looked at each other aghast. 'What have we done?' Rosen is reported to have exclaimed.

For most of us, the word *retreat* smacks of cowardice and carries many other negative connotations such as weakness, flight, giving up, and more. However, to military experts a well-conducted and timely retreat is considered a triumphant tactical move that requires great military skill. During a retreat the troops are up against heavy odds. First of all, they are usually trying to avoid annihilation by an overwhelming enemy. Secondly, an army in retreat is vulnerable to attacks in the rear; it is considerably harder repulsing an attack when you are moving away from an enemy rather than towards one.

In addition it is difficult to raise and keep morale high among retreating troops, as a retreat promises no glory, only maddening hardships. Further, it requires significant organisational and leadership skills to move large troops and heavy equipment without alerting the enemy.

While it may be easy for the retreating troops to lose sight of the fact that a successful withdrawal is half a victory, the attacking enemy will certainly feel like they have lost half a battle when they discover their opponent has flown the coop. Planning a grand assault only to find that your opponent has vanished in the dead of night, being denied a glorious climax, must be an emasculating experience – the disappointment of which is further compounded by the recognition that a new attack has to be planned from scratch.

There are many examples of successful retreats in military history, some of which were subsequently turned into victories, as they gave the retreating army time to regroup and prepare a new offensive. One example is General George Washington's historic retreat during the American Revolutionary War. Following a string of devastating defeats that culminated in a failed attempt to capture New York City, Washington decided to pull back in order to keep his army intact. Under cover of darkness, he fled with his men. Fortunately for the Americans, the victorious British decided against a pursuit. A few months later, Washington and his well-rested troops were able to beat the numerically superior enemy in a surprise attack at Trenton – the turning point of the war.

One of the most famous successful retreats of modern times is the near-miraculous French–British withdrawal from Dunkirk in 1940. Against heavy odds, most of the allied forces made it safely across the English Channel. By saving the troops, the allies were able to successfully strike back in the war's later phase.

But perhaps the most impressive – although not, ultimately, successful – retreat to date is that of the Nez Perce people, which took place in the north-western United States in 1877. The retreating tribe, comprising 600 men, women and children, managed under the expert leadership of Chief Joseph to escape the pursuing 2,000-strong American army under orders to capture and escort them to a reservation. The Nez Perce people managed to evade their pursuers for 3,000 kilometres before they were overpowered, only 30 kilometres from the Canadian border. Though Chief Joseph was eventually captured, he had managed to make complete fools of the American troops.

When the allied officers discovered that the Danish troops had escaped right under their noses, they were stunned and felt deeply embarrassed and humiliated. Crown Prince Friedrich, who was present at headquarters when Field Marshal von Wrangel received the news of the evacuation, described the moment:

> The sombre excitement that had filled us the night before the attack, in which we expected to suffer great casualties, turned to disappointment when at 8 a.m. this morning we received the news that the Danes had pulled back from Schleswig and were in retreat. We were all in the most miserable of moods. While we should have been thanking God for sparing us much bloodshed, we were embarrassed, as any battle-ready army would be in similar circumstances. We were expecting to launch an assault only to find the enemy gone – we did not even get a chance to size him up.

When one considers the many hardships the Danish soldiers suffered during the retreat, it is almost a pity they could not have been privy to the psychological impact their surprise withdrawal had on their opponent. As the Danes began their thirty-kilometre march (for those marching from the western section of the position, the march would be a staggering sixty kilometres) along icy roads, through a blinding snowstorm, they were completely ignorant of the pressure the Austrian and Prussian forces were under and of how humiliating it would be for their commanders to report back to Berlin that the enemy had managed to escape before they could attack. Their brilliantly devised plan of attack was now practically useless, and Bismarck, who had counted on a quick victory, would come under unprecedented political pressure.

What a surge of pride and energy knowing all this could have given the downtrodden and miserable Danish troops. Instead, they crawled along the frozen roads through heavy, wind-blown snowfalls, feeling as if they carried an entire nation's shame on their shoulders. None of them would ever forget this march.

Before leaving the fortification in the late afternoon on 5 February, the men had to spike the cannon and destroy carriages to prevent the enemy from being able to use Danish guns against them. The heavy transport wagons and field artillery were sent ahead, followed by the rest of the army – one unit at a time.

At noon a telegram had been dispatched from headquarters to Copenhagen. It reported that all was relatively quiet on the front; there was no mention of the planned retreat. At dusk another telegram was dispatched; it read:

After having convened a war council yesterday, the commander-in-chief decided to evacuate the Dannevirke before an expected large-scale attack. The army marches to Flensburg tonight.

The telegraph was immediately disconnected to prevent reception of a counter-order from Copenhagen. Shortly hereafter, the long train of men, wagons and horses began to move along the treacherous roads. All troops would eventually convene on the same road to Flensburg. The 4th army division troops, posted on the extreme right flank, faced the hardest trek, as they had to march sixty kilometres before morning. The heavy snow made it exceedingly difficult to press on at the necessary pace. The air temperature was eight degrees Celsius below zero, but taking the wind-chill factor into account, it became a bone-chilling minus twenty–thirty degrees. As the roads were soon trampled into hard sheets of ice, both men and wagons began to slip and slide, slowing the march even further. Wagons would often topple over or slide into ditches, spilling their contents all over the snow and causing even more delays. According to most first-hand accounts, the Danish forces escaped by the skin of their teeth. Private Peder Madsen of the 16th Regiment wrote to his wife, Hansine, shortly after:

The march was so painful, I ache just thinking about it, and I know that if the residents of Sletten [his home community] could have witnessed our retreat from Mysunde to Als, even the most hard-hearted of them would have been moved. And, my dear, if you could have seen us, you would never have been able to forget it as long as you live

– so many exhausted and starving people staggering along, trying desperately to summon their last ounce of strength in order to make it to Als and avoid capture by the enemy.

'It was a terrible march. No one who partook will ever be able to forget it,' wrote Adjutant Holbøll in one of hundreds of almost identical accounts written by soldiers about the retreat.

For every step we took, we slid back one. We were constantly brought to a halt. As we could not see our hands in front of our faces, we bumped into the man ahead of us when he stopped and were immediately thumped in the back by the man behind us … the first hour of the march, however, progressed without stops, but at midnight everything came to a standstill, and for a while we seemed unable to move forward … apparently a convoy of wagons had joined us from a western side road. It had been delayed and was supposed to be in front of our brigade. The wagons carried all sorts of things, from provisions to munitions and medical supplies … waiting in a standing position in the freezing cold was much worse for the men that were marching. They perched in the ditches, though they risked falling asleep and dying from exposure. The officers did everything they could to keep them awake … Finally, at 3 a.m., we were able to move on.

But it was still slow-going. An increasing number of men dropped from exhaustion on the road. Holbøll wrote, 'I heard an officer shouting to his men, "Get up or you will freeze to death or else the enemy will catch up with you and cut you down." But the men were completely dulled and said they would rather freeze to death than carry on. They remained on the ground, and we had to leave them to their fate.'

P. E. M. Ramsing wrote to his parents, 'We marched in this terrible weather; everything was a blur, so to speak. After literally having fallen asleep on my horse several times, I got off and travelled the last couple of kilometres on foot.'

Many suffered hallucinations as a result of extreme fatigue. Private Christian Bredsdorff was one. In a letter home, he said, he 'had been so tired I seemed to lose my mind. But when one of my comrades just wanted to give up, as did many, it seemed to spur me on to see someone in a worse condition than me. I grabbed him by the arm and began telling him a story from my travels abroad, but … just as I was sailing on the lovely Alpine lakes, an abyss opened at my feet, I seemed to have become suddenly paralysed; I could not move neither feet nor lips.

'I think,' continued Bredsdorff, 'that this march must have been like that of the French [retreat from Moscow] in 1812, when the starving troops moved slowly forward, men and horses collapsing from exhaustion; the roads littered with broken vehicles. No singing and no talking, everybody moved in silence.'

The most vivid and detailed description of the march was delivered by Danish war correspondent P. V. Grove, who marched with the men to Als:

I stayed in the town of Schleswig until 11 p.m. and so was towards the rear of the train. The position was still occupied at my departure, but by midnight the last battalions had left and would provide the rear-guard. It was a terrible march. Slowly the open wagons moved forward as in a funeral procession; the men, too, moved slowly and in complete silence. There was no morale-boosting good cheer. The Danish army, the nation's staunch defenders, were bowed by shame as they left the position that they had been charged with guarding. Some horses tripped over a cannon, the men hastened to right both horses and cannon and get them back in the train to minimise the enemy's loot. Suddenly the train came to a halt. Half an hour passed, then an hour, still no movement. Chilled to the bone, I jumped off my wagon to investigate. I ran past the long line of men. One battalion, bored with the wait, had set camp out on the road. With their knapsacks as pillows, the weary men had simply lain down directly on the frozen road and were soon covered in snow. I shouted a few encouragements to them and rushed on. After a mile [7.5km] I discovered the cause of our stopping. A couple of wagons had been overturned, some horses had suffered a fall and a cannon had tumbled into a ditch. Finally the train was on the move again. 'Form up! Form up!' the officers call out. The long column came into formation for a while until there was another stop in our nocturnal funeral procession.

20

Sankelmark

As the last Danish troops were leaving the town of Schleswig at one in the morning, a Prussian officer entered the Dannevirke. He and a bugler had been sent to the Dannevirke by the Austrian general staff to deliver a letter granting the Danes their request for a ceasefire to collect the wounded the following day. The request was of course a ruse meant to assure the opponent that 6 February would be like any other day at the front. The Danish subterfuge, however, nearly failed, as the allied envoys arrived later than expected, shortly after the Danes had evacuated the position. Had the envoys immediately alerted headquarters, a full-blown pursuit could have been set in motion and the retreating Danish troops routed there and then.

The two men had moved cautiously towards the position at around midnight; the bugler had signalled their arrival but all was quiet. The Danish soldiers, who were just then leaving the town of Schleswig a few kilometres to the north, heard the bugler's call and, believing it to be an assault signal, marched off rapidly.

The Prussian officer, confused by the silence, threw all caution to the wind and walked straight into the position, only to find it eerily devoid of life. But he did not raise the alarm. Instead the Prussian negotiator and his bugler continued north; on their way they came upon a group of residents from the town of Schleswig, who informed them that the Danes had evacuated the entire position and were heading north. Later that night, at about 4 a.m., the Schleswig residents were granted an interview with General Goblenz, the Austrian field marshal, at his headquarters in the village of Lottorf. Heavy with sleep and barely dressed, Gablenz met with the excited group. As soon as he understood what was going on, however, he was instantly wide awake and began barking orders left and right. 'A few moments later,' an eyewitness recounted, 'the whole village was in action. In the cold night [we heard] buglers blow to the assembly and saw orderlies run to and fro with orders from General Gablenz.'

Austrian troops soon drew up towards the town of Schleswig, which was in a state of great excitement. Austrian general staff officer Gründorf von Zebegény wrote in his memoirs that the town was 'lit and a festive reception for the Prussian arrival had been prepared. Even though it was very early in the morning … every man, woman and child was up and about. Young girls waved white scarves from candlelit windows, as we rode down the main street.' Schleswig's blue-and-white independence flag had been run up all over town to honour the German soldiers. A majority of the residents in this 'Danish' county seat clearly saw themselves as German and welcomed the Austrian troops as their liberators.

After arriving in town at about 7 a.m., Gablenz had dispatched a light cavalry unit, the Lichtenstein Hussars, to the north for reconnaissance and selected two brigades to pursue the Danish troops. They departed at a few minutes past 8 a.m. The rearguard of the Danish retreat was about two hours' march away. Would it be possible to run it down?

Gründorf von Zebegény, a hussar in the forward squadron, later remembered that:

> the main road from Schleswig to Flensburg, the Danish retreat route, was like a clear sheet of ice … the horses kept slipping and it was an agonising ride. We were terribly impatient and wanted to catch up with the Danish rearguard, which was rumoured to have more than 100 cannon that we were itching to get our hands on and bring back as war trophies. But there was no rushing it, we could only move at a trot.

The Danish rearguard did not have hundreds of cannon, but as the many heavy supply wagons ahead of them often stopped, the train moved at a sluggish pace. The Austrian hussars moved much faster – even at a trot – than the Danish troops.

Adjutant Holbøll of the 8th Brigade, which made up the rearguard, spotted the pursuers at dawn. 'At first light we noticed enemy riders following us at a distance, assessing our retreat,' he wrote. 'When the rearguard made a stop at Helligbæk, the hussars suddenly attacked our convoy of transport wagons. What a spectacle, and what confusion,' he continued. 'Wagons were scattered about, some toppled over. It was as if a massive whirlwind had struck. About fifty Lichtenstein Hussars darted through the rear line … turned wagons over, turned others around and then they disappeared as quickly as they had appeared. Everything happened so fast.'

In their surprise attack, the hussars had managed to take possession of several wagons and three cannon, as well as capturing some of the Danish soldiers who had lagged behind.

They also succeeded in causing so much chaos and mayhem that the retreat was halted for some time. Rather than risk further delays, the Danes decided to leave the rearguard behind to fight the attackers, thereby providing cover for the retreating army. At this point, the Austrians had set up a field battery: first two cannon, then four. A skirmish ensued between Danish infantry and the Austrian artillery and cavalry.

The battle progressed in accordance with old military rulebooks: the cavalry charged, forcing the Danish infantry to form a square from which their raised rifles with fixed bayonets protruded like porcupine quills. The cavalry then fell back to let the artillery open fire, forcing the Danish infantry to break up their formation to avoid the devastating impact a direct artillery strike would have on a packed-in square of infantrymen. Once they were spread out, however, the cavalry charged again, forcing them back in square formation, and so this exhausting death dance continued until the Prussian infantry brigades arrived at 2.30 p.m., at which point one of the war's most intense clashes began. The fighting took place in the wooded terrain between the village of Oeversee and Sankelmark Lake, about ten kilometres south of Flensburg. In the first phase of the skirmish, the Danish 8th Brigade had taken up the fight and were under orders to hold off the pursuers until relieved by the 7th Brigade later in the afternoon. With Austrian troop concentrations growing rapidly, the 7th Brigade would come to face overwhelming odds.

The commander of the Danish 7th Brigade (consisting of the 1st and 2nd Regiments, totalling 3,000 men) was the tough and offensive-minded Colonel Max Müller, who was known to react with unflinching harshness to all kinds of insults. According to a contemporary account:

If anyone treated him with disrespect or made his native land the target of ridicule, he would immediately require an apology or challenge the offender to a duel: 'Pistol, light or heavy sword?' he would ask in all seriousness. He was not gentle with his men either, but set as high standards for them as he did for himself. Still, he was respected and admired by his men, who all looked up to the tall, muscular and sinewy man with the dark brown hair and beard, chiselled features and rigid, uncompromising demeanour.

Max Müller's orders were to halt the Austrian troops' advance and ensure the retreating troops' cover until they reached Flensburg. Müller was delighted with his orders and told General Steinmann, who had passed them on, that 'halting the enemy is not enough, I must attack him'.

An attack was the best form of defence, according to Müller's rulebook, and to this end he was an avid proponent of the bayonet charge. His opponent General Gablenz was of a similar mindset, so the two opposing brigades clashed again and again: hussars lunging towards the Danish troops, who, standing in formation, aimed and fired volleys at the approaching cavalry. Several of the opposing companies met in close combat, clubbing each other with rifle butts, stabbing with bayonets, and some slugging it out with fists.

There was fighting on the open plains near the village of Sankelmark, on the heights of the Flensburg road, in fields, and even in the nearby woods, where the men fought fiercely from tree to tree.

By nightfall, the Danish 1st Regiment was broken and scattered. Max Müller, however, remained undaunted and pushed forward with the 11th Regiment, managing to repel the Austrian

At Sankelmark the battle progressed in accordance with old military rulebooks: the cavalry charged, forcing the Danish infantry to form a square from which their raised rifles with bayonets protruded like porcupine quills.

attackers, who chose not to launch a counter-attack as it was growing dark and the men were exhausted. Like the Danish troops, the Austrians had marched through the night and into the morning. They were hungry, worn out and overwhelmed. By 4 p.m. the fighting had died down. The Danish objective had been achieved: the retreating forces were able to make it safely to Flensburg and beyond. To further safeguard the Danish troops, outpost lines were established around the city.

The Battle of Sankelmark had been fierce, bloody and costly for both sides. A total of 800 dead and wounded lay scattered across the battlefield. The carnage was especially gruesome because both sides had been in a rush to leave the area, so had spent little time collecting the wounded. The Danes pushed on to Flensburg to prepare for an attack there; the Austrians were focused on moving forward as well. Hardly any medics had escorted the troops, there were no field hospitals and only a few doctors with but a modicum of medical supplies. While the battle raged, the Austrians had set up an impromptu dressing station near the combat zone. 'It was quickly over-crowded,' Austrian hussar Gründorf von Zebegény recounts in his memoirs. 'In less than an hour we had more than 20 officers and 300 men to tend to, not counting the 7 officers and 21 men who died in our care.'

As darkness fell, it became bitterly cold, and the need to find warm shelter for the wounded grew desperate. Most were housed in the nearby Oversee Inn. All furniture was removed and the floors strewn with hay to provide comfort. The severely wounded Prince Wilhelm von Württemberg was put in the inn's only bed. 'He was in need of an immediate operation,' Zebegény recalled, 'he had received a particularly serious wound in one foot, which was as dangerous as it was painful. His heel had been smashed up, and with barely any instruments, the brigade's chief surgeon had to try to cut out the damaged bone. There was no chloroform, and Württemberg suffered terribly.'

Local residents were asked to provide wagons for the wounded, and one eyewitness remembered that the day after the battle 'a train of creaking, swaying wagons carrying wounded moved down the road [towards the town of Schleswig]. The wounded suffered greatly in the cold, and the roughly built wagons offered little cushioning against the bumpy roads. Their moans and screams of pain filled the air on this winter day.'

The locals were also asked to help tend the wounded and cart off the dead. A group of people from the predominantly Danish city of Flensburg arrived the day after to help collect the dead and wounded. They retrieved about sixty dead Danish soldiers. The men and women involved in the humanitarian efforts milled about on the battlefield, but so too did looters eager to relieve the dead and dying of their valuables. Every now and then you could hear a shot ring out from a desperate wounded man trying to protect his belongings. To prevent further raiding the battlefield was cordoned off, though not to the amassing Austrian troops arriving from the south.

One of these Austrian soldiers, Private Wilhelm Varenkamp, visited the battlefield and described it in a letter to his parents:

We saw more than a hundred dead still lying in the snow. They had been suffering on the ground for twenty-four hours or longer, praying for their lives until they mercifully died from exposure. It was a terrible sight. I cannot get over how many horses, cannon and knapsacks there were; massive heaps had been gathered. Many men had already been buried.

In addition to losses incurred in the Battle of Sankelmark, the retreat had cost the Danish army 175 men who deserted (all men from Schleswig serving in the Danish army), 135 who were captured and 10 who died of exposure. At the Dannevirke, 135 pieces of ordnance were lost, many of which could have been saved had the available railway been used (only a miscommunication prevented this), together with 136,000 rounds of ammunition, half a ton of gunpowder, 6,500 shovels and pickaxes, several tons of bread and 50 wounded, who remained in hospitals in Flensburg.

On balance these losses cannot be considered extreme considering the nature and scale of the operation. The Danish army was intact and now divided into three fully manned divisions. One was deployed to Kolding and another to the position in Fredericia, with the main force to be stationed at Dybbøl.

Everyone was exhausted and morale was at an all-time low, however. In a letter to his parents, Lieutenant Storch briefly noted, 'We are in a most miserable condition, yet tasked with defending Dybbøl to the last man.'

21

The scapegoat

'This morning a vicious rumour spread that the Dannevirke had been abandoned,' Hans Christian Andersen noted in his diary on the evening of 6 February. From the street came the sound of loud angry voices, the thunder of cavalry hoof beats and the rhythmical fall of the Royal Life Guards' marching feet. Thyra's Fortress was believed to be impregnable, so news of the retreat was causing uproar. The residents of Copenhagen were bitterly disappointed and felt betrayed by king and cabinet. People began gathering on street corners to voice their outrage, many with wild gestures and angry shouts. As the day wore on, the situation intensified as more and more angry citizens took to the streets and began amassing outside Parliament and the royal palace. The Life Guards Infantry were soon ordered to patrol the city and prevent what looked like the beginnings of a riot.

Initially no one believed there could be any truth to the outrageous rumours. 'I was very upset that people were spreading this kind of news,' Hans Christian Andersen wrote. 'I drifted about all morning, hearing all kinds of rumours.' A writer friend joined Andersen on his walk, and together they headed for the Ministry of War, where Andersen spoke 'with several officers, who all attested to the fact that the Dannevirke had indeed been abandoned'. Some claimed that it had happened after a six-hour battle, others that there had been only a little action before they pulled back. A wine merchant named Münster joined in, stating that all the rumours were false and that, according to a recent dispatch, Napoleon and Great Britain had asked both the allied forces and the Danish army to pull out of the war.

None the wiser, Hans Christian Andersen continued his stroll through the streets of Copenhagen in search of a reliable source who could tell him what had happened. Someone somewhere was bound to know:

… in late afternoon while visiting the editorial offices of *Dagbladet* I learned the truth: General de Meza and his men had left the position without a fight. It all seemed like a bad dream. What was not supposed to have happened actually had. Dark, heavy mood. Dined with the honourable Mrs Neergaard this evening. After dinner we heard loud cheering and whistling from her street, where a huge crowd had gathered.

Later that night, escorted by a footman for safety, Andersen visited several of his friends. All of them were disheartened and indignant. 'I felt terribly anxious; in the streets there was singing and shouting.' Apparently the guardsmen and hussars patrolling the streets did not make Andersen feel any safer.

The following day he wrote:

Last night fourteen police officers and several people were wounded. Six were taken to barber Staal's, and one was hospitalised. I was in low spirits and felt ill at ease. I passed crowds of armed civilians as I went home through Vin-destræde Street. Still, everything seemed calm. There was one incident, though, where apparently some people had spat on the little princesses through the window of their carriage, and the Crown prince was deathly pale in church. The honourable Mrs Bille chose to walk home, as she was simply too scared to take a carriage.

The angry Copenhageners were infuriated, believing that their German-speaking king and the cabinet had negotiated a withdrawal with Bismarck behind everyone's back. They demanded a new cabinet and the dismissal of General de Meza.

The king and the prime minister, who had hurriedly left the front on 5 February, were still in Sønderborg when news of the retreat reached them. They immediately left for Flens-burg, where a composed and equable de Meza met them. Neither fatigue nor the scathing telegram he had just received from his minister of war, who furiously refused to recognise the abandonment of the Dannevirke, seemed to have ruffled his feathers. In the telegram Lundbye had stressed that he 'still believed the Dannevirke could be defended'. Quite an about-turn, as while they could still hear the roar of cannon from the action at Sankelmark both Lundbye and Monrad had given de Meza their full support. Monrad had in fact telegraphed the Ministry of War notifying them of his view that very day.

Once back in Copenhagen the following day, 7 February, Monrad was, however, shocked by the people's outrage, and quickly decided to abdicate any responsibility and deny prior knowledge of the withdrawal. On the boat back to Copen-hagen, he had, as he later recalled, been convinced he had the power to manage public opinion. But upon arrival, when the angry crowds shouted 'Traitor!' at him, he immediately sensed that swaying the public in his favour would be near impossible. The media launched a strident campaign against him and the king also came under attack. 'It is unimaginable that a retreat of this nature would have been conducted during the reign of Frederik VII,' the outraged editor of the *Fatherland* wrote.

Monrad realised that the situation was fast becoming critical: riots were likely to erupt and his own and the king's political survival was also at stake unless he changed course. Within a few hours of his arrival in Copenhagen, he gave a speech in Parliament cleansing himself of any involvement in the retreat. He appeared a little nervous at first but soon gained confidence and proceeded to give a remarkable performance, displaying all of his oratorical prowess. About the abandonment of the Dannevirke, he said, 'I cannot account for it' – extraordinary words from a man who, only a day earlier, had given his full support to the army commander and recognised that under the circumstances a retreat was the right decision.

After Monrad had assured both himself and Parliament of his blamelessness, he went on to support Lundbye's decision to recall de Meza and hold him accountable for the retreat. The eccentric General de Meza provided, Monrad soon discovered, the perfect scapegoat.

While in Copenhagen a lynch-mob atmosphere was created around de Meza, the Prussian military strategist Helmuth von Moltke was full of praise for de Meza's tactical leadership and acknowledged him as a brilliant and worthy adversary. Moltke even commended him publicly: 'The valiant General de Meza was strong enough to make the right decision, despite the public outcry from Copenhagen, where he is now being sacrificed.' The Prussian field officers shared Moltke's views: 'We were shamefully outmanoeuvred,' General von Goeben later confirmed.

The retreat caused exactly the kind of confusion and indecision in the Prussian–Austrian camp that Moltke had predicted would arise if a quick victory were not achieved. What to do?

There was general agreement among the Austrian and Prussian officers that the Danish positions at Dybbøl and Fredericia were too strong to be stormed. Memories of the humiliating defeat at Fredericia in the First Schleswig War lingered, and no one was eager to repeat this experience. Moreover, even if it had been possible to take Dybbøl by storm, a final victory was by no means a given, since the Danish troops would be able to retreat to the islands of Als and Fyn, where they would be protected by the Danish fleet. Further complicating the situation for the Prussians was the fact that they had gone to war on the pretext of forcing Denmark to comply with the 1852 London Protocol, and with an agreement in place stipulating that there would be no encroachment on Danish sovereign territory. The Prussian and Austrian forces could therefore not move beyond the Kongeåen River, which formed the natural border between the Duchy of Schleswig and the Kingdom of Denmark.

Austria was particularly anxious about violating the international agreement, fearing that it would prompt Great Britain and France to enter the war on the side of Denmark.

Denmark, however, was oblivious to its new position of strength. The country was too caught up in the debacle surrounding the retreat. Both de Meza and Chief of Staff

Kauffmann had been recalled to Copenhagen for an investigation. The subsequent hearings, conducted by a special inquiry board, lasted through most of February, a time that would have been better spent on initiating a peace conference – in which Denmark at this juncture would have probably been able to obtain very favourable terms – or on strategic military planning.

'De Meza and Kauffmann are sorely missed out here, as there is no real order under the current command,' wrote Major Ernst Schau to his wife, Friede, soon after their arrival at Dybbøl. De Meza, however, was relieved of his post as commander-in-chief of the Danish army and never returned to Dybbøl. The brilliant 'comeback soldier' was finally forced to confront defeat at the hands of political forces. The public feeling against him, however, had subsided somewhat by mid February. Moderate voices in the press were even suggesting that it had been a sensible tactical retreat, given the circumstances. King Christian IX was of the same opinion and advocated sending de Meza back to the front line as commander-in-chief of the Danish army. Minister Lundbye, however, perceived de Meza's actions as a personal affront. He was furious with de Meza for pulling back the troops without consulting him first. But what infuriated him even more was de Meza's threat to publish the heated correspondence which had taken place between them. This threat had been 'written in an unseemly tone, considering the general's subordinate position', Lundbye complained in a meeting with the king on 24 February.

In a desperate attempt to get de Meza reinstalled as commander-in-chief of the Danish army, the king vetoed his dismissal. Acting like a petulant child, Lundbye retaliated by threatening to resign, and received full support from the other cabinet ministers. No doubt Monrad for his part acted on the assumption that if de Meza took the fall for the unpopular withdrawal, the prime minister would stand clear in the public opinion. Thus, despite direct requests for de Meza's return from the Danish generals in the field, the king had no recourse but to accept his war minister's demand.

De Meza was relieved of his command and the weak-willed and more conservative General Gerlach installed in his place – a promotion he accepted with much reluctance.

De Meza had been aware that the retreat could cost him his command, but felt secure in the knowledge that abandoning the Dannevirke was the right decision. His thoughts regarding the retreat, contained in the following letter to his niece, were written as the withdrawal was still under way on 6 February:

> We are now departing the Dannevirke – more a romantic notion than a strong fortification – to our customary flank positions. It would have been irresponsible to try to hold the position considering the unfavourable weather conditions as well as many other unfavourable circumstances that our good-natured men, despite their brave perseverance, could not have withstood – half an army against two full armies would, even had our situation been different, have resulted in five days of harsh fighting, after which we would have to, with bleeding hearts and of our own volition – not fleeing – adopt the most favourable course of action – that's right, Fabius! [Fabius Cunctator was a Roman commander famed for successful delaying tactics

The theater of war: Dybbøl and Als

against Hannibal during the Second Punic War in 218–201 BCE.] Regardless of how the affected excitement may wish to present it, we have been brought into this delicate situation by the Eider cabinet. But a man must pay the price of his convictions.

While the Danes were busy waging war against their own in Copenhagen, a Prussian cavalry regiment pursuing a detail of Danish dragoons, crossed the border to the Danish kingdom on 18 February and proceeded to occupy the town of Kolding, which the Danes surrendered without a fight. The Prussian cavalry officers were not aware of breaching any international agreement.

As news of the occupation and infringement of the Danish borders came out, everyone seemed to hold their breath: in Berlin a high level of nervous anxiety spread among the cabinet ministers. The responsible field officers were severely reprimanded by Bismarck, who knew that if Great Britain and France now felt pressured to support Denmark, he would be in dire straits. If the Prussians were forced out of the war, he would be dismissed, the king would have to abdicate and Prussia would be plunged into a political crisis.

Great Britain and France initially reacted with as much outrage as Bismarck had feared. British and French envoys in Berlin summoned him to sombre meetings. Though Bismarck quickly intuited that their harsh words were nothing but inconsequential verbiage, King Wilhelm, fearing an imminent disaster, was deeply distraught.

As it turned out, Great Britain and France could not agree on a joint course of action and soon moderated their position on the infringement. Both countries, though particularly

France, were apprehensive about getting involved as they feared this relatively minor, and insignificant, Danish conflict could trigger a large-scale war and upset the current balance of power. Moreover, Denmark's passive surrender of Kolding slackened the French–British resolve to uphold the agreement regarding Denmark proper. Bismarck perceived this development as a tacit carte blanche to wage war against *all* of Denmark. Subsequently, he managed to convince a reluctant Austria to let their troops push further north. And as he had predicted, both Britain and France stood impassively by as large Austrian forces began crossing the Kongeåen River. This was a rude awakening for Denmark – their last ray of hope for international support extinguished.

Part Three

THE SIEGE

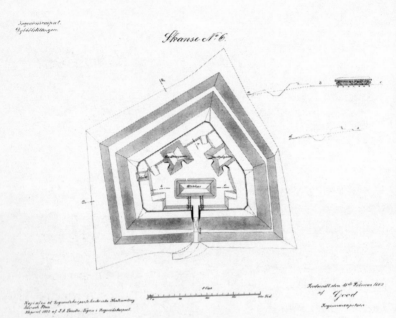

Drawing of a Danish redoubt (Redoubt 6)

22

Bloodshed

The Danish soldiers arriving at Dybbøl in February were not impressed by the two-kilometre defensive line, which appeared puny compared to the Dannevirke's extensive one. Dybbøl was a field fortification, situated on the crest of a hill, and since much of it was dug in, it was not much to look at on first inspection. There were only ten earthworks, which seemed inconsequential compared with the massive and elevated entrenchments (totalling twenty-seven redoubts) at the Dannevirke. Furthermore, since the bulk of the Danish military budget had been used to expand and strengthen the Dannevirke, the maintenance of Dybbøl had been gravely neglected.

'If the Prussians had known how weak we were, they might well have pursued our troops straight to Sønderborg [on Als]. One rapid strike and the position would have been theirs. They clearly believed us much stronger than we actually were,' wrote Artillery Lieutenant Castenskjold in his memoirs.

The sorry state of the redoubts was, however, soon to change. In the following weeks, during which the Prussians remained indecisive, more than 20,000 Danish soldiers got to work on expanding Dybbøl, building trenches and strengthening walls, ramparts and parapets. It was excruciatingly hard work, but the end result was a substantially stronger defensive structure.

The Prussians were losing precious time arguing over whether to attack Dybbøl, Fredericia or to go ahead and occupy the entire peninsula of Jutland. Following the latter course, some believed, would force the Danes out of their entrenchments and bring them into action on open ground, where the numerically superior Prussian army would have the advantage. In the open they could potentially strike a decisive blow against the Danes and win the war within a few hours, as was the original intent. Conversely, as long as the Danes remained strongly entrenched, victory at Dybbøl, if secured, was bound to require a long siege and would almost certainly be costly in terms of loss of life. Nonetheless, the Prussian command finally decided that an attack on Dybbøl was the only option: the fortifications there would offer the Danes a great launching point for a surprise rear attack on Prussian troops advancing into northern Jutland, and so it was necessary first to neutralise Dybbøl. But the Prussians were slow to concentrate forces there, and according to many war historians the Danes could in all likelihood have launched a decisive assault at this time. The Danish army command, however, was paralysed by the ongoing hearings against de Meza in Copenhagen. And as General Gerlach proved a poor substitute for his resolute and militarily astute predecessor, the initiative remained with the enemy.

The prospect of having to attack the entrenched position at Dybbøl, however, was not welcomed with open arms by the Prussian general staff, or by Prince Friedrich Karl, who had been put in charge of 'Operation Dybbøl' (in effect relieving the geriatric Wrangel of his duties as commander-in-chief).

Everyone realised that to secure victory a long siege would be necessary. The lesson from Mysunde had been clear: launching an impulsive frontal attack would likely end in a fiasco. But preparations for a siege operation involved time-consuming and strenuous work: there would be the digging of trenches (not only the main parallel trenches, but also the myriad zigzags of the communications trenches that would connect them all) in front of the Danish line, the heavy guns that had to be dragged up to the line for the systematic bom-bardment of the Danish position, and finally all the logistics involved in feeding the army during the operation.

Chief of Staff Blumenthal found the order to dig trenches an outrage. Blumenthal was not, he snorted, 'a gopher but a soldier'. The siege preparations were summarily delayed and except for a few clashes between patrols and one major skir-mish on 22 February, which the Danes lost, forcing them to pull back their outpost line, nothing of real consequence took place on the front until the beginning of March.

Though the Danish picket line had been pulled back, it was still at this time several kilometres in front of the fortification. Once the Prussians had their batteries placed on Broager by 15 March, they began bombarding the Danish position, but the Danes proved equal in strength and returned fire energetically by day. The damages incurred by the Prussian shelling were painstakingly repaired every night so they could be ready to receive another round of Prussian shelling the following day. On a surprise visit from King Christian IX and Minister of War Lundbye on the evening of 22 March, the men were com-mended for their relentless efforts, praise that did much to drum up morale among the troops.

The king's presence in the redoubts particularly boosted

While the Prussians were indecisive in February, more than
20,000 Danish soldiers were expanding and strengthening their
earthworks at Dybbøl and readying them for battle.

the men's spirits. The mood on the Prussian side, on the other
hand, was somewhat lacklustre, and Berlin was incensed by
the seeming impotence of the Prussian command. The Prussian general Manteuffel tried to spur Prince Friedrich Karl
into action with a letter in which he noted that:

> the eyes of the world are upon your Highness and your
> laurels must be earned at Dybbøl … Your Royal Highness
> must soon take Dybbøl by assault … if you postpone much
> longer, you will cast doubt on your ability to act decisively
> … the reputation of the Prussian army, and by extension the
> Prussian king, throughout Europe rests upon [you]. Should
> it require much bloodshed, so be it, and blood should be
> spilled by all from the highest ranking officer to the bugler.

The prominent and influential general Albrecht von Stosch
was particularly impatient. In a letter to a friend, he wrote, 'I'm
very displeased with Prince Friedrich Karl. After fifty years of

peace the Prussian state needs a good baptism by fire ... I would like to see the prince take both Dybbøl and Als ... during an assault much blood will be shed, but so it is with the history of man as with the land we toil over: only by our blood is it nourished.'

On 17 March, Prince Friedrich Karl finally managed to throw a noose around his enemy. Fighting had erupted in the villages of Dybbøl and Ragebøl, at the foot of Dybbøl Hill, a few kilometres west of the entrenchments. The Danes had sent a regiment of 1,500 men to clear out the enemy from the Ragebøl woods, but the Prussians responded quickly by sending in a large force with orders to take both villages, since they were important Danish defensive outposts.

The villages were fiercely contested and the battle was of the same intensity as the battles of Mysunde, Ober-Selk, Kongshøj and Sankelmark. In the end it came down to street fighting, with shells exploding all the while among the men. As one account notes:

> One especially gruesome moment occurred when a shell hit a Jäger [a type of German light infantryman tradition-ally deployed as scouts or skirmishers] and a Dane in the midst of hand-to-hand combat in a narrow village street. The two bodies were blown to atoms, and everyone around them was inundated with bodily matter: flesh, brains and intestines, so much so that they had to wipe their eyes to regain sight. Lieutenant Thiele, who had been lightly wounded in the calf, found bits and pieces of flesh on his coat the following day ... all that remained of the Jäger were his head and upper body, and of the Dane only his legs were still intact.

Yet, while the intensity of the battle was comparable to earlier engagements, the relative weakness of the Danish rifles was starting to become all too evident. In open terrain the Danish muzzle-loader could do little against the rapid Prussian breech-loader. 'The superiority of our needle guns made it impossible for the Danes to consolidate a victory, since as soon as they had gained a foothold in an area they immediately had to pull back because they did not stand a chance against our crossfire,' noted Prussian private Bubbe, who participated in the fighting that day.

On 17 March the Danish forces lost 153 dead, 253 wounded and 257 captured. The Prussians lost 33 dead and 105 wounded – a third of the Danish losses. The villages of Ragebøl and Dybbøl were nothing but smouldering ruins, and a fretful night awaited the homeless residents. Bubbe and his unit, camping near what was once the village of Dybbøl, got little sleep, as 'the night through you could hear the moaning and screaming of the wounded and dying nearby. When we took pity on the suffering men and tried to find them, we bumped into dead bodies everywhere and the smell of fire and blood permeated the air. It was disgusting.'

Having finally secured this, if not momentous then certainly significant, victory, things began to look up for Prince Friedrich Karl. The enemy was entrenched and he had occupied much of the terrain in front of their line. And while the Danes still held trenches 300 metres out from their own line and had a 600-metre picket line, it was obvious that Friedrich Karl had now not only noosed his enemy, but tightened the rope and was hoping to kick away the bucket from under him by the end of March. To achieve this objective, plans to make a crossing to Als and launch a large-scale rear attack were subsequently set in motion. The prince and his senior officers had chosen the widest part of the Sound of Als for the crossing, as it was assumed the Danes would not expect an attack here. And indeed, Danish troop concentrations were sparse on the northern side of Als.

Once again, however, the weather intervened. A magnificent storm rolled in just as they were getting ready to cross and the operation was called off.

Unlike earlier, though, the inclement weather was a blessing in disguise for the Prussians and quite unfortunate for the Danes, as the Danish general staff had long known about the Prussian plans. The many Prussian landing drills conducted in Nybøl Bay had alerted the Danes, who had immediately begun concentrating troops in the area and had also lined up several battleships along the coast of Als.

In spite of grave setbacks the Danes were not ready to back down just yet. They still had plenty of fight in them, which became apparent on 28 March when the Prussians launched an attack on the Dybbøl position in an attempt to secure some of the ground in front of the redoubts for the construction of their first siege trench. The attack failed. For a few days the Danes regained their confidence, beginning to believe that though the odds were stacked heavily against them, they might win this war after all. British war correspondent Edward Dicey commented:

> The officers were in the highest spirits. Every acquaintance I met came up and shook my hand until my arm began aching. Everyone was in good cheer; smiling and laughing broadly … the effect of the victory has been most favourable to the Danish army. It has raised the spirits of

the soldiers, who had been depressed by the capture of Avn-Bierg and Dybbøl village, and given them the well-founded impression that, with even a small force like their own, the position of Dybbøl may be successfully defended for a lengthened period.

It would not be long, however, before their luck ran out. Once the Prussians had given up on attacking from Als, they hunkered down and prepared for a lengthy war of attrition. The siege of Dybbøl was about to begin. On 2 April the Prussians commenced the digging of trenches and parallels. Constructing the web of zigzagging communication trenches and parallels that would eventually position the Prussians less than 200 metres from the Danish line was painstaking work. Siege batteries were placed along the Danish line, including all the cannon originally intended to have crossed the Sound of Als. Once this work was completed, the Prussians planned on launching a massive siege bombardment. The objective was to inflict as much damage as possible, including razing Sønderborg, silencing the Danish cannon and crushing the morale of the Danish troops. In short, Prince Friedrich Karl and his generals aimed to create an Armageddon.

Berlin was growing more and more impatient, however. Bismarck and his generals wanted their 'bloodshed' and they wanted it now: Prussia's role as a great European power hung in the balance. And as Prince Friedrich Karl knew only too well, his own reputation was as much at risk as Prussia's political status, so he decided to throw caution to the wind, set sail and drown any reservations in the sweat of their battle preparations in order to push for a large-scale all-out attack. If Berlin wanted a sea of blood, then that is what he would give them.

23

The bombardment

On 2 April the Prussians commenced a massive bombardment of Sønderborg. The heavy shelling, which took the residents by complete surprise, was primarily a diversionary tactic, as the Prussians were still considering a crossing to Als at this time. Frustrated, though, by the storm that forced them to call off the crossing, the Prussians opted to continue their relentless shelling of Sønderborg. Within a few days, much of the town had been razed.

There is no accurate account of how many civilian lives were lost during the bombardment, but British war correspondent Edward Dicey guessed it to be between fifty and a hundred people. The suffering of the inhabitants of Sønderborg is, however, well documented. Seaman Jens Christian Jensen and his comrades were in Sønderborg on the first day of the bombardment and witnessed a shell score a direct hit on the roof of a two-storeyed building. The impact of the explosion was so violent it caused the outer walls of the building to collapse. Jens Christian and his friends charged upstairs to the smashed top-floor flat, where they found 'a young woman lying dead across a crib with a whimpering infant spattered with its mother's blood but unharmed. The child was taken to a neighbour, who also took care of the mother's body.'

The Prussians had opened heavy fire on the entrenchments at Dybbøl, too, and the roar of cannon was overwhelming. The Prussian shelling became heavier as the days wore on. In the beginning the Danes were able to respond with will and vigour, causing much grief to the enemy, who also endured long, gruelling days on the front. In a letter to his parents, one Prussian gunner wrote that the early hours of 1 April were especially terrifying:

It rained as much as skies can, it was pitch-black, and I could not see my own hand. The road was almost impassable. One wagon toppled, another sank down in the mud to its axle and became stuck in a seemingly bottomless pit of silt ... We men were also kneep-deep in the heavy clay soil, and then there was an unexpectedly vigorous return fire from Redoubt VI and also from V, VIII and IX. The enemy's bullets leaped in front of, behind and above our battery. Our position was damaged in several places; the wall by no. 6 cannon was completely smashed. Private Hardow was wounded in the shoulder and carried off ... though we had our caps pulled down over our heads, there was a constant buzzing in our ears, rendering us almost deaf. Our chief gunner suffered the same affliction and finally the battery commander had to communicate with him in writing ... a gunner from no. 1 cannon [was] killed on the spot by an enemy shell. Another gunner lost both his arms.

In the first week of April the Prussians trained all guns on the Danish positions and quickly gained superiority as the Danish resistance drowned in their rain of destruction. All hope of being able to make a stand against their opponent, which the triumphant 28 March battle had kindled, was soon extinguished and life in the Danish trenches was fast becoming the Armageddon Prince Friedrich Karl had envisioned.

The redoubts on the left flank were falling into ruin. Embrasures were smashed. Palisades were shot away and the traverses collapsed. In Redoubt II a twelve-pound cannon was dismounted on 11 April. In Redoubt III the powder magazine was badly hit, and in Redoubt IV the blockhouse caught fire and a cannon was dismounted. In Redoubt V one door to the powder magazine had been cut to ribbons, the concrete panel of the other door cracked and a cannon rendered useless.

Redoubt VI had taken the heaviest fire and was severely damaged. This was the largest of the redoubts and had been nicknamed the Malakoff of the North by the Prussians. (Malakoff was the name of the main fortification in Sevastopol.) J. P. Hansen, a private in the 16th Regiment, recalled that:

> there was nothing left but a heap of rubble. Terraces had collapsed, gun platforms and the cannon had to be dug out every day ... there were almost no ordnance left which were still operable. Palisades were shattered and scattered about in the trenches, the drawbridge was so badly damaged, you could only cross it with greatest caution. The blockhouse inside, with its twelve-inch Pomeranian log roof, topped with dirt and sandbags, was destroyed many days ago.

Dybbøl Mill, which had somehow remained intact throughout the increasingly heavy shelling, was finally destroyed on 10 April by a direct hit. The Prussians cheered; the Danes were crestfallen. Splendidly white, the stoic edifice had towered over the landscape, stubbornly refusing to bow to the enemy, and had undoubtedly been viewed, whether consciously or unconsciously, by the Danish soldiers as a symbol of their own perseverance. Now, as it slumped to the ground, like a large grey bird with clipped wings, the Danish troops felt as if they too had had their wings clipped. The decisive shot had been fired by Premier-Lieutenant Millies from the no. 5 Prussian battery. Taking down the mill earned him 20 rixdollars, and after the war he was decorated for his excellent marksmanship.

During the night of 10 April there was the usual amount of outpost fighting in the strip of no-man's-land separating the two opposing lines – the Prussian entrenchments by this point were two parallels deep. Prussian troops advanced on Redoubts IV and V with the objective of forcing the Danish outpost line further back and taking their rifle-pits. The Danish men posted in these redoubts believed for a few frightful moments that the time had come for the long-expected grand assault. The alarm signal was raised – again. As they noticed a perceptible intensification of the Prussian shelling, more than 10,000 Danish soldiers were readied for battle in the cold morning air of the 11th. Approximately 4,000 shells fell on the positions that day.

'At daybreak on 11 April, the shelling increased in intensity at the Sundeved, so we thought the enemy had some operation in mind,' wrote one lieutenant to his brother in a letter, which continues:

Suddenly an orderly appears, announcing, 'I am here to inform you that the enemy is launching a grand assault' … all at once the whole staff was on the go, the horses were saddled while we got dressed and then on we went in full gallop through Sønderborg towards Sundeved. But our haste did little good; we arrived too late to make a difference. As soon as the enemy discovered we still had plenty of fight in us, they turned tail and began pounding us with more shells – worse than before.

On his way back, the adrenalin rush that had accompanied the sudden, intense action slowly subsided; the lieutenant drew in a deep, calming breath while looking out over the front:

The blue-grey smoke from the cannon wafted in thick plumes over the crest of Dybbøl Hill; near the sound there was a stirring of life in the camps, the men were going about their morning ritual, coffee was being boiled and the men huddled around campfires to warm up, others gathered in groups with mugs of freshly brewed hot coffee. Some of the units were moving back to Als. As these regiments moved down the road, rifles and uniform brass buttons shimmering in the sun, they looked like a shiny ribbon fluttering slightly in a breeze. On my left was the almost burnt-out town of Sønderborg, quiet and deserted, though from the northern section you could see coils of smoke rise from a few chimneys; apparently some people had decided to defy the enemy's fire, at least for a while, and stay in their homes.

It was on 11 April that Danish minister of war Lundbye informed his commander-in-chief, Gerlach, that 'Dybbøl was to be held at all costs'. Private Niels Larsen, one of the doomed soldiers we met in the first part of this book when he moved into the entrenchments with the 22nd Regiment on 17 April, wrote in a letter to his wife on 11 April that 'it would be so wonderful for me to come home soon, so we could enjoy our children whom I miss so much – your devoted husband, Niels Larsen'.

At the Prussian headquarters in the town of Gråsten, meanwhile, Prince Friedrich Karl was busy planning the assault on Dybbøl with his staff. The second parallel trench, recently dug, was 500 metres from the Danish line, but was it close enough to launch an assault from this distance? Or should they dig a third parallel even closer to the enemy's position? Most of the superior officers present agreed it was too risky to launch an attack from the current parallel, but the prince was under enormous pressure from Berlin and a date was therefore set, not for the construction of a third parallel, but for an attack: 14 April at 10 a.m. Assured that his uncle King Wilhelm I would be pleased and relieved that they were finally taking decisive action, the prince immediately dispatched a telegram to Berlin.

24

Seven long days

It is in fact seven more days, rather than three, before the Prussians are ready to storm the Danish positions. For both sides the days between 11 and 17 April are long and exhausting. The Danes are as eager for the moment of confrontation as the Prussians. The siege bombardment saps the energy of everyone involved: the relentless roar of the cannon, the uncertainty, the intolerably high danger of being killed by gunfire or shelling, and the utter discomfort of the trenches, are wearing them down. The Danish soldiers find it particularly stressful that they are unable to strike back and defend themselves. Whether crouching in the damp trenches or on duty in the redoubts, they are sitting ducks for the enemy fire. But both sides are under heavy strain.

On Tuesday 12 April a messenger arrives at the Prussian headquarters with a letter from King Wilhelm I to his nephew Prince Friedrich Karl, urging him to be patient. Though eager for a quick victory, the king is also aware that rushing things could result in a fiasco with catastrophic consequences. The Prussian army's reputation could be severely tarnished, his own position put in danger, and a political crisis made almost inevitable.

The king expresses specific concerns over the feasibility of successfully storming the position from the second parallel, 500 metres from the Danish line, a distance he believes to be too great. 'You will find it difficult to rout the enemy from that distance, as you may not get your timing right,' he writes, and relates a cautionary tale from the Napoleonic Wars about the Duke of Wellington's Spanish campaign. Though successful and eventually leading to Napoleon's defeat at Waterloo, Wellington, wrote the king, learned the hard way 'that you can only be sure – even with an overwhelming force – of capturing a fortification if you can launch your assault without having to cross a wide stretch of open terrain'. The king therefore advises his nephew to dig closer to the Danish line before attempting an assault.

The prince is relieved, as he had been very uncomfortable with the plan to attack from their current position. In his diary he writes:

> No one is happier than I to be governed not by political concern but, instead, by military prudence. The men were relieved to be attacking from a closer parallel – even my unruly officers General Manstein, Colonel Hartman and Major Krohn were so pleased they gave a cry of joy, as they had all feared that the operation could not succeed from our current positions.

Plans for the construction of a new parallel trench closer to the enemy line – preferably right under their noses – are formulated. Before construction can begin, however, another section of no-man's-land has to be cleared of the Danish infantrymen still holding the outpost line in the rifle-pits in front of the redoubts. It is decided that the remaining strip of no-man's-land, all but a few hundred metres, is to be taken the following night. To support this operation, the bombardment is intensified. On 12 April, 4,800 shells are fired into the entrenchment. Two Danish officers and twenty-seven men are killed, while seventy-one are wounded – another hundred of General Gerlach's men lost.

Our English war correspondent Edward Dicey reports that 'the object of the Prussian army is to make every man feel that at no time and in no place is he safe from destruction ... an object that has been pretty well attained. There is not a field or house or hollow where shells have not fallen ... the casualties of each day are as great as those in a serious engagement, and constitute no slight loss for so small an army.'

On the morning of Wednesday 13 April, a young eighteen-year-old officer sails into Høruphav and later describes his first impressions of Dybbøl:

We saw the batteries playing at Gammelmark: the white puffs of smoke preceding the boom of the cannon came at regular intervals and following the terrible precision of each volley a dark cloud of muddy dirt rose from the Dybbøl entrenchments. The hill looked bleak and charred, the mill scorched and the redoubts appeared quiet and dark – deserted.

This young officer, Wilhelm Dinesen, who would later father one of Denmark's most renowned writers, Karen Blixen, was born into a family with a rich military tradition and aristocratic aspirations. He was named after his father, an officer and landowner as well as a great adventurer. As a young man, his father had travelled far and wide, volunteering for duty in

several wars, notably France's colonial war in Algeria in 1837.
During the First Schleswig War, the by then decorated officer
commanded the no. 5 battery and participated in many of the
conflict's major battles at Bov, Ullerup, Isted and Mysunde in
1850. Dinesen junior remembered:

> During the cold winter nights at the family's manor in
> Jutland, as we children sat with mother in the living room,
> a big fire roaring in the fireplace, the wind howling in
> the chimney, rattling the windows and making the turret
> shutters squeak and moan at every gust, my father would
> sometimes be engaged in conversation with another of the
> area's landowners in the room next to us. He would pace up
> and down while explaining in detail about [officers] Hel-
> gesen, Krog and Krabbe, and about Bov, Ullerup and the
> Dannevirke – and we would all be listening. And when
> my father had concluded his account … he would some-
> times walk brusquely past me and poke me in the side and
> merrily predict, 'You will probably also be at the Danne-
> virke some day.'

Though he had inherited his father's love of adventure, the
young Dinesen had a troubled relationship with his father, who
was a taciturn and headstrong man. When he talked about
the war, however, his son would listen intently and formed
highly romantic and unrealistic mental pictures of what war
was like. Concepts such as honour, glory and courage loomed
large in his imagination of war, which he came to see as the
stage upon which a man proved his character. Throughout
his childhood, he desperately wanted, in one respect at least,
to be like his father: a formidable and heroic soldier. Now, on

Eighteen-year-old Lieutenant
Wilhelm Dinesen was the youngest
and one of the bravest officers
in the Danish army. Later, he
would become the father of one
of Denmark's most renowned
writers, Karen Blixen.

13 April 1864, looking out over the front from the railing of
the steamer, he feels a quick rush of excitement: he will soon
experience the action and drama of his father's past.

The 8th Brigade to which Dinesen belongs has just been
reassigned from Fredericia to Dybbøl. The 3,000-man brigade,
commanded by the esteemed Colonel Scharffenberg, is widely
considered the strongest unit in the Danish army. Scharffenberg is, according to a biography, 'the right man for the job;
he commanded his men with an iron fist, but he also looked
out for them and had their well-being at heart. His men wor-
shipped him not least because of his unparalleled ability to
remain calm and collected under duress – during the heat of
the battle on 18 April, he was seen calmly smoking his cigar.'

After the withdrawal from the Dannevirke, when the
brigade was posted at the Fredericia fortification, 100 kilometres north of Dybbøl, things were, for the most part, quiet.
A few skirmishes took place on open ground on the outskirts
of the city, which was under siege by Austrian forces. Unlike

Dybbøl, however, the siege here was neither close nor was there continuous shelling. In fact, there had only been two days of shelling. The biggest challenges for the men stationed there were the cold air, the mud and the boredom. When their marching orders for Dybbøl came, the men were overjoyed. Dybbøl: the name alone had a romantic ring to it. 'That was where the action was, and where there was no boredom.'

The first troops from the 8th Brigade landed on Als on 11 April. The rest arrived at noon on 13 April, and Dinesen comes in with this last embarkation.

As the assembled brigade march to their quarters on Als, a Prussian battalion gathers at Avnbjerg right behind the Prussian batteries, preparing to move into the most advanced Prussian parallel trench at 10 p.m. The 1,000-man battalion has been instructed to rush forward under cover of darkness to the Danish defensive line only 150 metres from the redoubts. They are to take the rifle-pits, dig them deeper and await relief by work details, who will then commence work on the new parallel trench.

As evening approaches, the battalion commander, Colonel von Hartmann, gives his men a pep talk: 'You have an opportunity to once again prove yourselves. Out there is a real Copenhagen regiment. Let us see who is the strongest – Copenhageners or Berliners!'

'His words had a great effect on us,' Captain C. Bunge noted in his memoirs:

With breathless expectation we stood waiting, my company making up the right flank by the water, with Redoubt I. We tried to make out the contours of the Danish defensive structure through the darkness. Suddenly we heard our commander whistle a high-pitched note in the night. We had barely run 150 paces before I came upon an enemy outpost, whose men looked on in surprise and fear as Prussian soldiers ran past them. A few shots rang out but we pointed our bayonets at their chests. Some fought back and were shot; others, too terror-stricken to do anything else, dropped their rifles and surrendered, shouting, '*Pardon, pardon, pardon!*' Without losing a single man, I was able to capture one officer and fifty-six soldiers.

For the other companies, however, it proves more difficult. In some sections the Danish sentries manage to fight back and alert the men in the redoubts. 'What followed,' wrote Bunge, 'was a lively exchange; there was a flash of light with each shot. Soon the redoubts began to return fire, sending shells and case-shot towards us. You could hear orders being shouted, cheering, and the cries of the wounded; the sounds of our skirmish broke through the night.'

The Prussians capture the entirety of the ground in front of the redoubts. But the Danish resistance has been fierce, and in several sections the Danes had made earnest, if failed, attempts at counter-strikes. Prussian losses total eighteen dead and twenty-six wounded. Among the dead is the popular Major von Jena. The news of his death is received with great sorrow by the Prussian troops. The Danish losses are not known, as records do not distinguish between the losses incurred during the day's shelling and the nightly skirmish. However, we know that in this 24-hour period, 7,300 shells fell on the Dybbøl positions with 114 dead or wounded Danes.

Thursday 14 April

At 4 p.m. the 8th Brigade march from their quarters on Als towards the front through Sønderborg. 'The road is dusty and full of potholes, the heat is oppressive, yet the march is in perfect formation, and everyone is in high spirits, singing one song after another,' Dinesen later wrote. He also noted that they marched for three hours, and the closer they got to Sønderborg the louder the din of cannon became. In Sønderborg they rest up until nightfall, at which point they are to march to Dybbøl for the relief, which is carried out as usual under the cover of darkness. The 8th Brigade's first rotation will be in Redoubts VII–X, as well as in the connecting trenches.

As darkness slowly envelops the redoubts, the Prussian bombardment intensifies and a Danish field battery responds with fire-bombs that draw long beams of light across the night sky.

As the newcomers from the 8th Brigade march towards the pontoon bridges in order to relieve the 8th and 15th Regiments, they are met by a transport of wounded soldiers on its way to the infirmary in Sønderborg. The sight is sobering and some of their cheerfulness evaporates. 'There were three stretchers,' one soldier later recalled, 'one of the wounded gave us a wave. The third stretcher, stopping ahead, was surrounded by men, who were talking loudly and all at once. The wounded man on the stretcher was screaming, his mouth wide open, so you could see far into his throat, his tongue was bluish-white and rigid, his legs an indiscernible mass of shredded blue cloth, black blood and flesh. A couple of the men were giving him a drink of water.'

In the trenches, Lieutenant Fabricius of the 8th Regiment

is desperately awaiting the relief, but is much surprised by the sight of them. 'It was obvious,' he wrote of the 8th Brigade in his diary, 'that they had never been to Dybbøl before. The companies marched in close columns, and the officers gave their orders in loud voices; in a word, they behaved as if there were no enemies nearby. Unsurprisingly, they suffered several losses before they reached the trenches. The rest of us would walk in small units with the rear spread out and not assemble our men until we were at the ravine [behind the redoubts].'

At the right flank's most advanced line, Dinesen gets a real sense of the famous Dybbøl cannonade for the first time. 'The battle took place over our heads, so we could take in the spectacle without fear of life and limb: there were long flashing arches in the sky, a deafening roar and men shouting, "Broager, take cover! Ragebøl, take cover!" and every now and then a scream and a shriek.'

Close to the Danish redoubts, pressed to the ground in the newly dug but still shallow Prussian parallel trench, are Captain Bunge and his men, tired from last night's skirmish and longing for their relief to come. Unfortunately, the scheduled daybreak relief is cancelled at the last minute because the relief regiment has suffered a minor delay. Once the sun is up, the Danish guns will be able to pick them off one by one on the open ground between the trenches and the redoubts. Bunge recalled that 'the second the relief troops started to emerge from the second parallel trench, the Danes opened a murderous fire' and the operation was postponed until nightfall.

It was anything but amusing: if we so much as stuck our hats up over the trench we drew a terrible fire, a dozen or more shots from the redoubts and the Danish communications

... our situation was especially perilous because a Danish outpost had dug in to our left at the same level, so we received a very disagreeable flank fire ... making matters worse, we could only move by crawling so as not to expose ourselves to enemy fire, and we could do little to alleviate the suffering of the wounded among us. I tried to cleanse their wounds with a handkerchief soaked in water from a little creek running through our ravine, but my ministrations afforded only scant relief.

Not until darkness falls and it is safe enough to carry out a relief can Bunge and his men leave their uncomfortable posts in the new trench. As they are leaving, the 8th Brigade moves into the Danish redoubts. While they settle into their posts, Prussian engineering and work details set to work on finishing the construction of the third parallel trench, which is to be the launching point for the grand attack. By 2 a.m. a 650-metre parallel trench has been dug out, and the last shovel of dirt before the assault thrown.

Friday 15 April

Late in the afternoon, the Danish army is close to a spontaneous collapse as two regiments suddenly, in the middle of a street in Sønderborg, refuse to continue their march to the entrenchment. The immediate fear among the officers is that the mutinous mood will spread to the rest of the army.

Insensitive management is at the heart of their mutiny. Following the arrival of the 8th Brigade, the regular rotating roster is changed, affecting among others the 16th and 17th Regiments of the 3rd Brigade. After six excruciating days at Dybbøl, they have only just settled in for their customary four days' rest on Als when new orders come in for them to march back to Dybbøl. It should be noted that not only are these men exhausted from enduring many days of heavy shelling, they have also suffered extraordinary losses: 250 dead or wounded, about 10 per cent of the Dybbøl troops. The 16th and 17th are the worst hit regiments, and it is not difficult to imagine their exhausted outrage at their new orders. Not only were they going back on duty, they also had to march twenty kilometres to Sønderborg before they could move into position. A large percentage of them are older reservists, many of them husbands and fathers with heavy responsibilities who, like Niels Larsen of the 22nd Regiment, just want to go home. And now they are heading back to Dybbøl, where death and destruction await.

In Sønderborg they pass the 8th and 15th Regiments, who have been as lucky as they themselves have been unlucky: they have had their trench duty cut short. The regiments heading for Als, made up primarily of young men, immediately sense a rumble of discontent as they greet their relief regiments. So does Brigade Commander Colonel Wørishøffer. 'I noticed a negative change in mood,' he later writes in a personal account of the incident. Initially there is merely an angry murmur, then outright shouting: 'Why do they get to go on leave so soon? The young are to be spared, while we are sent to the butcher's block, is that it?'

Heckling and calls from a group of labour and artillery details goad them into outright mutiny. When the colonel orders them to forward march, nobody moves. According to an official report:

> once the order to 'fall in' was given, the men in the 1st and 2nd company began cheering and soon everyone was

cheering. The brigade commander arrived and asked me to order 'Shoulder arms, march!' Nothing happened. The company remained standing in a position of order arms. Colonel Wørishøffer then orders his aide-de-camp, First Lieutenant Colding, and my orderly to First Lieutenant Heyn to draw sword and to strike down any soldier who did not obey my command ... the premier lieutenants drew their swords and the men shouldered arms.

With their officers' threats ringing in their ears, the regiments grudgingly begin to move. But they have not come far before several more soldiers from other companies begin shouting for them to stand down and not follow orders. According to a report written up by one of the brigade's officers, 'One of the gunners in the crowd turned ringleader. Every time I spoke, he hollered and screamed, inciting the men to disobey… neither orders nor strong admonishments could make them budge.'

Once again the assertive action of Colonel Wørishøffer is called for. He gives a talk that is part threat, part encouragement. 'I asked them,' he recalled in this memoirs, '"Your officers, do they not share in the danger and hardship, do you not see me with you in the trenches every day as well?" When one shouted "No!", it had a magic effect. Soon hundreds of voices countered this outright lie by shouting, "Yes, yes!"'

Finally the columns move, until the march is halted once more, this time by the ailing General Gerlach and his chief of staff, Stiernholm, who arrive at great speed in a closed carriage. They have, of course, heard of the 3rd Brigade's mutinous behaviour. The chief of staff bolts out of the carriage, and immediately launches into a tirade. In his memoirs,

Wørrishøffer writes diplomatically that when the chief of staff spoke to the men his 'choice of words was unfortunate and the rumblings of discontent were soon heard again'.

With a last-ditch effort Wørishøffer, however, manages to get his men in line and finally the 2,500-men column moves forward towards Dybbøl.

Private J. P. Hansen from the 16th Regiment writes in a letter to his family:

[As we proceeded towards Dybbøl] a reinforcement from the 17th Regiment was marching with his head bowed and not participating in our conversation. Once we got to the bridge, he seemed suddenly to wake up; he raised his hand as if in salutation and shouted, 'Good bye, everyone' then he fell silent again and joined the rest. His words, or perhaps more his tone of voice, expressed such sorrow and hopelessness, it is difficult to describe.

Saturday 16 April

In a letter to his beloved Friede, Major Ernst Schau notes:

The atmosphere is not great ... last night the 16th and 17th Regiments mutinied when they were ordered back into position ... it is becoming more and more frightening here ... and we will see our army disgraced if we do not withdraw in time. Upon my recommendation, our general has gone to headquarters to give them a full report of our situation. Whether he will succeed is, however, doubtful, as the Ministry of War has ordered that we fight to the bitter end; the question is, though, whether this bitter moment has not, in fact, already come.

Schau's superior is Major General Peter Henrik Claude du Plat, one of the army's most capable and clear-headed officers and in every respect the archetypal general: tall, imposing, with impeccable manners, perfect military bearing and a calm yet firm demeanour. According to a contemporary biographical article, 'His kindness towards his subordinates, whom he was always happy to help in any way possible and easily forgave for youthful folly, combined with high expectation of his officers … made him very well liked by everyone who served under his command.' No one could agree more with this assessment than Schau, who reveres du Plat, not least for his courage to stand by as well as articulate his convictions. During the war council on 4 February, for instance, he never wavered in his support of the decision to vacate the Dannevirke.

His innate military instincts have been refined during his many years of active service, not only in the Danish but also other armies. He served in the Russian army in 1847, for example, participating in a campaign in Caucasus; and in the First Schleswig War he served with distinction, quickly rising to the rank of general. It would no doubt have been to the Danish army's advantage had he been promoted to commander-in-chief in place of de Meza. But seniority carried the day in the Danish army, as it did in most European armies, and generals Gerlach, Luttichau and Steinmann were advanced ahead of him.

As he rides through the streets of the now razed Sønderborg towards the Danish headquarters in Ulkebøl to meet with the worn-out and weak-hearted Gerlach, du Plat undoubtedly decides to disregard all military conventions and speak his mind.

General Peter Henrik Claude du Plat was one of the most
capable and clear-headed officers in the Danish army. In vain
he tried to convince his superior, General Gerlach to withdraw
the army from Dybbøl before the Prussians could attack.

There is no word-for-word record of the conversation
between the ailing and bedridden Gerlach and the strong,
decisive du Plat. But we do know that du Plat did not beat
around the bush. He urges Gerlach in no uncertain terms to
abandon the position immediately. Gerlach claims it cannot be
done. He feels obliged to carry out the Ministry of War's order
to hold the position at all costs. Next du Plat suggests that
since Gerlach is ill, he should report sick and allow du Plat,
the most senior divisional general, to replace him and order
the withdrawal of the army. Du Plat argues that this way he
would be the one to take the fall. Gerlach, however, does not
have the courage to take him up on this gallant offer. In the
end du Plat suggests that they at least withdraw the troops

from the left flank, which is so damaged it can no long
be defended. These troops could then man the line direct
behind the redoubts.

Not even this compromise, however, appeals to Gerlach. (
perhaps at this point he is simply too weak in spirit to do an
thing but blindly follow orders from Copenhagen. If a pupp
general was what Minister of War Lundbye had wanted, I
certainly had one in Gerlach. Du Plat takes his leave, resig
ing himself to the unfortunate state of affairs. The followin
day, du Plat, Schau and his chief-of-staff, Major Rosen, ta
up their position at Dybbøl to do their duty, as the saying go
None of them survive.

Sunday 17 April

The Prussian soldier Wilhelm Gather is attending a servi
for the men at Nybøl. His head is bent: he is praying he w
survive the battle. Prince Friedrich Karl is putting the finis
ing touches to the details of the battle plan with his gene
als. He feels confident that they will succeed and can almo
taste victory. Meanwhile, Gerlach is in the midst of his la
fevered, yet curiously half-hearted, attempt to get the Minist
of War to give him an authorisation to withdraw the troo
to Als. The Red Cross delegate van de Velde is still tryin
to process the ordeal of the night before, when he observe
several amputations; a tired, unwashed and hungry war co
respondent Edward Dicey is walking through the streets
Sønderborg, where he comes across work details on the squa
in front of Sønderborg Castle building coffins just as the 21
and 22nd Regiments march past on their way to Dybbøl f
the last time. Skipper Larssen is trying to soothe a mortal
wounded comrade in Redoubt IV, while desperately callin

for a medic. Major Ernst is writing what will be his last letter to Friede. Before sunset the next day, she will be a widow and her mother-in-law, Dorothea, will have lost her two remaining sons. Niels Larsen's wife will become a widow with two small children, the youngest christened Marie in accordance with the wishes of a father she will never meet.

A blockhouse in Redoubt II takes a direct hit and is set on fire. Thick smoke billows out from the redoubt and the raging flames sweep towards the powder magazine, where, had it not been for the resourceful artillery lieutenant Ancker, a massive explosion would have erupted, razing the entire redoubt line. Ancker, however, organises a work detail that manages to build a barrier of sandbags and dirt to protect the powder magazine. Despite intense shelling, the men sing while they work.

On the Prussian side, two officers, Captain von Hoffmüller and Lieutenant Hasselt, launch a rowing boat with a handful of seamen in the late afternoon and cross over to Als. Without drawing the attention of any of the Danish troops, they sneak out to the Danish field artillery position, where they manage to spike two cannon before they are discovered. They escape and make it back to the Prussian side of the front unscathed, with a few Danish tools as war trophies. The story of their courageous deed is immediately wired to King Wilhelm I, who sees it as a good omen for the upcoming battle and awards the brave men the highest Prussian military order, the Order of the Red Eagle.

Soon tens of thousands of Prussian troops will advance on the Danish line. General von Goeben, meanwhile, will be carrying out his own separate mission: a few hours before the time appointed for the assault, he and his brigade are to march to Sottrup Woods near the Sound of Als. Their objective is to ready two pontoon bridges and almost a hundred rowing boats for launch. Goeben's standing orders are then to occupy the opposite bank if he thinks it militarily sound, and if at this time the assault is proceeding successfully, encircle the Danes and attack them in the rear. If all went according to plan, the Prussians would, by the afternoon of 18 April, not only have won a decisive victory, but also have completely wiped out the Danish army.

25

Night

On the evening of 17 April, the Prussian ordnance at the Gammelmark and front batteries open fire; the weight and intensity of the bombardment is no different from any other day. The Danish artillery emplacements on Als return fire. Shells arch through the sky over the redoubts like deathly meteors, tracing streams of light behind them. The Danish trenches are in the midst of rotating the troops. The 2nd and 22nd Regiments move into Redoubts I–VI on the left flank, while the 4th Regiment march back to Als and the two mutinous regiments, 16th and 17th, grudgingly take up position on the line's right flank in Redoubts VII–X. Posted at the barracks line are the reserve regiments of the 8th Brigade with standing instructions to draw up to the Danish second line, behind the redoubts, if the alarm is sounded. Two additional reserve regiments (the 9th and 20th) are posted behind them at the bridgehead to the two pontoon bridges.

The military routines this evening do not vary from previous nights; they are as normal as normal can be during an intense siege. At around 11 p.m., however, there is an unusual lull in the Prussian shelling, and after a while both the Prussian and Danish cannon have ceased firing. By midnight an eerie silence has enveloped the area. Prussian private Bubbe is able to hear the bells of Broager church strike twelve, and thinks to himself, 'The witching hour has struck.' Though every now and then a flash and a boom pierce the darkness, it is thick, ubiquitous silence that presides, and, as it turns out, heralds the day of doom for the Danish army.

Later in the night, from an observation post at Bøffelkobbel, Bubbe becomes aware of the moon breaking through the clouds; the light is now bright enough for him to make out the contours of the Danish redoubts and the ocean far beyond. In the gentle breeze, the clouds drift lazily across the sky, and as they momentarily cover the moon, the private finds it strange to be sitting in complete darkness. 'Normally the sky is lit up by shelling, but not tonight,' he writes.

Bubbe shivers in fear. 'An uncomfortable feeling of anxious anticipation came over us in this quiet hour, as over a ship's captain calm before a storm,' he later recalls.

The Danish soldiers on duty in the trenches feel a similar dread. According to gunner Christian Christensen – one of Lieutenant Ancker's most trusted and experienced men – you can hear 'the hoarse croak of predatory birds along the line. All gun crews were at this time in position in the redoubts; the atmosphere was gloomy as if we all knew we were nearing the end.'

Shortly after midnight, Prussian private Bubbe and his company draw up to the large camp at Bøffelkobbel, where some try to snatch a few winks of sleep. A campfire is lit, and groups of soldiers gather round to warm up. Though it is a mild night, the soldiers are cold. Bubbe huddles closer to the fire, but the wood is too fresh to burn properly and provides little warmth.

The time passes slowly. Finally, at 2 a.m., the order is given:

Prussian 'storm-troops'; one of the Prussians companies
that was part of the first wave of attack.

the 5th column, which will conduct the first wave of attack,
is to assemble and form up. Bubbe and his company line
up and are told that from this moment on there will be no
spoken commands given. The men are led as if by an invis-
ible hand through the woods and into an open field, where
they take off their helmets and packs, put on caps, load their
rifles and receive rations of food and ammunition for three
days. To their great surprise, the men are also asked to bring
a sack of hay each, to be used as a pad to sit or lie on in the
cold, damp trench, where they will spend many hours before
the attack. The sacks are also intended to be used during the
storm as protection against the many obstacles the Danes have
laid out to impede attackers. Finally they are each given an
empty sandbag, which they are to fill with sand once they have
moved out into the front-line trench. These are to be used as
shields against enemy bullets while approaching, and as material to build a wall behind which they can take cover if they
are brought to a halt.

Armed with hay sacks and loaded rifles, the Prussian troops await their order to march out to the front-line trench through the myriad communications ditches. 'It was,' Bubbe later writes, 'an eerie position to be in.' He continues:

> The flickering flames of the dying campfires sent small and large shadows dancing among the trees; now and then we could hear an owl shriek, almost as if it were trying to warn the enemy of our coming. The soldiers were gathered in groups debating the possible outcome of the morning's battle. One man conjured up a terrible scenario, involving all the obstacles we had to negotiate before we got to the enemy: the wolf pits, abatis [sharpened stakes], chevaux de frise [spiked fences], harrows and wire.

As Bubbe looks around at his comrades, he notices a sergeant, an experienced and highly decorated soldier, whose face, lit up by the flames, is bathed in tears. 'He is holding a photo of his wife and child. They all try to comfort this – under normal circumstances very brave – man, but to no avail. When the marching order is given they have to hold his hand and lead him like a child.'

They move as quietly as possible out to their position, which is only 150 metres from the Danish line. It is a cumbersome march, as they are carrying heavy hay sacks and cartridge pouches as well as their rifles through the narrow passages, and they make slow progress. The columns are often forced to stop when equipment is dropped, which elicits a lot of swearing and cursing. It is tough-going and Bubbe can feel drops of sweat trickling down his forehead.

Other companies follow close behind. Private Kaspar

Honthumb – a gunner in the 53rd Regiment, 1st Company, designated to attack Redoubt IV – is among these soldiers:

> We walk soundlessly in the moonlit night and despite the seriousness of the situation, I cannot help but find it amusing to think of us with our bales of hay being like the Norwegians in *Macbeth* [i.e. decked out in branches, fulfilling the prophecy that Macbeth will be vanquished only when Birnam Wood comes to Dunsinane Hill].

Once down in the front-line trench, the Prussian soldiers begin filling their bags with sand and spreading the hay out for comfort and protection against the damp ground. At the fire step, which is large enough to accommodate an entire unit, the soldiers lie down to rest before the big battle.

Once everyone is in place in the frontline-trench there 'begin the endless hours of waiting', writes Bubbe. The assault is to commence at exactly 10 a.m. All Prussian batteries will open fire on the Danish position at 4 a.m. and without pause bombard the Danish line for six hours.

As the Prussian infantry bed down in their trenches, Danish war correspondent P.V. Grove from *Dagbladet* is on Als, more than ten kilometres from the front. He has taken lodgings in a farmhouse and has become all but inured to the steady, daily rumble of cannon from Dybbøl, but it is nothing compared to the infernal noise that awakens him at 4 a.m. on 18 April. 'If you were not there,' he later wrote, 'you will have no sense of how intense this shelling was. It was as if heaven and hell were doing battle and all demons had come through hell's gates, and were flying all around mocking us and set on destroying all of mankind. It is shocking to realise that death thus beckons yet not knowing to whom.'

Close to the Danish headquarters in Ulkebøl is van de Velde, the Red Cross delegate, trying desperately to get some rest. But the noise from the front keeps him awake. Anxious and restless, he thinks of the men out here, so many of whom will be suffering horrendous injuries as they lay down their lives for their flag.

Carl Bunge, the Prussian captain who on 14 April had participated in the night skirmish that secured occupation of the ground in front of the redoubts, is just moving out towards the second trench, right behind the front-line trench, with his company as the bombardment commences. 'The noise from the batteries gets worse by the minute,' he remembers. 'The thunder of the cannon is unbearable, the shots howl and hiss, and it feels like the sky is going to fall. You cannot hear what the man next to you is saying. In a heavy mood we lie pressed to the ground while the hellish din keeps up.'

Seven Danish officers from the 22nd Regiment sit huddled together behind an embankment at the rear of Redoubts II and III. An explosive shell suddenly hits the embankment; six officers are hit. A shell fragment pierces the neck of a captain, killing him instantly. A premier lieutenant's spine is crushed. A colonel receives a blow to the head and falls to the ground unconscious. Three lieutenants are wounded and carried off. For an army with so few officers, the losses are serious.

The shelling is by now so intense that the redoubts on the left flank are cleared of men; only a few gunners and lookout men remain. Most of the Danish soldiers are placed behind the redoubts in ditches, hollows and behind ramparts with orders from Lieutenant Colonel Wilhelm Dreyer to remain in a state of readiness and keep their rifles loaded. The soldiers are either lying down with their rifles close or sitting with their backs against the embankment with their rifles in their laps. The shells flying overhead seem, as they later describe it, 'to sometimes collide in mid-air'. A medic becomes emotionally overwhelmed by it all and breaks down in tears.

At the barracks line, 8th Brigade is put on red alert from 4 a.m. The men perceive the heavy bombardment as a forewarning of an impending attack, which they think will commence while it is still dark. But as the bombardment continues through the early morning hours, the Danish general staff assumes that the shelling, even if unusually intense, is just the Prussians carrying on with their customary siege bombardment. The alert is therefore called off.

Private Bubbe has a view of the sea and the majestic Dybbøl Hill from where he is sitting in the second-line trench. While the shelling thunders overhead, he enjoys the sunrise. Whilst the area is still enveloped in darkness, he sees the first hesitant rays of sunlight break through on the horizon. First there is a pale stripe of sky. Soon it is mixed with a rose colour that continues to intensify until it is a brilliant crimson; as the sun rises out of the sea, all the light and colours are reflected in the glassy waters.

From one of the lookout posts, Danish guards notice hectic activity in the Prussian trenches. A message is immediately sent to Lieutenant Colonel Dreyer about the mass of columns seen in the enemy's front-line trenches. Dreyer, however, assumes the Prussians are at work expanding their front trench, but he does send a runner to headquarters to let them know of the unusual activity. Headquarters have received no reports from other sectors of the front of anything out of the ordinary, and the general staff chooses to ignore Dreyer's intelligence.

It seems quite remarkable that only a few guards pick up on all the activity taking place only 150 metres away, where 10,000 Prussian soldiers have amassed during the night. Given the intense bombardment – about twenty shells were fired every minute and closer to forty at some points – it would have been hard for anyone to notice anything. Still, it remains a superb feat of organization and logistics on the part of the Prussian troops.

A German lieutenant from the 5th attack column later wrote, 'We were very lucky that the Danes stopped their shelling this morning as they had done every other morning. Had they known what was going on, had their batteries continued firing and concentrated even briefly on our third parallel, it would have been disastrous for us.'

26

18 April 1864

Prince Friedrich Karl swings himself into the saddle bright and early on the morning of 18 April and heads for the lookout point on Avnbjerg Hill with an entourage of bigwigs from Berlin: the Crown Prince of Prussia, a host of noblemen and staff, as well as Field Marshal von Wrangel. Prince Friedrich Karl is a bit anxious; he is worried that the Danes may have retreated during the night, but his brigadier general assures him that they are still entrenched in their positions. Relieved, he climbs Avnbjerg at 9.30 a.m., thinking to himself, 'I've got them now! I've got them now!'

Once on Avnbjerg, he settles in to await the spectacle soon to be played out before him. To accompany the performance, he has engaged a 300-man military orchestra, posted in the second front-line trench, which at exactly 10 a.m., and at full blast, will play a piece called the 'Düppler Schanzen-Marsch', written for the occasion by the prince's favourite composer, Gottfried Piefke.

Though their assault would be set to music, none of the men in the Prussian trenches feel particularly cheerful. What awaits them is not a glorious performance but a play of life and death. Their fear is palpable. Kaspar Honthumb, the rifleman from 53rd Regiment, 1st Company, peers nervously

Lieutenant Peter Frederik Grünewaldts sketched his
comrades during the bombardments at Dybbøl.

over the top of the trench wall and sees the shells pounding the redoubts. Dropping back into the trench, he studies the faces of his comrades. Some wear expressions of terror, others quiet resignation. A third group seems to have gone almost insane, their eyes flickering madly. Army chaplains move through the trenches, trying to soothe the men's fear. Honthumb remembers the regimental chaplain walking among the men: 'In a few words he told us of our duty and our goal, made the sign of the cross and forgave us our sins. Eyes welled up, and solemnly we contemplated our mortality and eternity.'

Wilhelm Gather later remembers the army chaplain who visits his unit: 'His voice quivered with sadness. Our hearts softened, and some had tears in their eyes. We shook hands and said, "Goodbye, comrade," asking each other to bring messages to loved ones for us, should we not make it.'

There are now less than five minutes before the assault. The air is so full of smoke the men can no longer follow the trajectory of the individual shells across the sky.

At each Prussian battery, watches are checked for synchronisation several times during the night to make sure that everyone is on schedule. At exactly 10 a.m. on 18 April a deafening silence falls upon the area. The sudden quiet is as surreal as it is brief. A few seconds of shattering silence. For the Prussian troops, who have been anticipating this moment with dread all night while lying pressed to the ground in the front-line trench, these seconds make an indelible impression. They will never forget this quiet before the storm. Within seconds, they know, all hell will break loose, Armageddon will come, and a collective madness will set in; that grinding in the men's heads will begin.

The order to attack is called. At the top of Avnbjerg, Prince

Friedrich Karl stands up in his stirrups, pulls his sword and cries, 'Attack!'

Officers all along the line cry, 'Forward!', 'Forward!', 'Forward!' A cacophony of battle cries is heard as the mass of Prussian soldiers erupt from the front-line trench and swarm the Danish position.

Soon they are supported by heavy artillery as all Prussian batteries now open fire at full blast. To prevent retreat, their first target is the second line of the Danish position, behind the redoubts. Danish batteries immediately return fire and case-shot pours into the approaching attack columns. A tremendous fusillade follows and bullets tear through the air.

The Prussian troops 'are barely out of the ground before dead and wounded fall to the ground in a splattering of blood', recalls Private Adalbert Rosenkötter, who is right behind the first attack column. In a few seconds it will be his turn to brave the hail of Danish bullets.

The [dead and wounded] are immediately carried off by medics, so we will not have to look at them. We are not very comfortable. Everyone is pale. One corporal begins to cry, and I have to force him to get it together – we cannot stop now. Orders fly about. There is a mad beat from the calfskin drums; the buglers are blowing their horns and wild war-cries are heard from all sides while bullets whizz past our ears. Left and right our comrades fall, screaming in pain and for help. We give them only a sideways glance as we push on.

In the first few moments of the assault, Kaspar Honthumb hears Colonel von Buddenbrock bellowing, 'Forward!'

In an instant 1st Company is out of the trench and immediately there are casualties, as we are met by a dense hail of bullets from the redoubts. But as the order to move forward has hit us like an electrical shock, we push on without a moment's hesitation, stirred by all the hollering and shouting. At one point we fall to the ground in exhaustion, but just for a moment, then we are [catapulted] forward by another loud command.

'As soon as we reach open ground,' Gather later writes in a letter to his parents, 'we hear the wretched groans and moans of the wounded and dying scattered left and right as well as behind and in front of us. You see men swaying as if dizzy, then fall to the ground in a pool of their own blood.'

On the Danish side, Gunner Christian Christensen in Redoubt II remembers the first few seconds of the storm:

The sudden silence hits like an electric shock, quiet as in a tomb. The contrast is stark. 'What will happen, now?' someone asks, but instinctively we all know, and somebody answers, 'The enemy is attacking.' We look out over the parapet and quite so, breaking forth like a storm-flood, comes a wave of enemy soldiers at us. Right then, we hear the crackle of a volley of musketry from the trench on the right side of Redoubt II; it sounds like a wagonload of small pebbles being unloaded. The effect, however, is not nearly as devastating as so many bullets tearing into a dense column of men should have been, though some do suffer mortal wounds and fall. We hear them cry out in pain. The approaching column holds back for a few moments, and I say to Lieutenant Ancker, 'They are pulling back!' 'Yes, damn it, they are,' he replies. But then the column moves forward again with renewed vigour.

At the stroke of 10 a.m. a Danish corporal in Redoubt V hears someone shouting, 'The enemy is coming!' but no one believes him, though they all run into the trench to see for themselves. There, before their eyes, is:

a white mass on tiny black legs approaching at great speed; it is a column of men in which each man is holding a sandbag; behind them follows the real work column. The enemy overcomes our obstacles with ease, employing an ingenious method by which the first men cut the wire, the next pillow our caltrops with sandbags, and the whole column then pushes forward without a minute's pause ... all this, I think, happens faster than I can write it. Bullets fall close together like a bowl of peas poured on a plate. Though the enemy leaves a trail of dead bodies in their wake, the size of the column does not seem to shrink.

The Danish infantry, who have taken up position in the second line behind the redoubts, now throw themselves into a mad race with the enemy. Who will reach the redoubts first, the Danes or the Prussians? Only a few of the redoubts are fully manned at this point; in most there are but a handful of gunners, who run to load the cannon that are still operational. Gunner Christensen from Redoubt II recalls:

Right in front of the redoubt, I do not see many men. Only a few are heading towards us. Yet we fire case-shot out into the ravine; once the smoke has cleared, I peer through the embrasure and suddenly I see a mass of Prussian men on the outer edge of the moat, all pointing their rifle muzzles at us. Whatever it takes, we have to sweep the area clean of enemies. In a hurry we load the cannon and direct it so it will rake the area where they are [...] As the smoke lifts, we see no one in the far distance, but heads appear close by, looking in at us over the parapet.

On the hills above the battlefield an audience looks down on the action. Among them is Prussian military artist Wilhelm Camphausen, whose favourite motif is battle scenes. Camphausen has taken up position near the Gammelmark batteries, from where he has the perfect view of the Danish left flank. As he trains his binoculars on the redoubts, soldiers that looked like tiny black figures with the naked eye become distinct, and Camphausen is able to make out their features and follow the course of events.

Demonically the earth seems to spew out [enemies], thousands jump from hidden ditches and on to the parapets. Marker flags are unfolded and the hitherto deserted wasteland is already specked with storming soldiers. In feverish excitement, heart pounding, I alert everyone around me that it has begun. Then I press the binoculars to my eyes. Unstoppable and at great speed the enemy advances in a loose line, and in what seems like only a few seconds they have covered the distance to the redoubts; none of the infamous obstacles seem to have slowed or impeded their approach ... in still denser lines come more and more soldiers; some of their bayonets are clearly visible, others have fascines with scaling ladders. The Danes meet the shells, case-shot and volleys of musket-fire with angry [resistance] ... there, I see some get hit and fall, some remaining immovable on the ground, others getting up, but then stumbling and falling again, writhing [in agony] in the yellow dirt – still others, lightly wounded or perhaps with lethal lead in their chest, drag themselves to the dressing stations. At this point the redoubts have already been mounted and occupied.

On the battlefield, a Prussian lieutenant is moving on Redoubt V with his men, and about to cross a ravine:

We run past dead and wounded ... in front of me a man falls. Perhaps it is at this moment, or perhaps it is when I cross the ravine, that I feel a quick, sharp blow to my left upper arm? There is no time to worry about it. We push on, get past the road, when I am suddenly overcome by dizziness and my arm becomes heavy and hangs lifelessly at my side. Instinctively, I know I can no longer move forward, but to fall here in the shower of bullets [does not seem practical]... a few paces away I spot a rifle-pit, probably part of the former Danish outpost line. I stagger towards it and discover that other wounded have sought refuge here; they lie crouched together, but there is room for me too, I see. And however tight and flat the pit is, it offers some protection against the furious rifle fire. My mouth is bleeding profusely; there is an odd prickling sensation in my fingertips as if my arm has fallen asleep. There is no question that my bone is broken; I can feel the fractured ends rub against each other.

Kaspar Honthumb, the gunner from 53rd Regiment, later remembers that as he makes his way to Redoubt IV:

I notice my comrades falling all around me, and suddenly there is a jolt and I fall to the ground ... it feels like I have been wounded in the left hip, but I do not know whether I have just been grazed or whether the bullet is lodged deep inside me. To the best of my knowledge, I have just been grazed, so I try to get up and move on, but cannot, I have no strength left, more because of the last few minutes of exertion and my agitated state of mind than because of my light wound, I think. My situation out here in the open terrain is frightening; I am exposed to the increasingly heavy fire and scattered around me are dead and wounded men, the latter moaning. The wounded in particular make me uneasy.

While Kaspar Honthumb is on the ground, he is aware of his company forcing their way up the embankment of the redoubt, and he sees hordes of Danes fleeing to seek cover behind it. Anger courses through his veins at the sight, an anger so strong he reaches for his rifle. In a wild blood frenzy, he begins shooting into the mass of Danish soldiers. 'And when I run out of cartridges, I try to get back on my feet again.'

Wilhelm Gather has reached the moat in front of Redoubt VI and is facing the palisades. He jumps into the moat, 'and right there are two dead men. One of the men who led the assault lying down, and one from our regiment in a crouched position; both have been bleeding profusely.' Once he has passed them, he runs up the rampart.

Captain Bunge and his men, a reserve unit, are also on their way into battle. They approach the trenches between Redoubt

I and II at the same time as the attack columns are heading up over the ramparts. From the time Bunge and his men spring out of the second front-line trench, 'more men are either lightly or severely wounded. Next to me our regiment's right-flank man, who is a tall, skilled soldier, is hit by a shot just as he makes it over the parapet; I hear his teeth splinter and see him touch his wounded mouth, then fall to the ground with a gurgling scream, a jet of blood gushing from his mouth and nose.'

Private J. Bubbe, approaching Redoubt V, sees his comrades on the top of the parapet: 'they are received with bayonets and the first line have to fall back. But still more are coming and finally the crown of the earthwork can be mounted. A terrible fight ensues: man-to-man combat. There is stabbing with bayonets and clubbing with rifle butts.'

'It would be terrible,' Bubbe later writes, 'if everyone was not fighting with the utmost fury. To my left, a sergeant from the 64th Regiment, 12th Company, tries to plant the black-and-red marker flag, but he is shot dead. Not until a group of soldiers join forces do they manage to plant our flag and pull down the Dannebrog [the Danish flag].'

A Danish corporal who is on the crown of the breastwork recalls that:

a fight arises with some really brave Prussians: there is bayonet fencing, clubbing and a mad medley of sounds – rifle shots, men's screaming and death cries. Most of the Prussians pull back to fire at us; we, of course, can't fight and load at the same time, so we can't do any real harm. One of the most daring of the Prussians closes in on us and shoots a Dane engaged in a hand-to-hand fight ... once we lose almost half of our garrison and are encircled by the enemy, who have broken through our line further down and are coming at us from the rear, we surrender.

Private Bubbe recalls the next sequence of events as follows: The Danish infantry is driven back and tries to break away through the redoubt gate, but the gunners have not been defeated. They can't bring their guns with them, and apparently they do not want to leave them. So they have no other option but to draw their swords to defend themselves and their ordnance. They fight until crushed, falling to the ground with mortal wounds.

Though few hear it through the din and strife of the fighting, Prince Friedrich Karl's military orchestra plays from the moment the battle begins. Afterwards, Friedrich Karl pronounces the conductor and composer Gottfried Piefke a 'musical hero'. Positioned close to the parapet, Piefke conducts his orchestra, swaying his baton, to which a Prussian flag is attached, with alacrity. Even before they have come to the end of the 'Düppler Schanzen-Marsch', Piefke spots the Prussian flag flying on Redoubt III, and he joyously launches into 'Heil dir im Siegerkranz' ('Hail to Thee in Victor's Crown'). At this point, however, a shower of Danish bullets pours over the orchestra; the men are relatively safe in the trench, but the conductor, standing above ground, is exposed, and as case-shot begins to whizz past Piefke's baton, the men plead with him to take cover. 'When we are in the midst of our third march, a shell strikes the edge of the trench, showering the oboists with dirt, and as if by magic the music stops,' Piefke later reports to Friedrich Karl. 'The air pressure flings the cigars from the left breast pocket of my tunic. Though at my call, the oboists begin to play again only a few moments later, and the rest of the orchestra soon joins in … as the men beseech me to take cover in the trench, I oblige and from here I continue to conduct.'

The music plays, the cannon roar, and while most of the soldiers try to destroy as much life as possible, there are others, namely the medics, who try to save as many lives as they can. Several hundred medics on both sides of the front move hurriedly back and forth on the battlefield, carrying and collecting the wounded. It is a back-breaking job carrying the blood-soaked men through the narrow trenches and across the open ground to the dressing stations, and all the while bullets are whizzing by their ears. Considering the impressive number of medics present at Dybbøl, it is remarkable that there are practically no accounts relaying the hardships they endure and the horrific mutilations, amputations and deaths they witness. Though perhaps it is exactly because they see only the horror of the war that so little has been written by or about them.

In the 1800s the ugly side of war was largely ignored, even considered taboo among the public at large. With the exception of Jean-Henri Dunant, no one wrote about the shadow side of war. In fact, it was not until a couple of years into the First World War that the true horrors of war received any attention beyond soldiers' diaries and letters. There are thousands of the latter from the war of 1864, too; curiously, however, I have been able to find only one first-hand account from a medic who was on the battlefield on 18 April: a vivid description of the events of the day by a Prussian medic, in Theodor Rehtwisch's chronicle of the war, *Um Schleswig-Holsteins Freiheit* (1912). Unfortunately, as was the custom in the early 1900s, the men quoted in this work are only mentioned by title, so we do not know the name of this man; Rehtwisch refers to him simply as 'the Medic'.

From the moment the storm begins, the Medic is in constant motion between the battlefield and the dressing station. After carrying the first wounded men to the dressing station, the Medic hears a man shouting 'Jesus, Mary and Joseph!', his voice full of pain. It is an infantryman who has just been brought in. 'Half of his arm has been shot off and the sound of his voice goes right through you. At the dressing station there is a Danish soldier calling for his wife and children – he has been shot in the shoulder.'

The Medic hurries off to the battlefield again:

... through the trenches, where the sun is beating down on me as if it were July not April. In the third parallel [the third front-line trench] there are wounded everywhere. We collect one, carry him to the dressing station and then return to the trench. Just how many we bring back, I do not know. We do not talk at all. And the impressions of the day erase all numbers. We walk – no, we run – to and fro. Always two at a time with a stretcher between us. Sometimes we get so exhausted we have to lie down for a rest. Then we continue, passing rows of Danish soldiers who have been taken prisoner; and then we come upon the Prussian military band – or not band exactly, there were about 150 musicians – and above the din of cannon we can hear them play 'Heil dir im Siegerkranz'.

27

The left flank

Thousands of soldiers are fighting across the battlefield; by the afternoon, thousands will have soaked the ground with their blood.

The Danes are outnumbered almost five to one during the battle's first phase: 10,000 Prussians against only 2,200 Danes. The odds are overwhelming, and there is little the Danes can do to stem the Prussian deluge. But the Danes are not thinking about numbers or odds at this time: they are fighting, energised by the pure, raw force of man's primordial instinct for survival. Kind-hearted students, millers, farmhands, bakers, schoolteachers, noblemen, theologians and stationmasters have turned into roaring, carnivorous animals who club, beat, bite, thrust and shoot, killing to survive, sometimes armed with rage alone; some fights last only a few minutes, others half an hour.

Redoubt I is overrun by 10.06 a.m. Almost a thousand Prussian soldiers have moved on this redoubt. It is defended by only seventy Danish soldiers. The Danes were taking cover behind the redoubt when the storm began, and only just made it inside as the enemy poured in over its parapet. There is but one usable cannon in the fortification, and the gunners never get a chance even to load. In the connecting trenches

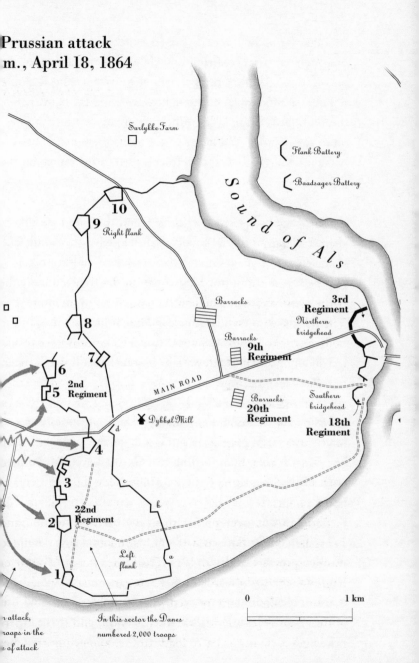

Prussian attack
m., April 18, 1864

Surlykke Farm

Flank Battery

Baadsager Battery

S o u n d   o f   A l s

10

9   Right flank

8

Barracks

3rd
Regiment
Northern
bridgehead

Barracks

9th
Regiment

7

6

2nd
Regiment

5

MAIN ROAD

Barracks

20th
Regiment

Southern
bridgehead

18th
Regiment

Dybbøl Mill

d

4

c

3

b

22nd
Regiment

2

a

Left
flank

1

0   1 km

attack,

roops in the

e of attack

In this sector the Danes
numbered 2,000 troops

between Redoubt I and II, First Lieutenant Johannsen puts up a fierce resistance, firing one volley after another into the oncoming mass of enemies enveloping and entering Redoubt I. There are too many of them, however, and the battle inside the redoubt is brief. 'When the first enemy column stepped on to the parapet … a fierce battle with rifle butts and bayonets ensued,' writes Captain Johannesen in his report on the fighting:

> The redoubt is quickly encircled, and the garrison, who have already suffered much, find themselves in too tight quarters to put up an effective resistance and are taken prisoners and disarmed. The men in the trenches under the command of Lieutenant Renonard make an attempt to pull back to the Danish second line near the beach, but the number of approaching Prussian columns is too overwhelming and only a few make it; some are killed and the rest are taken prisoner.

Inside the redoubt a resourceful Danish gunner 'tries to torch the powder magazine, but is stabbed by a bayonet before he can set it ablaze', according to a German account. Almost none of the Danish troops who are in Redoubt I and on the beach escape; they are taken prisoner, wounded or killed. The Prussians suffer losses of nine dead and fifty wounded.

Lieutenant Storch, the artillery commander in Redoubt I, is taken prisoner and writes in a letter to his parents shortly after his capture, 'I was almost unconscious, having been beaten repeatedly by enemy rifle butts, when I was led out of the redoubt by a Prussian officer, stepping over the many dead bodies.'

Corporal Rasmus Nellemann was a thirty-four-year-old estate manager and one of the Danish army's older reservists. At home he had a wife and a two-year-old daughter. He longed for the war to be over but was killed during the short, fierce defense of Redoubt II.

The fighting in Redoubt II is even fiercer. The gunners in this redoubt are among the best and most experienced in the Danish army. They have been under heavy shelling for weeks and are by now guided by an angry, determined fearlessness. These rough and resourceful men manage to fire several rounds of case-shot at the enemy. The infantry, seventy men under the command of Peter Grünwaldt, are likewise skilful men, who manage to get inside the redoubt before the enemy. However, while the soldiers manning Redoubt II have fought gallantly up to this point, the tiny garrison does not stand a chance against the almost 2,000 enemies pouring into their fortification. The Prussians' superior numbers have a devastating effect. Still, the gunners continue their fire undaunted until the Prussians plant a marker flag on the crown of the earthworks; at this point in the fight, the Danish gunners set to work spiking their cannon to render them unusable by the enemy. Corporal Rasmus Nellemann, whom we met earlier while on the march up to the redoubts on 17 April, is seemingly seized by a mad fury. Nellemann charges up the slope of the earthworks, towards the hated Prussian flag. Weeks of exhaustion, fear, untold hardships and excruciating longing for his wife and two-year-old daughter find relief in his final act of courageous defiance. In a letter to his brother, written the day before, he writes of how he finds it 'almost unbearable now to lie passively awaiting death by those hellish shells ... can no longer bear it'. The enraged Nellemann turns into a blazing one-man army when he sees the Prussian flag atop his redoubt. He tears it down and hurls it into the moat. The Prussians plant yet another flag, but Nellemann manages to tear this second one up as well before he is hit by a shower of enemy bullets and is mortally wounded.

A portrait of Rasmus Nellemann taken before the war shows a young man dressed in his Sunday best with fancy neckwear, his hair neatly combed back. He looks directly at us; his head is slightly tilted, a faint half-smile on his lips and a faraway expression in his eyes. Looking at this gentle face, it is almost impossible to imagine him charging up an embankment to fight flag-planting Prussians.

It is equally difficult to imagine Lieutenant Grünwaldt, a gentle aspiring artist, seized by bloodlust, fighting and clubbing the enemy while shouting wildly. But this is exactly what happens to him. Unlike Nellemann, he survives the battle.

In the 1864 archives held at the Sønderborg Castle museum, in the folder marked '22nd Regiment', you can find a letter from Grünwaldt, along with some of his sketches. Though a lieutenant and a professional soldier, Grünwaldt's big dream was to become an artist. He had considerable talent and studied at the prestigious Royal Academy of Arts in Copenhagen from 1861 to 1863. After the war he would go on to study with the world-famous Danish artist P. S. Krøyer, later exhibiting at the prominent Charlottenborg Gallery. In his day, he became known for his 'beautiful paintings featuring motifs from the Copenhagen Fort', according to a contemporary biographical sketch.

Grünwaldt brings a sketchbook to the war and often draws during the tedious hours of waiting in the trenches. On one sketch of his comrades, Grünwaldt has jotted a note: 'From the trenches at Dybbøl, 64'; he may well have drawn these portraits on the morning of 18 April. His sketches clearly show – better than most visual accounts from the war – how gruelling life in the trenches was. On this particular sketch we see the men's faces empty of expression, as if they have withdrawn from life or resigned themselves to their fate. Their caps are pulled down over their ears, coat collars turned up to cover most of their dirty faces. Their hair is long, beards are scraggly, and their uniforms wrinkled and soiled. A self-portrait archived in the current Defence Ministry's records shows a man seemingly prepared for imminent death. Yet, despite his quiet despair, the drawing seems to show a man of strong character and fortitude.

Certainly he seems to have been made of the right stuff, as he directs the defence of his assigned redoubt on 18 April with fierce determination. Like Lieutenants Ancker and Castenskjold, who also survive, he was later hailed as a war hero. However, we know from a letter he sent to his parents while in Prussian captivity that he attributes no heroism to his own actions: 'The Prussians assaulted us with a might many times ours, and after half an hour I had to surrender the redoubt.'

After a short but vigorous resistance, Grünwaldt and the handful of his men who are still alive surrender. The official report has noted the time of surrender as 10.10 a.m., the time at which the Prussian flag is planted on top of the redoubt. But undoubtedly there is fighting inside the redoubt well beyond this time.

There are many Danish and Prussian stories about the capture of Lieutenant Ancker: one claims that he is captured while holding a fuse in his hand, ready to blow up the works, and is allowed to survive because the Prussians have orders to take him alive. Others say that his captors let him keep his sword as a sign of respect. A third account reports that his sword is torn from him and that he receives a severe beating before being hustled over to the other prisoners.

When it comes to 'war stories', however, even official military reports are often pure fiction; hence the use of this term in popular parlance for all that is far-fetched. But fabrications of this nature probably cannot be helped. For one thing, in the heat of battle it is almost impossible to get a clear sense of what is actually transpiring. Time, place and even the sequence of events become a blur. Not only are the soldiers under enormous pressure, but they may easily become disorientated in the dizzying, centrifugal forces of a battle in full swing. In addition, memory is fickle and our recall often influenced by wishful thinking. That's why the Danish accounts feature mean and brutal Prussians, while the German accounts feature noble Prussians treating Ancker with the utmost respect.

One of the great patriotic myths later told by the Prussians involves the heroic, self-sacrificing actions of a soldier from the 3rd Brandenburger Battalion who was in the first wave of troops to storm the Danish position. According to the legend, Carl Klinke sacrificed his life to save his comrades trying to get into Redoubt II.

The official story (in accordance with the report given by the Prussian general staff, a report collaborated by the battalion's officers) is that the men in the ditch in front of Redoubt II have some difficulty clearing the palisades but agreed that there is not enough time to use axes, so they decide to blast their way in. A thirty-pound sack of dynamite is lit, but because the sack had been bumped about during their hectic approach, the explosion is quicker and more violent than expected. The blast creates a hole in the palisade, but several of the soldiers are also severely burned, including 23-year-old farmer's son Carl Klinke from the village of Bohsdorf in the south-eastern part of Prussia. He is on the ground for a few moments, then tries to get up but is immediately killed by a Danish bullet.

In the heroic version, Klinke straps the bag of explosives on his back and detonates it while charging the palisade. This story was most likely spun by regimental commander Major General Canstein, who, though he was not present, began referring to Klinke as a hero soon after the war. Dead heroes have often been more useful than live ones, as they cannot dispute the stories told about them. Klinke did not receive any special attention until after the war and was buried in an unmarked mass grave.

German newspapers carried Canstein's version of events in mid May 1864, and Klinke immediately became a war hero, a status he would keep well into the next century. During Germany's unification in 1871, the story of the hero from Redoubt II was used politically to foster a common German identity and boost patriotic feelings of loyalty to the state among the new nation's citizens. Henceforth all German schoolchildren would learn of the patriotic hero who sacrificed his life for his country. Statues were erected in his honour and he has

A realistic rendering of the intensity of the man-to-man
fighting following the entry of the Prussian troops into the
Danish redoubts, by German painter Friedrich Kaiser.

been immortalised in songs and poems. It was not until the
advent of the First World War, when Europe nearly drowned
in the blood of her sons, that Klinke began fading from the
collective German memory. In a conflict that saw mass kill-
ings by armies of a million men or more, the heroic actions of
a single soldier in a war effort fifty years in the past suddenly
seemed irrelevant. Furthermore, after Marne, Verdun and the
Somme, it no longer seemed credible that one single soldier
could influence the outcome of a battle. Warfare had become
industrial and the individual soldier played a minor role.

Though the story of Klinke has little merit, it is certainly true
that the skills and courage of individual soldiers made a difference in the war of 1864. This is especially apparent in the
fighting taking place in Redoubt III. Only nineteen defenders

meet the enemy there, supported by guns in Redoubt IV and heavy rifle fire from the trenches. And while the redoubt is taken within five minutes, the Prussians suffer 148 casualties, 48 killed – a big loss considering the size of the garrison, and a testament to the courageous and tenacious resistance by the nineteen men, commanded by the skilful young Corporal Smidt, who shoots the first Prussian who tries to plant a flag on the parapet of the fortification himself. Seconds later it is swarmed by Prussians and intense hand-to-hand combat ensues, but the Danes are swiftly encircled and when only nine are left alive, they surrender. Contemporary German historian Count Waldersee noted in his book on the war, *Der Krieg gegen Dänemark*, that 'it required a rare combination of energy and skill to defend a position so successfully with so few men'. Or perhaps more accurately, it required a rare degree of courage and madness.

The bloodiest fighting took place in Redoubt IV. Upon closer examination of the fighting here, it becomes apparent that had the circumstances for the Danish troops been better, the redoubts would in fact have presented a strong defensive line. Moreover, we come to appreciate the wisdom of the decision by the Prussian field officers to delay an attack until a new front-line trench had been dug. Redoubt IV is the most recessed of the works, and the attackers have to cover a distance of 400 metres to reach it, giving the Danes ample time to spray them with volleys of case-shot. The Prussian 53rd Regiment, 1st Company, loses a third of its troops – 150 dead or wounded – in this action alone. Their loss in numbers per company is comparable to the losses incurred during trench assaults on the Western Front in the First World War – though, of course, the

Prussians were gunned down by muzzle-loaders and breech cannon, which take half a minute to load, rather than machine guns, which could pour forth a continuous wave of deadly fire. In view of the killing capacities of our modern weaponry, it is difficult to fathom the destruction and mayhem wrought by the more primitive weapons of the 1860s, but the losses were great.

At Redoubt IV, Danish casualties are as extensive as the Prussians', and soon the ground is littered with mangled bodies – 300 in total. A blind fury seems to take hold of both Prussian and Danish soldiers inside Redoubt IV. The first Prussians to enter are fuelled by a mad rush of adrenalin, killing without mercy even the Danes who surrender.

But let us start at the beginning, so we may get a sense of what drove the Prussians to conduct such a mad killing spree. As previously noted, the attack gets off to a bad start because of the considerable distance to the redoubt, which allows the seventy defenders to get into position, line up the sights, fire, reload and fire again. At the same time a Danish company of 140 infantry are firing at the approaching enemy from the trench between Redoubts III and IV. The Prussians are thrown into confusion when two of the column's commanders are killed in the beginning of the attack. The column is ordered to split into two sections and flank the redoubt, but in the confusion one section is diverted and ends up advancing on Redoubt III. Unawares, the next columns moving up behind them blindly follow them to Redoubt III. The defenders in Redoubt IV are thus facing a relatively small group of attackers, which they are able to hold off for a while. At one point it even looks as if the Danes have the upper hand: riflemen are able to mount the crown of the defensive works and pick off the approaching attackers one by one.

Among the attackers is Lieutenant Spinn, commander of the hard-hit 53rd Regiment, 1st Company. In a bitter account of the attack, he recalls:

As soon as we spring from the third parallel, two men fall to the ground, wounded. Case-shot explodes left and right. I am about thirty metres from the redoubt when most of my men drop to the ground, out of breath. 'We have to rest, sir,' they announce. They proceed to cover themselves with sandbags as best they can. Looking back over my shoulder, I see many of my men lying dead or wounded on the ground ... to the best of my abilities I try to encourage the men. They finally spring up, but some immediately fall, landing on the pointed stakes of the abatis. I fall too. I hear someone shouting, 'Oh no, the lieutenant is wounded.' But I let them know I am still alive by shouting, 'Fix bayonets ... charge, charge' ... a roar erupts from the men, the sound mingling with the screaming and moaning of the wounded. They pour through the hacked-down palisades, and I squeeze through a hole between two palisades that our guns had blown to pieces, but my upper body is barely through when a shell fragment strikes and splinters the palisade right next to me. A Danish soldier charges me, luckily with his rifle slung. I grab him by the throat, and he drops his gun and begs for mercy. All the Danes who put up a fight instead of surrendering are brutally massacred ... dead gunners, officers and privates lie scattered in the area around the cannon.

The battle is out of control. The Danish commander, Captain Lundbye, orders his men to surrender. A Prussian soldier charges him and shoots him in the chest. According to some accounts, he is clubbed with a rifle butt. Regardless, the fighting resumes and turns into a massacre. Those Danes who wish to surrender throw down their rifles, but the Prussian soldiers do not seem to understand the gesture and they are viciously gunned down. A volunteer Swedish lieutenant and his handful of men keep up a fierce resistance until he is shot in the cheek and falls to the ground. The gunners too refuse to surrender, as they have not yet had time to spike their cannon. The Prussians turn their intense fire on the gunners and the killing spree continues until a Prussian officer finally manages to stem the blood lust.

Redoubt IV falls after half an hour of fighting, at which point Prussian flags are waving from everywhere along the Danish line of fortifications. Redoubt V is overrun in all but five minutes, but as attested by Private Bubbe, the fighting, though brief, was as fierce as in any of the other battles. The Prussians suffer 130 casualties here. Redoubt VI, which Wilhelm Gather has helped take, is the first to fall. Almost none of the Danish soldiers make it into this redoubt before the enemy, so it takes only four minutes and thirty seconds to overpower this defence. It is a low-intensity fight and the Prussians suffer their smallest number of casualties here. Wilhelm Gather, who has not participated in any other fighting during the campaign, survives the brief battle. Perhaps his fervent prayers at the service in Nybøl helped protect him, or perhaps it is the amulet of protection which he clasped around his neck before the battle that saves his life. In any event, Gather is ecstatic with relief to make it out of the attack alive. With his comrades he looks on as the fighting rages in the remaining redoubts. In a letter to his parents he dryly notes hat 'it is no doubt more fun watching the battle than being n it'.

The Battle of Dybbøl, however, is far from over. After Redoubt IV falls, the fighting moves into the trenches between he works and is as fierce here as it was in the redoubts. There s violent fighting from trench to trench and rifle-pit to rifle-pit. The Swedish volunteer Lieutenant Knorring, who joined he Danish army five days earlier, comes to his less than glori-ous death in one of the trenches.

The Danish forces are overwhelmed, and what is left of he 2nd and 22nd Regiments make a fighting retreat. The regiments are dissolved – nine out of ten soldiers have been killed, wounded or taken prisoner. The scattered elements hurry down towards the withdrawn defensive line, pursued by Prussian soldiers. Drunk on victory, they charge forward, ntent on eradicating the last of the enemy.

The Danish forces are subsequently driven back from he withdrawn line. The Prussians are surging forward at such great speed that their ranks are thrown into disarray. The companies get mixed up and no one follows the well-thought-out and detailed Prussian attack plan any more. According to the plan, the first attack columns were to take he redoubts and stay there, while fresh reserve troops pre-pared to conduct the next wave of attack on the Danish bridgehead positions.

Captain Bunge is among the men who charge forward. His company has defeated the Danish troops in the trenches between Redoubts I and II and proceed to engage in a mad race with the Danish soldiers towards the withdrawn line. He writes:

The retreating Danes are pursued by our fire … on our way, we pass many Danish cannon, which we spike before moving on towards the bridgehead. From all sides minor [Danish] detachments attempt to drive us back or halt our advance; we take fire from all sides. It is a mad chaos, and in the end we have no clear sense of where we are and how we got there.

As it turns out, Captain Bunge and his men are near Dybbøl Mill, where they are suddenly met by a massive Danish force, 3,000 men moving quickly towards them in dense columns and battle formation. It is 10.30 a.m. and the 8th Brigade has just commenced what will be a much-lauded counter-attack. At this time the silhouette of *Rolf Krake* is seen on the horizon, steaming in to support the Danes. The battle's greatest encounter is about to begin.

Unfortunately for Edward Dicey his uncanny sense of timing fails him on this pivotal day. For weeks he has camped out with the Danish soldiers on Als and sharing in their suffering. He has visited the redoubts, though he later admits that they had not been much to his liking. Like the soldiers, he has managed to overcome many privations, sleeping in his clothes like everyone else so he could be ready to jump out of bed at a moment's notice should the attack begin. Dicey has been deeply immersed in his work, obsessed even, and dead set on reporting all events at Dybbøl and Sundeved to his readers. The fate of the Danish army has become a passion. Most days his colleague from *The Times*, Antonio Gallenga, joins him, as is the case on the morning of 18 April.

On this morning of all mornings, however, they ride in the

opposite direction, away from the action rather than towards it. Instead of going to Sønderborg, where they could have followed the events of the battle, they ride to Hørup Hav Harbour to send their latest articles to London.

The intense bombardment has of course not escaped their attention, but although, like everyone else on the Danish side of the line, they believe at first that the bombardment signals an imminent attack, when it continues through the morning they assume like the Danish officers that this day is going to be like any other. Without any concrete evidence to back up their theory, the Danish command is convinced that when the Prussians attack it will be early in the morning while it is still dark.

And as it is a beautiful morning, a ride to Hørup Hav on the north-western side of Als seems like the right thing to do. 'I rode leisurely about my business, sauntering along through the pleasant lanes and wood-paths of this Alsian island,' Dicey writes.

On his way back, however, it soon becomes obvious that something out of the ordinary is going on. 'I meet orderly after orderly galloping hastily by. Something is evidently stirring, and the whole face of Dybbøl Hill, and the banks of the Sund, are now covered with smoke … I have not gone many steps before I meet a Danish gentleman, resident at the same house as myself, who tells me that the Prussians have already captured Redoubts Nos. 4 and 5 and that "all was lost".'

As soon as Dicey reaches a lookout with a good view of Sønderborg and Dybbøl Hill, he is able to see for himself:

The centre batteries have already been turned against the town, and the shells followed each other so rapidly that their sound is like that of a steam-hammer striking constantly ... the Laarder-Gaarde [where Dicey is staying] itself is surrounded by spiral columns of smoke rising into the air, and then dying away into the clear blue sky, as shell after shell strike the ground in its neighbourhood. The *Rolf Krake*, which is moored almost opposite our dwelling, is being fired at fiercely by the enemy's batteries. Great waterspouts spring up on every side of her as the shot fall in showers about her; and every now and then there is a fearful crash heard above the roar of the cannon and the constant crack of musketry, and we can tell that a shot has hit her iron sides.

Dicey hurries to the farmhouse to save his belongings. 'Inside the house everything is in confusion. The officers whom I had left sleeping at breakfast-time are all away in the battle, prisoners, or wounded, or killed.'

Dicey quickly packs up his few things and stows them away in a nearby hedge. He hitches his horse and hurries back to find a spot from where he will be able to follow the course of events on the battlefield. He is in place at about the same time as the Danish 8th Brigade moves up Dybbøl Hill.

A magnificent scenario plays out below him:

The scene itself ... had about it a strange beauty. On the face of Dybbøl Hill, looking eastwards, the morning sun shone brightly. To the right, along the Sund, vast columns of smoke rose straight into the air from the burning cottages of Ulkebøl Westermark. On the left the cliffs of the Wemming Bund shores were enveloped in the haze caused by the ceaseless puffs of snow-white smoke which were belched forth by the Broager batteries. From the crest of the hill a belt of flame flashed constantly; and the clear blue sky overhead and the still blue sea underneath encircled the whole of this picture of fire and flame and smoke in a gorgeous setting. The noise was fearful, greater even than I ever yet have heard it.

Ten thousand Danish soldiers now leave their encampments on Als and march forward to take up their reserve positions along Sønderborg's coast. The civilians panic and flee as shells land on not just the already bomb-torn town but also the surrounding areas. The small country roads on the island become clogged with masses of fleeing civilians, soldiers, military transport wagons, horse-drawn carts carrying wounded, and medics carrying stretchers from Dybbøl. Van de Velde's mission to help tend the wounded could now have begun in earnest, just as Dunant helped out in the Battle of Solferino. But as usual van de Velde is overwhelmed by the condition of the many badly mangled men and unable to take action. So instead, he decides to go back to his lodgings to, as he phrased it in a letter to Dunant, 'get something to use in the field'. What this 'something' was is never revealed.

However, after having been to his house, he realises he is wasting his time. The battle is in full swing, and he must quickly return to Sønderborg. In his letter to Dunant, he writes:

With great effort and after much time, I manage to procure a wagon and drive to Sønderborg. On my way I meet two wounded officers, who can barely walk. They ask me to drive them to Hørup Hav [where wounded are taken before being transported to Copenhagen]. Unfortunately the roads are crowded with farmers and troops and everything is covered by dust, so we make slow progress.

Thus while the Danish army is fighting a desperate battle on Dybbøl Hill, half of the world's first Red Cross delegation is riding away from the battlefield and the many wounded in need of assistance. No doubt van de Velde is relieved to have a somewhat legitimate excuse for distancing himself from the hail of shells pouring down over Sønderborg.

28

Counter-attack

The rush of excited enthusiasm the men of the 8th Brigade had felt as they marched to Dybbøl on 14 April wore off quickly. The brigade lost forty men, dead or wounded, during their first three days at Dybbøl. Even the otherwise spirited Lieutenant Dinesen became subdued, even though he had seen combat earlier in the campaign at the Dannevirke, and was aware of the harsh realities of the war.

Dinesen later recalled that day on 3 February, when the Austrians took the ground at the centre of the Dannevirke line: 'It only took a few minutes before I was seized by fear, a fear akin to that of a man sentenced to death upon seeing the axe descend.' During this skirmish, Dinesen saw a man from the 1st Regiment coming towards him from up the road:

As he reached me, he stretched out his arms, dropped his rifle, spread out his fingers and fell flat on his face in the middle of the road – a bullet hole was visible in the back of his head. I can still recall the surrounding scenery: the cosy houses with smoke rising from their chimneys, bounded by yards and trees, the stone wall lining the road up over the hill, the snow-covered fields sparkling beneath the sun – how lovely it would have been to sit and enjoy all this!

– however, in a minute I might well be lying face down, like this man, in a pool of my own blood, a bullet hole in the back of my head! And all would be pitch black, eternal night!

On the morning of 4 February, Dinesen had participated in the collection of casualties in front of the redoubts. The corpses were frozen solid. The bodies were laid out in long rows and Dinesen had assisted in burying them in a mass grave and given the eulogy, as there was no pastor to hand. Dinesen, however, made a conscious effort not to think about the darker side of the war and maintain an outwardly cheerful demeanour.

On 17 April, after their first night in the redoubts, the 8th Brigade had been moved into reserve positions at the barracks line east of Dybbøl Mill. Its standing orders were to move up to the second line behind the redoubts to support the troops when the Prussians attacked.

'The shelling was particularly intense on the night of the 17th; we took cover as best we could in any depression in the ground,' Dinesen later wrote.

After being on red alert from four until six in the morning on 18 April, the men now try to catch some sleep, but the shelling is so intense that most manage to get only a few hours of fretful rest. Dinesen eats breakfast with a group of officers, though cooking during the heavy bombardment is no easy task.

At close to 10 a.m. the men started cooking their breakfast. Every so often a man was carried off; one man, leaning against a stone wall enjoying the sun, got his head shot off.

The 8th Brigade, approximately 3,000 men, counter-attacked in close formations like these. Although successful at the outset, the brigade was heavily outnumbered and forced to retreat. It had a casualty rate of almost fifty per cent.

The shelling kept increasing.

At exactly ten o'clock the shelling comes to a sudden halt. We are startled by the silence and spring up, alert and listening. A rumbling sound like that of a wagon on frozen ground: it is volleys of musketry. The storm has begun!

The whole brigade rises immediately to their feet. 'Within a couple of minutes … all companies are combat ready, arms ordered and formed up in the ditch behind the embankment, awaiting further orders. Now the enemy's bombardment recommences, shells fall close, bullets scream. Orders must come soon if we are to support the redoubts.'

But nothing happens. The brigade is held back in their reserve position while the battle rages on Dybbøl Hill. Not until 10.30 a.m. is the brigade dispatched to the redoubts with orders to launch a counter-attack. Why the hesitation?

Accounts differ. Some military reports and eyewitness testimonies claim it is not until 10.30 that anyone knows the storm has begun, because the lines of communications from the redoubts to the reserve troops have been severed. Many of the buglers posted along the main road from Sønderborg, who have orders to sound a 'long bugle call' when the Prussian assault is launched, have been killed. And if there are any calls, they cannot be heard over the rising din of the battle. Critics of this account have argued that no one could have remained oblivious to the onset of the assault. At the very least, the men themselves would have been alerted a few minutes after the fact. There have been debates and controversies among war historians and participants regarding who gave which orders and when. Did the division commander General du Plat order a retreat when he realised that the entire left flank of the position had fallen, and did brigade commander Colonel Scharffenberg subsequently give a counter-order? Or did du Plat actually order the counter-attack, but then try to stop it once he realized the opponent was too overwhelming? Or did he acknowledge that once it was under way he was helpless to stop it? Some sources later claim that they heard him say, 'But what can we do? It seems now to have taken on a life of its own.'

There are many questions, to which there are but a few clear answers. In correspondence between two brigade officers, Adjutant Holbøll and Captain Redsted, who twenty years later were still trying to reconstruct the details of the brigade's counter-attack, Holbøll writes, 'I do not think anyone will ever be able to give a completely truthful and reliable account of the battle ... as in my opinion we will all of us only be able to give an account of the events we participated in ourselves.'

What we do know for sure is that at 10.30 a.m., the 8th Brigade, comprising 3,000 Danish troops, enters the fray and launches what would later become a celebrated counter-attack. The brigade charges the advancing Prussian troops, who by this time have reached Dybbøl Mill. Though the attack later becomes a cultural marker in the collective Danish imagination of the small nation's ability to fight against heavy odds, the Danish soldiers charging up Dybbøl Hill this morning are not concerned with lofty symbolism.

As the massive column moves forward, the men turn into mindless, wild animals acting on pure instinct: their senses sharpen and their eyes focus only on the enemy up ahead. The 9th Regiment, which includes Dinesen's 1st Company, makes up the Danish right wing. On the left is the 20th Regiment. The two regiments are practically sucked into the maelstrom on Dybbøl Hill. 'The entire line lunges forward,' Dinesen later writes. 'We tear along, through bogs, puddles, hedges and thickets; despite [a hailstorm of the enemy's] iron and lead, we keep moving forward. There is a determined seriousness to our attack.'

At about the same time as the 8th Brigade commences its counter-attack, the formidable ironclad *Rolf Krake* belatedly steams into Vemmingbund to support the troops at Dybbøl. Captain Rothe has for some time been aware that large numbers of Prussian troops seem to be swarming over the Danish positions, and he and his men can hear unusual fire from the fortifications at Dybbøl. The assault must be underway, Rothe concludes, and decides to rush to support the troops. Upon entering Vemmingbund, *Rolf Krake* immediately attracts enemy fire from the Prussian batteries as well

1864

The 8th Brigade's counter-attack, 10.30 a.m.

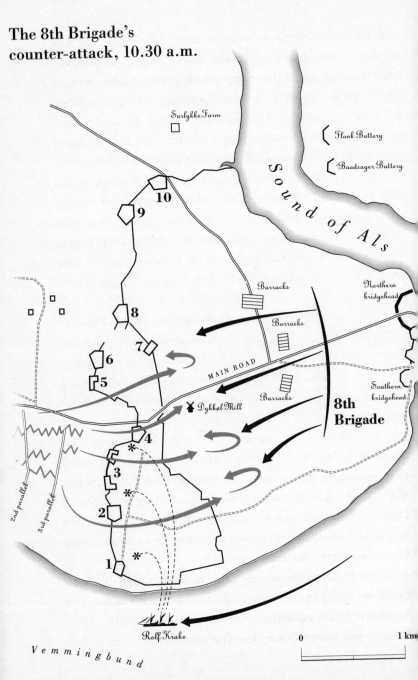

Surlykke Farm

{ Flank Battery

{ Baadsager Battery

S o u n d   o f   A l s

10

9

Barracks

Northern bridgehead

8

Barracks

7

6

MAIN ROAD

5

Barracks

Southern bridgehead

Dybbøl Mill

8th Brigade

4

*

3

*

2nd parallel

3rd parallel

2

*

1

*

Rolf Krake

0   1 km

V e m m i n g b u n d

as from a captured Danish 84-pounder in Redoubt II, which is quickly turned on the Danish warship. *Rolf Krake* reciprocates, hurling shells into the redoubt line, concentrating on Redoubt IV, where the warship has observed intense enemy activity.

Just as *Rolf Krake* opens fire, the bedraggled Prussian 53rd Regiment, 1st Company, is assembling in a corner of Redoubt IV. A shell strikes, killing Private Flügel and wounding two men. 'I was just talking to him and with tears in his eyes he was telling me about his best friend, who has died during the storm, and then a few minutes later he lies dead at my feet,' writes Kaspar Honthumb. Hastily the Prussians seek shelter from the warship's fire.

The sudden counter-attack takes the advancing Prussian troops by surprise. So far only minor detachments from the Danish 2nd and 22nd Regiments have been trying to halt the Prussian advance, when suddenly a tsunami of Danish soldiers rises out of the ground and travels towards them at great and fearsome speed. The Prussians are thrown back over the crest of Dybbøl Hill, where they turn around to try to repulse the attacking Danes. They fire again and again into the wave of men, and the Danes suffer massive losses, though it seems not even the hail of enemy bullets can stop the determined Danish attackers, who keep surging forward, inflicting serious damage. 'The battlefield is covered with dead and wounded Prussians,' Dinesen later writes.

The companies on the left flank manage to beat back the Prussians as far as the withdrawn line, and the Danish 20th Regiment on the right flank advances on Redoubt IV, which has only just been taken by the Prussians.

For a while it looks as if the brigade will be able to repel the Prussian advance and perhaps even retake the redoubts, but the odds are stacked heavily against them. Several thousand Prussian riflemen lie in wait behind the second line and, when the Danes are near enough, they open fire. The enemy's fire is 'extraordinarily deadly', according to a contemporary and otherwise dry Danish military report of the 8th Brigade's attack. This report – currently archived in the museum of Sønderborg Castle museum – further notes that the 20th Regiment loses 'its commander Colonel Tersling, the 1st battalion commander Count Ahlefeldt-Laurvig, and almost all company commanders as well as a large portion of its lieutenants and non-commissioned officers'. In total 300 men are killed within a few minutes by the Prussian riflemen.

At the redoubt line Prussian reinforcements move up and prepare for a major assault. The 27,000 Prussian reserves amassed here dwarf the Danish 8th Brigade. Once the two forces clash there will be nine Prussians for each Dane. While the Prussian reserves are moved forward, on the Danish side of the line Captain Redsted tries to retake Dybbøl Mill with the 1st Company, in which Dinesen serves. Several Prussian units are holding the mill at this time and the battle that ensues is fierce and costly.

'Redsted moves up to the mill itself with the 1st and 3rd Brigades; with the rest of the men I move up to the area in front of the mill, which we storm with fixed bayonets and loud cheers despite being met by a hail of enemy bullets,' Dinesen writes.

Knauer falls right outside the mill, but his men join Redsted and we storm the mill from all sides, killing and crushing all resistance we encounter and forcing the remaining enemies into the mill itself. In these close quarters there is no room to aim or use bayonets, so we drop our rifles and fight with our fists and swords. Outside the mill, Redsted pulls himself up by the arms to peer in, just as a Prussian presses the muzzle of his rifle against his head and pulls the trigger.

Redsted, though shot through the neck and shoulder, survives and describes the incident later while in Prussian captivity:

I move forward, reach the corner of the building. My faithful men follow me. It's here, as I try to enter a window, that I receive my current wounds. Still, I try to stay on my feet and encourage my men with looks and gestures as my voice has gone, but within a few seconds I fall backwards, landing on the ground, unconscious. I come to a few minutes later as two enemy soldiers are robbing me, and see that a section of our company is still putting up a good fight. The Prussians now move great masses of troops forward. What happens after this point, I do not know.

Dinesen remembers:

The Prussian charge is overwhelming. Complete destruction. Of the men from 1st Company who enter the mill, only Corporal Blinkenberg and Lance Corporal Vestesen survive, though the latter is mortally wounded and dies later. When the mill falls, we are just outside, locked in a firefight with the enemy. We know we will not be able to hold out much longer as the enemy is also moving up on our flank and we are beginning to receive enfilade fire as well; we soon understand that the Battle of Dybbøl has come to an end.

Though the battle has indeed been decisively lost, the fighting is far from over. The remnants of the 8th Brigade now in retreat face a perilous journey. Dinesen and his comrades exist in what is generally perceived as the most dangerous place and time in Danish history. The horizon is black with the oncoming mass of enemies. Dinesen remembers: 'The enemy was getting closer fast. Scattered elements from dissolved companies had joined me, but more and more of my commanders were falling prey to enemy fire. I had thus far carried a swagger stick but dropped it now and drew my sabre.'

The entire Danish line is retreating. The Danes are holding down two farmsteads, Jensen's farm and the Sney farm, on the left flank. They bravely try to hold out against the overwhelming enemy. As the last remnants of the Danish troops pull back here, dead and wounded cover the road and fields. 'Some of the wounded just lie still on the ground,' Dinesen writes, 'others are sitting up, looking frantically around them, and still others are scrambling for cover behind anything that will provide shelter. The enemy reaches the barracks at the same time we do; we make our last effort to repulse the enemy, but are routed and retreat in wild confusion.'

Dinesen tries to round up his men, but many soldiers have become separated from their units and are running around frantically in complete confusion. It is utter pandemonium. One of these men, Private Frederik Hansen, has left a vivid account of the event. (His handwritten and unpublished memoirs are archived in Sønderborg Castle museum.)

The retreating Danish forces tried to hold out against the overwhelming
Prussian forces from the ruins of farmsteads like this one.

I pull back as best I can, making my first rest stop in a ditch
full of water, where I am soaked through; my boots fill
with water, and on my next stretch I am weighed down
by the heavy boots. I make it to a burnt-down farmstead,
where I hide for a while behind the naked walls, which are
still standing. Many Danes are captured here, but I escape,
running in a north-easterly direction, where I find shelter
behind a fence. Here seven or eight men and one officer are
also taking cover. The officer orders us to fire, but before
I can get my wits about me I am the only one left. I get up
and begin running along the fence until I come to another
and cross it. Here I link up with a comrade and we take
cover as best we can. We cannot move further forward as
Danish troops have taken up their positions at the bridgehead, and we are therefore in as much danger of being
killed by friendly fire as by enemy fire. I lie with my nose
pressed to the ground, too afraid to get up. I lie there for
about an hour when I hear my comrade ask, 'What should

we do?' I tell him that I think we should stay until night
fall as it is too risky to leave now. I lie back down, listening. Hundreds of bullets whizz overhead from both sides.
Finally I hear voices; they are speaking in German, and I
immediately shout, 'I surrender.' I shout this three times
before there is an answer. 'Kom mal hieruber' ['Come over
here'] the voice says; I jump the fence, Danish bullets whistling past my ears. I stay there with the Germans for about
half an hour before we pull back to the redoubt line, where
we are in grave danger of being hit by the Danish shells.

At 11 a.m., at about the same time as the 8th Brigade begins
its wild retreat, *Rolf Krake* pulls out of the battle after taking
a direct hit that pierces the ship's iron-plated deck, killing an
officer and wounding nine men. Though menacing to look at,
Rolf Krake never becomes a decisive element in the battle. It
is pulled out because it is deemed more important to keep the
ship intact for the defence of Als, should that become necessary.

By the barracks line, Dinesen meets up with the division
staff: General du Plat, Major Rosen and Major Ernst Schau.
For some time du Plat has been aware that the enemy is too
overwhelming, and he is concerned it may not be possible to
hold them off long enough for the men to retreat to Als. He
is also aware that the 8th Brigade has pushed too far forward
and that the Danish army may be close to a total collapse. He
has therefore ordered the only remaining cohesive brigade,
which is still in position on the far right flank of the Danish
line, to retreat. Dybbøl is lost and he recognises that sending
in reserve troops is futile. Du Plat sends a message to that
effect to headquarters, informing them also that the retreat

has begun. The focus now for the Danish troops is to hold the bridgehead until all troops have been moved to Als. The 3rd and 18th Regiments are deployed at the pontoon bridges to cover the retreating troops and halt the advancing Prussians, as it is believed they will try to occupy Als.

The situation is critical. But, as it turns out, the worst is yet to come.

In the barracks line, everything is chaos. Dinesen recalls:

Our strength is spent. The once 140-man company is now down to thirty-three. The men are exhausted and no matter how much I beg, plead and coax them they can run for only brief stretches before resorting to a slower walking pace; the enemy's fire, coming at us from rifles and the newly positioned Prussian batteries, takes them down one by one. Just before reaching the barracks line we are stopped by Major Rosen, who is supporting the head of General du Plat; du Plat's white hair is covered in blood, and I realise he must be dead.

Dinesen initially attempts to get a few of his men to carry the general with them. But two of the bearers are shot and killed and there is nothing to do but leave the general behind. Major Rosen takes a hit, 'his right arm shoots up and he clamps his hand to his side and falls with a moan into the ditch on the right side of the road.'

Rosen is seriously wounded and only a few paces away lies the mortally wounded Major Ernst Schau, who has taken a bullet to the hip. Dorothea Schau is about to lose her sixth son. Her seventh will die in just a few moments. Emil is with the 6th Regiment and in full retreat from the right flank.

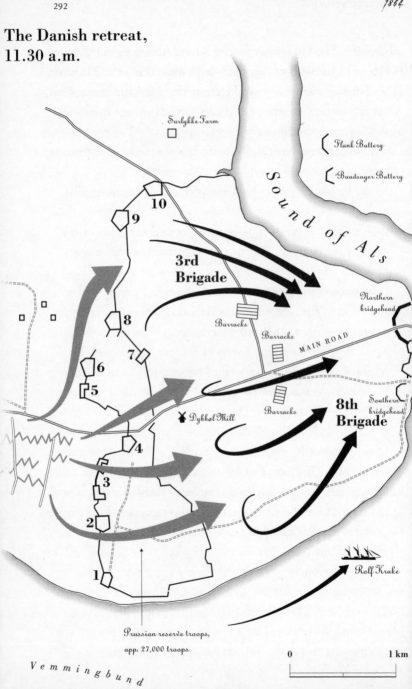

1864

The Danish retreat,
11.30 a.m.

Surlykke Farm

Flank Battery

Baadsager Battery

S o u n d   o f   A l s

10

9

**3rd
Brigade**

Northern
bridgehead

Barracks

8

Barracks

MAIN ROAD

7

6

5

Barracks

Dybbøl Mill

8th
Brigade

Southern
bridgehead

Barracks

4

3

2

1

Rolf Krake

Prussian reserve troops,
app. 27,000 troops

0   1 km

V e m m i n g b u n d

The Medic and his four comrades have finally been informed of the whereabouts of the wounded major, but he resists when they try to get him on to a stretcher. The Medic later recalled, 'We had to leave him and return to the dressing station. The road is strewn with wounded men begging to be picked up.' Instead they decide to carry a severely wounded, bulky Danish officer, who has been shot in the arm and leg.

He is in bad shape and has already been there for more than an hour and a half. It is hard work carrying the heavy man. Even though there are four of us and we have every possible cause to hurry out of range, we are forced to pause every few minutes. We are so exhausted and our last ration of water is given to the wounded. But, oh, what we would not have given for a sip of water!

Slowly the medics make their way back across the redoubt line with their heavy burden, all the while bullets and shells from Als striking down like giant pieces of hail all around them. Not until they reach the trenches are they able to breathe again. 'We were able to carry the enemy – or rather friend – safely to the dressing station. He was so grateful. The dressing station is full to bursting with dead and wounded; the screaming of the latter goes right through you. We quench our thirst by lapping up water from a puddle.'

29

Burning bridges

A man can handle only so much turmoil. Even just reading about the battle, you find yourself needing to take a break. Many of the men on the battlefield, though in the midst of a hail of bullets and shells, suddenly give up and throw themselves on the ground, completely spent and resigned to their fate.

We, however, have to take a deep breath and move on: the battle is far from over. The Danes still need to get their brigades across the Sound of Als. Only if they succeed in this feat will they have prevented total annihilation.

The Danish right flank, comprising the 16th and 17th Regiments – approximately 2,500 men – suffer the lightest casualties, though they lose more than 200 dead and wounded before the day closes, almost 10 per cent of the command; a further 500 are taken prisoner. Even in the Danish sector with the fewest casualties, about one in four of the troops there do not make it back to Als.

At around 11 a.m. the 16th and 17th Regiments commence their retreat from Redoubts VII–X and barely escape being encircled by the Prussians – a fate they avoid due to the 8th Brigade's fierce counter-attack. While that battle is in full swing, the right-flank regiments retreat towards the bridgehead.

If it were possible to ask Lieutenant Jacob Bang what it was like to be on the Danish right flank on 18 April, he probably would not have been very sympathetic to the notion that their fight was undramatic compared to others that day. When the Prussian storm troops swarm the left flank, he and his outposts rush back to the trenches, which are being subjected to heavy Prussian shelling. While running to the trenches, Bang witnesses the killing of a young seventeen-year-old bugler, who falls to the ground with the words, 'Dear lord, help me.'

> As soon as we make it into [the trench] we are greeted by the sight of two comrades sitting on the banquette, one without a head and the other torn lengthwise from head to foot. We have to sit next to them, and although I have curled myself up as much as possible, a shell strikes near my neck and I am so overwhelmed by the noise that for a few moments I do not know whether I am alive or dead.

Two of Bang's comrades, sitting next to him, are hit, one of them seriously. From the trench they fire volleys at the Prussians storming Redoubt VII. Just as the regiments receive orders to retreat to the bridgehead, the company commander Captain Gandil is wounded.

Supporting Gandil, Bang and his men venture out into the open, where they are easy targets for the enemy bullets. Worst of all, they have to get across a ravine. Once down there, they receive heavy fire from a group of Prussian riflemen who have taken position on top of the ravine. Prussian troops have also taken hold of the ruins of the Steensgården farmstead situated on relatively high ground, allowing them to fire directly on the retreating Danes.

By the mouth of the stream we see several dead soldiers alerting us to the danger waiting ahead. The Germans have taken up position so as to prevent our crossing the stream, shooting at us down the length of the ravine. But we out-smart them: some of us storm up the embankment next to the ravine with loud cheers, firing our rifles; the Germans are taken in, allowing some of us, including the captain and me, to get across, while those behind us surrender.

Many never get a chance to surrender, however, and are killed or wounded during the firefight. Some tumble down the slope and are trampled by the soldiers coming up behind them. Lieutenant Emil Schau is shot in the foot, but manages to hobble all the way back to the bridgehead. Once there, however, he takes a bullet in the gut and is killed instantly. Dorothea's last living son departs the earth.

Another man who never makes it back is Private J. P. Hansen, 16th Regiment, 7th Company. He survives but is taken prisoner. His company is holding position on a hilltop close to the Sound of Als. In a letter, written only a few hours later, he notes, 'We are completely surrounded and take fire from all sides. Lieutenant Fisher, 6th Regiment, falls next to me, hit by a bullet in the mouth, though he does not die. A sergeant falls to my right, hit by a bullet in his left hand and another in his abdomen. I never learn whether he makes it.'

The situation for the Danes at this time, nearing noon and scarcely two hours after the battle commenced, is grim. The entire redoubt line has been lost, the withdrawn line has been lost, and two entire regiments have been wiped out. The 8th Brigade, though having performed gallantly, has sustained losses of such magnitude that it has basically ceased to exist. The 16th and 17th Regiments are in full retreat, hastily moving across the pontoon bridges.

Elsewhere the battle still rages. The 3rd and 18th Regiments, holding the bridgehead – Denmark's last stronghold – are now fully engaged in the battle. Behind the entrenchments and embankments they are firing away at the advancing Prussians and managing to hold them off. The various batteries in and around Sønderborg have joined in too. In intensity and volume, nothing seems changed for the spectators on the Sønderborg side. Dicey writes about this phase of the battle:

> As the Danes retreat down the hill, the Prussians turned the whole force of their fire full upon the bridges and the streets [of Sønderborg] through which the retiring troops would have to pass. The Danish batteries on the Sønderborg shore opened fire to cover the retreat, and with some effect. The immediate result, however, was to bring down upon them the fire of Broager with fearful accuracy.

The bullets strike the Sønderborg church battery, and the windmill behind it is set ablaze. Shells explode near the pontoon bridges, some producing giant water columns. Masses of Prussian troops are advancing on the 3rd and 18th Regiments, and the Prussians are also deploying field batteries on Dybbøl Hill.

One of the soldiers manning these Prussian batteries is Gunner Robert Bochmann. As soon as the redoubts have been taken from the Danes, Prussian troops – Bochmann among them – immediately move four batteries of field artillery

forward and position them on Dybbøl Hill to repel the counter-attack and later sweep the attackers as they retreat.

The ride out to the battlefield in the artillery wagon is anything but pleasant for Bochmann:

> The battery commander rides in front with his trumpet.
> Lieutenant Vohs follows with his battery on the main road,
> where they receive fire from Redoubts VIII and IX. Ahead
> of us is the four-pound mobile battery. We take rifle fire,
> and one gunner from the mobile battery is shot. He is in the
> ditch when we drive by, his head nearly severed.

As they pass the dead gunner, the soldier sitting next to
Bochmann is cheering loudly. He is thrilled by their speedy
progress. To Bochmann there seems scant cause for cheering.
The combat zone is cluttered with obstacles and so torn by
shelling that the gunners keep falling off the swaying wagons.
'We jump off and walk behind the cannon, while holding
it steady. One cannon topples over when the horses react to a
shell that strikes nearby. We take up position behind Redoubt
VII ... but first we have to remove the dead and wounded
Danes.' From their position close to this redoubt they engage
in battle with the Danish Sønderborg batteries and fire at the
retreating Danish troops.

Bochmann later notes in his diary:

> An enemy shell explodes close to Gunner Hensel's head
> and his uniform is torn in several places by shrapnel, but
> though he is not wounded he loses his hearing in one ear.
> A cannonball rolls out from the barrel of our 5th cannon,
> explodes and wounds non-commissioned Officer Hinze in

the thigh. Senior Lance-Corporal Ganzert from our 4th cannon gets his leg crushed. He collapses behind a fence and dies.

In a letter to his parents, Bochmann describes their engagement with the Danish artillery at Sønderborg:

After a few rounds a fortification in Sønderborg explodes. With our smooth-bore cannon we are unable to reach targets on Als. Our shells strike the water, so instead we focus our fire on the bridgehead by the Sound of Als. After an hour the pontoon bridges are on fire. All corners of Sønderborg are in flames as well.

This makes for perilous circumstances for the retreating remnants of the Danish army, who are trying to cross the pontoon bridges to Als. The 3rd and 18th Regiments are putting all their resources into providing sufficient cover and repelling the advancing Prussian forces. Prince Friedrich Karl dispatches an order from his post on Avnbjerg for his troops to attack the bridgehead if, and only if, they deem it feasible.

When the 3rd and 18th Regiments of the Danish army had taken up their position at the bridgehead two hours earlier, just as the assault commenced, they had, according to Christian Bredsdorff, been convinced that 'it would be our last battle, as the order given was "to hold the bridges at all costs and to meet the enemy with fixed bayonets". A hailstorm of bullets and shells pelts us and it seems incomprehensible that we can walk about with impunity, which we do for a few hours.'

Once the retreating troops arrive and are led through the bridgehead and across the pontoon bridges, the two regiments focus all their energy on holding off the enemy. At a few minutes past one, all retreating companies have crossed the bridges to Als, and the 3rd and 18th Regiments can begin their retreat, one unit at a time, a particularly hazardous endeavour as it gradually reduces the number of Danish soldiers available to provide covering fire. Lieutenant P. E. M. Ramsing of the 18th Regiment writes in a letter a few days later that while the retreat was under way, 'a shell rushed in along the breast-work, killing and maiming six men; the others looked on in horror, but none pulled back as much as an inch. They just clutched their rifles tighter and mumbled, "You just wait until you get within shooting range, then it will be payback time."'

After large parts of the Danish army have made it across to Als, a massive column of Prussians suddenly advance on the bridgehead trench. 'Captain Svane and his company are posted here,' Ramsing writes. 'When the enemy is thirty metres from us, a single loud cheer rises from the trench; surprised, the Prussians stop short. "Fire!" sounds a command behind the rampart and whole rows of Prussians fall to the ground. The rest turn around and flee, but many fall prey to the next volley of Danish fire.'

The time has now come to get the remaining companies across the bridge, and this is done under intense fire from the Prussian batteries. Swedish volunteer Lieutenant Axel Ivar Key describes this dangerous situation, in which the last units to retreat are at great risk of being attacked in the rear while on the bridges. 'Our progress is slow and our ranks break because everyone is eager to move ahead quickly. There is chaos on the crowded passage, made worse by the fact that we have no time to dispose of our comrades' dead bodies and so have to negotiate our way over them.'

But even these last units make it across, and the Prussians have to content themselves with looking on as the last Danish troops leave the mainland. Not even General von Goeben, who has been posted near Sottrup Woods all day, waiting for the chance to cross the Sound of Als, has at any point during the battle found the opportunity to launch boats or pontoon bridges. Facing him all day have been two vigilant Danish regiments, the 1st and 11th, commanded by the unwavering Colonel Max Müller, who had clashed with the Austrians at Sankelmark on 6 February. Since the early morning, Müller's battery has met Goeben and his men with fierce resistance, leaving the Prussians no choice but to stay put. Certainly Goeben has not felt inclined to risk a fiasco that would cast a shadow over the Prussian victory.

Since mid-morning the Danish engineers have been hard at work scuttling and burning ferries, other vessels and bridges which the Prussians could use to cross the sound to Als. At noon the northern pontoon bridge near the bridgehead is destroyed, and by 2. 30 p.m. the second of the two bridges is badly hit by heavy Prussian fire. Four Danish engineers row out to the bridge to complete the job. As if by miracle none are wounded by the intense enemy fire.

Four and a half hours of brutal battle are over and Dybbøl has been irretrievably lost. The bridges to mainland Schleswig have been burnt down. The triumphant Prince Friedrich Karl dispatches a telegram to his uncle King Wilhelm I in Berlin. It reads: 'Ten redoubts at your feet, Your Majesty.'

30

The dead

While the bridges burn away, Dybbøl Hill is quiet and enveloped in a thick smoke that, over the course of the afternoon, slowly lifts and mixes with a fog which rolls gently in across the entire area, down towards the Sound of Als, Vemmingbund and Broager, where more smoke from the smouldering barracks and ruins mingles with the miasmic clouds from the battlefield. A peaceful atmosphere, however, does not descend over the theatre of war until nightfall, as the Prussian and Danish cannon still play furiously across Als Sound. The Prussians have moved their batteries down there and are pounding the Danish batteries on the island. Intent on preventing the enemy from attempting a crossing, the Danes return fire with fierce determination. Still, the din of this battle seems like nothing more than a soft humming compared with the thunderous roar of the day's earlier bombardments.

The battle of 18 April is definitively over. But for many of the survivors, the worst is still to come. While the fighting is in full swing, the men, infused with adrenalin, are focused only on survival, but now, as the immediate danger has passed, they begin to feel the full impact of the battle, recognising the degree of destruction and suffering it has wrought. For some, like eighteen-year-old Wilhelm Dinesen, the emotional scars never heal. His fate, however, is for another book; let us now join the Prussian soldiers as they take in the wasteland of the battlefield, strewn with unburied foes and friends.

After shaking off the worst of his agitation, Private J. Bubbe, who took part in the storming of Redoubt V and in repelling the Danish counter-attack, walks across the battle-field. In his memoirs, he describes the wasteland of human death that meets him here:

What a mess! Doctors and medics with stretchers are busily occupied bandaging and carrying the wounded off in ambulances and transport wagons. There is much moaning and misery for such a small area of land. There are dead soldiers everywhere, lying where they have fallen and struggled with death. Next to and underneath the ordnance are the bodies of the brave Danish gunners, who fulfilled their duty heroically. The majority of the men on the ground have expired, but some are still in the last throes of death, suffering most terribly. Their muscles twitch and their already distorted faces are twisted, their eyes bulge and their frantic expressions become more and more glassy. It takes a lot to finish off these young, strong-hearted men. Their breathing becomes more and more laboured, their chests heave, yet another heavy contraction of the muscles, and then the body gives one final spasmodic jerk and the man is at last at peace. On top of the corner of the breastwork, where the Prussian flag is now planted, under a heap of dead men, lays the Prussian sergeant who carried our colours during battle. Next to him is the young Danish infantry officer who plunged his sabre through the sergeant's chest and whom death has also taken. Both have fought with vigour for their country, and both have fought each other bitterly. Now they rest peacefully next to one another. When passing through the gate of death, we are no longer opponents.

Bubbe continues his walk, passing a small heap of Danish soldiers who have met their maker in front of the powder magazine near a trench:

One lies with his feet on the banquette of the breastwork, his head resting on the edge of the trench. In his right hand he still clutches his loaded rifle, finger on the trigger. Death has got to him before he has had time to fire the deadly lead in his gun. A bullet has penetrated his forehead just as he was about to fire. On a table nearby are the remnants of a scanty breakfast, two opened letters and a shoe brush – by the entrance are the four bodies.

Once past this little group of Danes, Bubbe is met by a sight that makes him stop short. The experienced sergeant who had so surprised Bubbe by breaking down just before their march to Dybbøl in the early hours of the 18th, crying and clutching a photo of his family, lies right in front of him, dead. 'He lies with an almost peaceful smile on his face as if he was trying to tell us that it is really peaceful in heaven. His forehead has been perforated by a shot. Presumably he made no sound as he fell. It seems his premonition that he would be among the dead was correct.'

Wilhelm Gather, who participated in the relatively easy storming of Redoubt VI, is also walking about on the battlefield and is much affected by what he sees. In a letter to his parents, Gather writes:

The dressing station is a terrible sight. The dead have been gathered in a rush and the wounded have received only hasty bandaging, just enough so they can be safely transported. On the main road there are entire wagon trains carrying wounded, whose facial expressions are so horrible that it is as if death has already toyed with them. Once you have seen all this, you must conclude that we live in a terrible world; only a terrible place can allow people to butcher each other like that and then attempt to patch up their wounds.

In the late afternoon, Gather and his company are ordered to march back to their quarters at Nybøl. On the march they see dead and wounded everywhere. The bodies of dead Prussian soldiers are deposited in a giant heap at Nybøl church. 'Among them are five officers, including our major. There is also a foot without a body.'

The march across what until the First World War is without shame referred to as 'the field of glory' will be forever etched on Captain Bunge's memory. The burning bridges are visible on the horizon, the barracks are in flames, and the landscape he and his men march through is enveloped in smoke-tinged fog which is slowly lifting. In his memoirs he writes:

At about five in the afternoon, we are ordered to pull back to our quarters; the march leads us through the battlefield to the redoubt line where we relive the horrors of the past few hours. The indefatigable doctors and medics carrying stretchers are busily tending the wounded. All is misery and pain, dead bodies and ruins. Behind the redoubts and the defensive line's breastworks as well as behind fences there are rows of dead bodies, and there are also rows of prisoners being led away.

Louis Appia, the Swiss Red Cross delegate, goes out to the battlefield in the afternoon in order to be able to describe the scene to Jean Henri Dunant, the Red Cross commissioner in Geneva. In a letter to Dunant, he writes:

Blood flows in the streams, and bits and pieces of the men's uniforms and toiletries are strewn about. The landscape is heavily scarred by shelling and littered by all kinds of shells: case-shot, conical shells and bullets the size of my head. There is a jumble of Danish and Prussian cartridge belts everywhere, you can just bend down and pick one up as a trophy … and there are fragments of letters, probably written to parents or sweethearts. Down by one of the redoubts I pass twenty-five bodies, which have been lined up on a plank, ready for burial in a mass grave. There are already more mass graves next to this one, along with a cross that reads: 'Here lie 308 brave soldiers, who died for their country'.

The civilian painter Wilhelm Camphausen also takes a walk across the battlefield and describes his experience with an artist's sensitivity and attention to detail. While the battle was in full swing he had observed it with binoculars from Broager, but the day after the battle, he gathers enough courage to visit the battlefield. The first sight that meets him is a row of dead soldiers being readied for mass burial. Camphausen has never seen a battlefield before, nor has he ever witnessed the kind of effect shells and bullets have on the human body:

Among the dead officers were the two Danish brothers (above) Emil Victor
and Ernst Schau and the two Prussians, Arthur and Louis Rabenau.

With a shiver I move closer to the row of dead bodies and only after a while am I able to take in the horrible spectacle. There are the bodies, most laid out side by side and prepared for burial, their faces motionless and ashen white, their eyes glazed and wide open, staring emptily at the blue sky above ... I look at one, then another, and soon I am able to view them with a steadier gaze. To my great consternation, I discover how quickly we become inured to that which is shocking and horrifying when there is much of it. When I grab my pencil to sketch the distinctive groupings of bodies, the revulsion that had at first filled me dissipates. All I see is the angles and shapes of the sad mess of twisted limbs, which I proceed to sketch as I would tables and chairs. I, who have grown up in quiet and peaceable circumstances, am afraid to think how emotionally desensitised soldiers must become, being exposed to such scenes all the time.

After a few sketches, Camphausen moves on down the row of bodies. There are hundreds of them:

While some are horrifically mutilated, either completely crushed or with limbs torn from their bodies, most have been shot through the head by rifle bullets. The majority have a calm, almost gentle expression, their bluish lips pursed and ringed by reddish-blond beards, their fingers oddly locked as if about to scratch an itch. The most mutilated bodies are covered by coats. I lift one, covering a head, and behold an unshapely mass, a crushed head with no face ... I see piles of bodies being loaded on to farmers' carts and driven to mass graves. Between 100 and 200 men are buried in deep graves. The dead lie atop and between one another, on hay, and are finally covered with dirt. The grave is marked by a simple wooden cross with the inscription 'Here lie 150 brave Danes' and a small painting of two entwined hands within a palm wreath.

What Camphausen does not tell, but what his drawings show and many first-hand accounts further attest to, is that most of the bodies have been robbed of all valuables by the victors. The most highly prized loot is Danish army boots. Most of the dead Danes lie, row after row, in bare feet or with their stockings exposed. A few have even been robbed of their uniform trousers.

Though Camphausen may have become relatively anaesthetised to the gruesome sight of dead soldiers, much of what he sees on that day bears witness to the horrendous human suffering of the battle.

It's in the trenches between the redoubts that the number of thick pools of blood are most pronounced, presumably because the fighting here has claimed the most victims. There is an abundance of odds and ends in the trenches: a blood-soiled letter, which I pick up and am able to read in parts. It moves me to tears. It is from a small boy – the letters are lopsided and immature – to his father on the front. The boy tells his father of little events at home – when he last had sweet fruit soup [a traditional Danish dish], when he played with his toy pony – and, in conclusion, 'We are so happy that you are doing well and will be coming home shortly. Please write again soon.'

Colonel Paul Scharffenberg was considered one of the most fearless officers in the Danish Army, however in the hours after his counter-attack with the 8th Brigade he suffered a mental breakdown.

While we do not know exactly how many dead there were on Dybbøl Hill on the late afternoon of 18 April, we are now sure that both armies' official body count is considerably lower than the actual number of killed. According to the records, 379 Danish soldiers were killed, 39 of whom were officers. The Prussians have listed 263 as killed in action, with 17 of those officers. Denmark recorded 646 as missing, most of whom had presumably been killed during the battle and buried in mass graves. Thus, the total number of Danish soldiers killed in action were closer to 1,000 men, a number that corresponds to an estimate provided by the meticulous Prussian chief surgeon, F. Loeffler, who collected data from his field hospital and the battlefield on 18 April. The Prussians listed 29 as missing, all presumably dead, which brings their total number of men killed in the battle closer to 300. The actual count of Prussians killed in action is probably even larger if we are to believe the many eyewitness accounts from the redoubts, the counter-attack and the fighting at the bridgehead. The most credible low estimate is 1,100 dead Danes and Prussians on the battlefield. There were 2,500 wounded. Of these, 1,500 were, according to Loeffler's numbers, Danes (the Danish estimate was 1,000) and 1,000 were Prussians. Several hundred of these were seriously wounded and died either within hours of the battle or some weeks later. So, if we include men who subsequently died of their wounds or complications arising from their wounds, the overall death toll is closer to 2,000 men.

In addition to losses incurred on the battlefield, Denmark lost 3,300 men taken as prisoners of war. About 430 of these were wounded and have been included in the number of wounded mentioned above. The total Danish casualties totaled then some 5,500 whereas the total number of Prussian casualties was at least 1,200 men. That number roughly corresponds to every other Danish soldier present on Dybbøl Hill that day – a loss which in and of itself is crushing – but the losses incurred by the 2nd and 22nd Regiments, who bore the brunt of the assault, and the 8th Brigade (9th and 20th Regiments), who conducted the counter-attack, were unprecedented. The 2nd Regiment lost 864 men, including officers, out of a force of 1,268. Only 400 of the dissolved regiment made it safely to Als. The 22nd Regiment lost 921 men all told, out of a force of 1,104. (The regimental report estimated 500 dead or wounded – almost half of the force.) The 22nd Regiment was also dissolved. The 8th Brigade lost 1,416 men in total – approximately half of the force. The remaining troops were moved to the Island of Fyn later that evening. Their otherwise calm and collected commander, Colonel Scharffenberg, suffered a nervous breakdown sometime during the early evening. 'He was,' his adjutant, H. Holbøll, wrote in his memoirs, 'emotionally distressed ... the loss of several of his dear friends and many well-liked comrades affected him deeply. In the evening he was seized by a nervous fit that rendered him unable to move. I managed to get him on to a couch, but as his condition did not improve, he agreed to go to bed. But he was unable to walk from the couch to his bed. He was completely paralysed and had to be carried by a couple of orderlies.'

31

The dying

Though the battle was over, the ghastly suffering of the wounded seemed never-ending. In the hours and days following the assault, medics continued to find wounded men strewn pell-mell throughout the theatre of war. In chilling detail both the Prussian chief surgeon F. Loeffler and Chief Surgeon Julius Ressel of the Order of St John provide in their field reports from the battle long lists of the gruesome wounds their patients had sustained. Scores of men had severe head trauma, many with their faces torn up, eyes shot out, crushed jaws and necks, or gaping wounds to the throat; some had spinal cord and nerve damage, shell-splintered ribcages, perforated lungs or shattered shoulders, arms, elbows, hands or fingers; limbs had been torn off; shells and shrapnel had been lodged in guts. Several hundred soldiers had had their hips, thighbones, knee caps or calves crushed; feet were partially or completely smashed or toes shot off. Many soldiers suffered multiple wounds. The Swedish volunteer Lieutenant Lundgreen of the 22nd Regiment is perhaps the worst recorded case of multiple wounding. According to Loeffler's report, a bullet had 'pierced his jaw, passed through the root of the tongue and exited just to the right of his larynx. A bullet struck his left shoulder, grazing the collarbone. A bullet struck his right shoulder. A bullet ripped through his stomach. A bullet penetrated his right hip. Smashed fingers on the right hand.' After lingering in great agony for over nine days, he died at a field hospital in Stenderup village near Ragebøl.

In his report on the battle at Dybbøl to Jean Henri Dunant and the Red Cross committee, Louis Appia noted that although the Prussians had more than five times the normal allocation of medical personnel, their field surgeons and medical orderlies were overworked and worn out. They had 1,500 wounded in their care, while the Danish side had 800 to 900. Danish and Prussian doctors alike dressed wounds, amputated limbs, stopped haemorrhaging and in general patched up the men as best they could until they themselves were near death from exhaustion. The diaries of T. D. Reymert, a volunteer doctor from Norway, give a clear picture of the many hours the steadfast doctors worked. Reymert had been deployed to the field hospital at Hørup Hav and on 18 April he writes only a short entry: 'Terrible shooting. The number of wounded today cannot be processed.' On the 19th he wrote:

Until 2 a.m. [last night] the Swedish doctor and I were busy dressing the wounds of the many soldiers that came in from Sønderborg to our facility before being shipped to Copenhagen for further treatment. At Hørup Hav the wounded were received and bandaged on the floor of a large warehouse. At some point after midnight the Swedish doctor and I were so tired we lay down among the wounded to catch a little sleep. I found a spot between two seriously wounded soldiers; one of them, a guardsman from Copenhagen, drew his last breath at my side. Shortly before he

died, he asked me if I would accept his sabre as a remem-
brance ... he had used it bravely against many enemies of
Denmark, he told me.

Many years later, Reymert wrote, 'Whenever I see this weapon,
the memory of that unhappy night is upon me.'

Edward Dicey was also in Hørup Hav on the 19th and
could observe the state of the men as they left Reymert's field
hospital and were hoisted aboard the steamer for Copenhagen. Dicey told his readers that although he had become quite
callous at seeing so much suffering, he was greatly affected by
what he saw that day:

> The scene was terrible. As the cart jolted down to the
> wharf, soldier after soldier was borne out on stretchers
> and placed on the deck of the ship. The men were well
> wrapped and covered up, and all their wounds seemed to
> have been attended to carefully ... Some of the men lay so
> quiet that you could scarcely tell whether they lived or not;
> others tossed from side to side constantly in the restlessness
> of pain; and others literally writhed with agony as the carts
> swayed to and fro. In more than one case, which I observed
> in the course of a few minutes, the occupant of the cart was
> found dead when the bearers came to remove him, and his
> body, instead of being taken on board ship, was replaced in
> the straw and covered over with a soldier's coat.

W. F. Besser, a Prussian pastor, came in even closer contact
with the wounded. He arrived at Dybbøl a few days after the
battle, and it was his job to comfort the wounded and admin-
ster last rites to the dying in the Prussian field hospitals. For

Wounded Danish and Prussian soldiers, side by side at a field hospital
in Flensburg. Although the Prussians had more than five times the
normal allocation of medical personnel, their field surgeons were
severely overworked and the dying continued weeks after the battle.

Besser the following days became a journey into human suffering such as he had never seen before.

On 19 April his congregation had commissioned him to go
to Dybbøl. He felt a pressure to make haste to the site of the
battle 'because hundreds of wounded and dying were laid up
in the field hospitals'. He travelled by train from Waldenburg
in southern Prussia through Berlin to Schleswig-Holstein and
finally from there on to Dybbøl. Through the train windows
he saw several troops of Danish prisoners being transported
en masse, and large crowds of people gathering on the train
stations to stare at the defeated. In Berlin the streets teemed
with victorious soldiers, but there were also a great many civilians with black armbands, showing they were in mourning
and had lost a son, a father or a husband.

Still, what struck Besser most forcibly in Berlin was the level of euphoric energy palpable in the streets of the city, compared with when he was there three months earlier. All people wanted to talk about was *the victory*.

Driving through the streets of Berlin everything seemed so changed from three months ago. You could actually see [the victory] in the way people walked, they seemed to have more of a bounce in their step. It was certainly obvious that it had re-instilled true national pride and unity in people here.

On the train from Berlin to the duchies, Besser, however, was to become acquainted with the darker side of the war: he travelled north with relatives of mortally wounded soldiers too badly mangled or too close to death to be able to make the journey home. One officer with whom Besser shared a compartment was quite disheartened as he had two brothers in the field hospitals on the front and neither of them, he told Besser, was likely to survive their wounds. These were Lieutenants Louis and Arthur Rabenau. Besser also spoke to the father, brother and brother-in-law of a young wounded soldier who, as if by divine intervention, had been pulled out from under a heap of dead soldiers at the bridgehead with no severe wounds. 'It was as if he had been given a second chance.'

Though Besser arrived several days after the action, the shell-torn battlefield was still covered in the blood of the dead and wounded. Walking across the battlefield, he was shocked by 'the pools of blood still soaking the ground … there were still dead bodies hidden in rifle-pits, behind fences and in ruins'.

Besser quickly began his work of bringing consolation to the wounded and dying. The first field hospital he visited was in Stenderup village. 'I could not restrain an involuntary shudder when a nurse shouted at me, "Please be careful not to step on that leg there!" as I walked down the aisle between the two rows of beds in the first room.' The leg had been amputated from a Danish soldier fifteen minutes ago and was to be buried in a soldier's grave. Next to the leg lay another Danish soldier who had had both of his arms amputated. Besser had learned Danish as a student years ago but only well enough to be able to read it, and had never practised speaking the language. Once he realised there were several wounded Danes in the hospital, he saw it as his special mission to comfort them as they had no one else to talk to. So he turned to the man who had lost his leg, and said, 'It is better that you step into life lame, than have both feet and end in hell.' The soldier understood his halting Danish, and gratefully held out his hand, saying 'Your words have been enough.'

Besser also consoled the dying Swedish volunteer Lieutenant Lundgreen. In a whisper he told the chaplain that his father was a minister. 'And it was as if,' noted Besser, 'the thought of his father gave him peace.' Besser was then taken to the adjoining stable, where a Danish soldier with a serious thigh trauma had been laid up due to his uncontrollable outbursts of rage. A lantern flickered in the corner of the stable, and the young man's wild eyes fixed on Besser. The Prussian pastor had got hold of a Danish Bible, and he began reading passages out loud. Though it took a while, the wounded man slowly calmed down, folded his hands and began to weep at the chaplain's final words: 'Behold, I stand at the door, and knock.' The Dane died shortly afterwards.

At one of the larger field hospitals, which had 180 beds and where at least ten men succumbed to their wounds every day, Besser was led into an operating theatre where the doctors were preforming what they call 'a bullet search', that is, they had opened up their patient and were using their fingers to probe around inside him, looking for bullets that had been lodged deep in the gut or penetrated a bone. Just as Besser entered, the doctors were removing a large piece of shrapnel – weighing about a kilo – from the gut of a very pale young Prussian soldier.

Besser was also taken to console two seriously wounded Danish men who had been put in a small room upstairs. One clearly only had a few hours of life left in him, and Besser noted that 'his pallid face bore the unmistakable mark of death. There lay this young man, like a seedling crushed before reaching maturity.'

The other Dane said to Besser, 'Oh, Reverend, if only you could have been here earlier. He has been begging for an army chaplain to give him his last rites.'

But now it was too late. Or was it? The soldier who had just spoken heaved himself out of bed, made for his friend's and shouted at the top of his voice, 'Comrade, comrade!' 'And suddenly he was back,' Besser wrote. 'The wounded man opened his eyes and looked questioningly at us … I immediately began to perform the sacrament. Finally I blessed the two men, who both died shortly; the one who had been in a coma within a few hours, the other within a few days.'

The kinds of wounds incurred by the two Danes and the thousands of others who had fallen victim to the storm of steel that swept across Dybbøl on 18 April are meticulously described in the medical reports. Loeffler, for instance, describes all of his seventy-four amputations in detail, and reading his case files is much like travelling with each bullet as it tears through human tissue, shatters bone and severs arteries.

Loeffler's report also covers 200 representative cases of battle wounds caused by all kinds of shot and shells. Being a stickler for order, he begins with the various head injuries and then moves on down the body to the shoulders, lungs, abdomen, legs, and finally concludes with a section on foot injuries. In keeping with standard medical practice, each case is identified by a number. Below are excerpts from cases 8, 9 and 13.

Case 8: Danish Private M. Christensen, 2nd Regiment, shot through the head – bullet passing through the skull and brain, exiting the other side. Bullet has passed through both eyeballs, puncturing them and causing swelling. Patient unconscious. Involuntary muscular movements of arms and hands, hitting face and causing ice packs and bandages to be displaced from the wounds. On 19 April the patient becomes delirious, restless and his speech is incoherent. From 20 April he is quiet, mouth open, rapid breathing and bloody discharge from his nose. He dies on 22 April.

Case 9: Prussian Private Leppin, 24th Regiment. Shot through the skull. A bone splinter lodged deep in the brain. Brain matter and splintered bone around entry wound. Bullet not located. The wounded babbles but is conscious. He is able to answer questions with nods and can move all limbs. Leppin has also received a wound to the left arm. All muscle tissues shredded and the bone exposed. To relieve his pain, lower arm is amputated. 20 April: patient complains of a headache, tosses and turns in his bed, unable to control bladder and bowels, faecal matter and urine pouring forth unimpeded. 25 April: amputation wound has begun to suppurate. The patient thrashes about in his cot, breathing is heavy. Death came.

Case 13: Prussian Sergeant Ritter, 18th Regiment, 11th Company. Shot through the skull. Bone destroyed, blown off … he has trouble speaking. Left side of his face paralysed. Tongue retracted to the left. The right arm is stiffening and immovable. 2 May: right leg also completely paralysed. Patient has an unnatural bluish pallor and is passive. He dies on 5 May.

The medical report penned by Julius Ressel is equally rich n gruesome and bloody details. The Order of St John had wo field hospitals: one in Nybøl, near the redoubt line; and a econd at the Bellevue Hospital in Flensburg, just south of the present-day German–Danish border. The Order, a voluntary elief organisation, had many of the most prominent German physicians on staff during the engagement in Denmark, notably the world-renowned Friedrich von Esmarch. The Order mainly took care of wounded officers, but as their 200-case report attested, bullets tore with the same death-dealing violence through the bodies of the commissioned officers as he private soldiers. One badly wounded officer was a second ieutenant of the Prussian 60th Regiment. He was brought to he field hospital in Nybøl and his case is described in detail in he Order's report: a bullet had passed:

through the shoulder blade to the throat, crushing the 5th and 6th cervical vertebra as well as the spinal cord. The bullet exited just above the right clavicle. The neck is becoming deformed and there are signs of paralysis, evident in his speech. He is losing muscle control in all limbs, but it is especially pronounced in the legs. There is also a problem with bowel control. Conversely urine has to be drawn off with a catheter. Abdomen swollen. Urine is turbid from organ secretion and there is a strong ammoniacal odour. The patient is thirsty, but not hungry and sleeps poorly. His strength is beginning to wane, paralysis sets in. On 29 April at 10.45 a.m., death follows.

The dying Danish Major Ernst Schau is in the care of the Order of St John, too.

The patient was shot through the right thigh during the defence of the Danish positions. A careful examination of his wound showed the femur was fractured and the joint crushed. A temporary dressing had been applied. 20 April: an amputation at the joint performed by a circular incision. 21 April: the patient runs a high fever, is restless and sleeps only a little. Thirsty. Ice packs are still tolerated. 22 April: the patient complains of severe pain in his stump, which is swollen and very tender. 23 April: the patient sleeps fretfully, is restless, pulse is regular but weak. Pain in the stump is severe and gangrene is developing in several areas of the wound. Gangrene is spreading. Morphine is administered. At about three o'clock the patient begins to vomit; to prevent further vomiting he is given ice cubes to suck. In the evening the vomiting resumes. The patient collapses and dies at four in the morning.

Before the amputation Ernst Schau had managed to pen a letter to his wife, though his writing is barely legible; by this time, Schau was almost too weak to hold his pencil.

> My most dearly beloved Friede! Yesterday I was too weak to write words of comfort to you, but today, after a few hours of sleep, I feel strong enough to write. [The doctors] still cannot assess the seriousness of my wound and whether an amputation will be necessary, but we hope for the best. Have you had any tidings of Emil? He was very much in danger of being taken prisoner that day. I am in the care of the Order of St John at Bellevue Hospital and it is excellent. A thousand warm regards from Your Ernst.

On 20 April a delegation of Prussian negotiators sailed to Als with the bodies of about twenty Danish officers, including the body of General du Plat, who was the only one to have been given a casket. Field Marshal von Wrangel had seen to it himself that du Plat's body be adorned with a laurel wreath. Du Plat's body was also the only one that had not been looted. Ernst Schau was not thus honoured by his foes, but he was delivered to the Danish army, allowing his grieving wife, mother and children to mourn their loss at a proper burial.

32

The prisoners

Residents of Flensburg followed bulletins from the battlefield closely throughout 18 April. The town was half Danish, half German. News that the battle had begun reached Flensburg early in the day, and as one eyewitness phrased it, 'anxious crowds soon flocked into the streets'. By noon a rumour was going around that the redoubt line had fallen. But was it true?

Everyone was in a state of tension and sought desperately to get accurate news from the front. The outcome of the war would have a huge impact on the lives of all residents in Flensburg, so one and all were eagerly awaiting updates. If the Prussians won, the large Danish population would most likely come under German rule; conversely the pro-Germans perceived the war as a war of independence, which would, if a victory was secured, free them from Danish oppression.

The people of Flensburg had been close to the war efforts from the beginning, as it was located on the major route for troop movements. First the Danish troops marching to the Dannevirke; then the Danes again as they retreated from the Dannevirke positions; and finally their Prussian pursuers: they all marched straight through Flensburg. The Prussians established their biggest field hospitals here. The townspeople were called upon to supply not only lodging for the regiments but also housing for the wounded, who came in large numbers by boat or ambulance wagon.

When it became clear that the Prussians had won, 'German soldiers and residents cheered and celebrated, while the Danes walked about with eyes downcast in deep mourning, but as usual they behaved with dignity and self-possession, not wanting to give the Germans more reason to exult over them,' wrote one eyewitness.

By about 8 p.m. the townspeople had learned the full extent of the battle. Another eyewitness, high-school history teacher Karl Friedrich Schumacher, wrote to his son:

> At Franziska Petersen's house the street suddenly filled with Prussian lancers and hussars, who rode at full gallop through town, so we had in haste to seek refuge in the nearest houses. Once we felt it was safe to go outside and walk home, we encounter large masses of prisoners. There were so many of them the procession had come to a halt. Some were on foot, others were carried in wagons.

At Dybbøl, as previously noted, the Prussians had taken 3,300 prisoners, who were force-marched in long, straggling columns to Flensburg, thirty kilometres south of the Danish positions. Eyewitnesses noted that the prisoner's uniforms were worn and torn, their boots, faces and hair covered in dust or mud. Their expressions were despondent, eyes vacant and downcast.

'Every Dane who experienced 18 April 1964 in Flensburg will always have a vivid recollection of that day,' Reverend Vilhelm Gregersen wrote in his memoirs. Though he was just a child in 1864, he remembered the day vividly:

During the war more than 7,000 Danish soldiers were taken
as prisoners. They were taken to camps all over Prussia
and Austria and were generally well treated.

I will always remember this young woman in a dark dress,
who stood outside Nørre Port [the town's northern gate],
grief-stricken and inconsolable. Tears flowed freely and
her chest heaved with gut-wrenching sorrow ... like so
many she had gone to meet the prisoners and it was the
sight of them that had moved her so deeply.

Column after column of prisoners marched through the town
and, wrote Gregersen:

[Their] calm, sad faces affected me deeply ... one-two,
one-two – marching forward in a steady beat, and in
silence like sodden leaves falling one by one on a fog-filled
and rainy day in harvest time.

Only in a few exceptional cases were we able to exchange a couple of words with the men in the outermost rows; yes, only rarely, as Prussian hussars and lancers rode with loaded guns, carbines and pistols along each side of the rain of men. But though words could not be spoken, there was communication through the eyes, and messages of comfort flowed from us to them and back.

In the morning the prisoners were to be moved to military prisons further south, but that evening they were kept in large public buildings in Flensburg. On the streets out in front, large crowds of Danish residents gathered in a show of support.

Suddenly the first few notes of the Danish marching song 'The Brave Foot Soldier' broke through the gloomy atmosphere. At first the singing was soft and tentative – then louder and bolder and finally everyone was singing at the top of their voices despite orders [to quieten down] and rearing horses; like a giant wave of warmth the now liberated voices rose above us into the dark evening sky. The soldiers joined in from their enclosure in the lofts of the big building and people on the street below sang.

Later that evening Gregersen's father took him to the town's residents' meeting house, where the captured officers were kept. The air was thick with smoke. Gregersen junior wanted to meet the famous Lieutenant Ancker, who was among the prisoners, and his father soon spotted him.

A moment later we stood in front of him. My father told him in a kind direct manner that we would like to talk to him – and what father's words did not express, my eyes certainly did. I am sure that all the glowing enthusiasm my young heart held and the expression of devotion and admiration in my eyes washed over him like a warm wave. He stood puzzled for a moment. Then his gaze grew gentle. And suddenly he bent down, grabbed me and lifted me to give me a kiss.

33

Berlin

On the morning of 18 April, King Wilhelm I of Prussia was on Tempelhof Common near Berlin, inspecting a selection of elite Royal Guard battalions. He was aware that the battle at Dybbøl was in progress, but had not yet had news from the front. On his way back to Berlin he received the very telegram he had hoped for: 'The Dybbøl position has fallen.' The king immediately turned around and drove back to the guardsmen on Tempelhof Common, where the telegram was read aloud to the men. All broke into loud cheers, as did the greater populace of Berlin when the news reached the city. The king rushed to his castle and his queen to deliver the good tidings in person. He also dispatched a telegram to Prince Friedrich Karl that read: 'I would like to thank my wonderful army and you and your leadership for the glorious victory achieved today. Express my sincere acknowledgement to the men and relay my royal gratitude for their efforts. Wilhelm.'

In Berlin, people were gathering in the streets to celebrate the victory. The *Berliner Börsen-Zeitung* newspaper reported that there was an 'upbeat atmosphere':

Flags, lit up, waved from many public and private buildings. A little after eight, six cannon fired 101 shots in the park. A large crowd of people massed on Unter den Linden and in front of the royal palace. At about 9 p.m. the king appeared on the balcony, leaned over the balustrade towards the crowd and spoke these words: 'Let us salute our brave troops.' The response was thunderous and people began singing the 'Schleswig-Holstein meerumschlungen' ['Schleswig-Holstein, sea-girt land'] battle song. Later they sang 'Heil dir im Siegerkranz' ['Hail to Thee in Victor's Crown']. There was partying in the streets till after midnight.

While people were celebrating in the streets of Berlin, the king received a deputation of inhabitants who congratulated him on behalf of the entire city on his victory. This took place at about 10.30 p.m. The daily newspaper *Die Kreuzzeitung* reported that a visibly moved king had said, 'This victory fully makes up for our many earlier disappointments; the glorious achievements of our army attests to the strength of our Prussian character.'

The king then went on to convey the latest news from Dybbøl. A joyous atmosphere erupted and the king 'graciously allowed the deputation to retire', in the words of the reporter from *Die Kreuzzeitung*.

The following day the king travelled north with a large entourage to survey the battlefield and celebrate the victory with the troops. Prussian minister-president Otto von Bismarck also immediately set off for Dybbøl to see with his own eyes the battlefield upon which his political career had been saved.

34

The ghost ship

While Prussian dignitaries and high-ranking military personnel were eagerly travelling to Dybbøl to rejoice in the glorious achievement of their army, most Danes, like war correspondent P. V. Grove, were fleeing the area, wishing nothing more than to put the horrors of war and defeat behind them.

Grove had managed to get passage to Copenhagen on the steamer transporting the wounded. The quick escape he had longed for from the haunting experiences of violence and brutality on the front, then, was not to be had just yet. On board the *North Star*, he was confronted head on with the war's devastating human cost. Grove would never forget this passage – the steamer's cargo of wounded and dying men made the *North Star* more like a 'ghost ship' than a transport vessel, Grove later recalled.

Grove had followed the long train of wounded bound for Copenhagen all the way from the battlefield at Dybbøl to the large dressing station set up at Hørup Hav Harbour. Here, near one of the bridges, the *North Star* and two cutters lay at anchor.

'The steamer's once elegant lounge had been reserved for the worst cases and the red velvet sofas would soon gain an even darker hue,' Grove wrote to his readers. Straw covered all floors of the steamer and the cutters. On the wharf 'loving hands carefully placed one wounded man at a time in a barrel with one side cut out and hoisted him aboard'.

It was a beautiful day on 18 April and Grove found himself enjoying the mild weather despite the mass of wounded men surrounding him. 'The sea was as smooth as a millpond, there was no wind, and the waves lapped gently against the beach; yet the black smoke rising above Sønderborg and the roar of cannon reminded us that we were still at war and had no right to indulge in tranquil meditations.'

The *North Star* was not scheduled to weigh anchor until nightfall, which left Grove time to study the hundreds of wounded – 500 in total – before they were hoisted aboard the steamer and the two cutters.

In this wagon there is an officer of high station; he is severely wounded – you can tell from his sallow pallor and the tired, pained expression in his eyes. If you move in closer, you can hear his rasping breath, an indication of damaged lungs … and there is a young lieutenant with a bandaged arm. His greatcoat is perforated with bullet-holes, and he has taken three shots to the arm, but still he jumps nimbly off the wagon and walks on board without assistance, while smoking a cigar … An older reservist in a blue greatcoat is gently lifted off the wagon; he limps aboard aided by a couple of men and crawls into the hold.

On deck the wounded are soon spread out and a host of doctors, 'pale, exhausted and covered in blood run about. "Is there anyone on board who has not had their wounds dressed?" is their first question, and as many answer in the

War correspondent P. V. Groove wrote a number of captivating eyewitness accounts from the theater of war. He followed the Danish army from Dannevirke to the battle of Dybbøl, and returned to Copenhagen with a large steamer full of severely wounded soldiers.

affirmative, they get out their dressings and continue the work started at the dressing stations [near the battlefield].'

By 8 p.m. the ship is packed tight with wounded soldiers.

Most of the wounded officers were on deck, smoking and eating their dinner while talking about the events of the day ... non-commissioned officers and privates were seated on benches, lying down or pacing back and forth wrapped in white woollen blankets. From the lounge came the sound of quiet moans; in there the men were struggling with death and every moment we expected to hear that yet another had lost his final battle.

The three ships weigh anchor and set their course towards Copenhagen. Grove described the journey in vivid detail to his readers:

Twinkling stars were scattered across the nocturnal firmament; now and then we passed a lighthouse with flashing beacons. The sailors went quietly about their work, and every so often the medical orderlies would come out from the lounge or the cabins to empty buckets filled with water bloody from washing fresh wounds. Once in a while one of the wounded would come on deck to get a breath of fresh air. As his wounds prevented a quiet rest in his bunk, he had to get up and walk to alleviate the pain.

'It was,' concluded Grove, 'a long, sad night, a night of much pain and suffering – for some their last.'

The following afternoon, 'we were able to make out the outline of Copenhagen's towers in the distance, and we arrived by sunset. We passed the Langelinje and neared our final destination: the Toldboden, enveloped in a golden light.'

On the wharf hundreds of people were gathered to pay their respects to the wounded. The news of their impending arrival had reached the city earlier in the day. 'In silent deference,' Grove wrote, 'people would uncover their heads as the ships passed by.'

Epilogue:
The groundswell after the storm

The Battle of Dybbøl did not end the war. Although the Prussians had successfully stormed Dybbøl, they had not yet gained control of the entire Duchy of Schleswig. In fact, by the time the last Danish troops had withdrawn across the Sound of Als on 18 April 1864, all the Prussians had succeeded in capturing was a bit of muddy, blasted land. With the Danes still in possession of the island of Als, the Prussians could not yet claim to have conquered the duchy, which was after all the crux of the crisis.

To the Prussian generals, Denmark's decision to remain at the fortifications at Dybbøl, even after they realised it could not be defended, seemed rash, particularly considering they had the option of pulling back to Als. Commander-in-chief Prince Friedrich Karl noted in his memoirs that 'although Dybbøl was a great moral victory, it was strategically unimportant'.

If the Danes had withdrawn from Dybbøl in time, the Prussian commanders would have been faced with another humiliating blow, similar to the one they incurred at the Dannevirke. The political ramifications of such a humiliation would have been large for Berlin, possibly impeding Prussia's chances of achieving a favourable decision at the peace negotiations in London on 20 April.

Denmark for her part would have been able to enter the peace conference mediated by Great Britain from a much stronger position had she decided to abandon Dybbøl. The defeat was therefore a double tragedy for Denmark: she lost not only political leverage, but also the lives of many brave men. Defending Dybbøl was, from the outset, a lost cause.

The string of events following the defeat on 18 April plunged Denmark into an abyss of political difficulties from which it would take her many years to fully extricate herself. The Prussians may have conquered only a few kilometres of bomb-torn land that day in April, but the psychological effect of the victory was great. It boosted Prussian confidence and pride in her military capabilities, as was evident by the wild and spontaneous scenes of jubilation that erupted in the streets of Berlin when news of the successful assault reached the city. King Wilhelm I and his ambitious minister-president, Otto von Bismarck, had suddenly gained wide popular support and were in great shape for the coming international peace negotiations in London.

The negotiations lasted two months, during which time the warring parties and the Great Powers attended several sessions. The realpolitik, hidden agendas and double-dealing on display could fill an entire book in their own right, but in short the skilful poker player Otto von Bismarck emerged as the great winner. It was most likely during these negotiations that the international community first discovered what a powerful and talented politician Berlin had at its helm.

Great Britain, who had initiated the conference, was eager to broker a peace, as the Danish–German war presented a serious threat to the delicate balance of power in Europe. A strong Prussia with access to the Baltic was not in Great

Britain's interest, as this could well end up threatening her supremacy at sea. In addition the war was causing political tensions domestically. The opposition, led by Tory politician Benjamin Disraeli, openly reproached the government for not intervening militarily on Denmark's behalf – a view that had considerable popular support in Britain, where many were moved by pro-Danish stories in the media. As previously noted, British prime minister Lord Palmerston and Foreign Secretary Lord Russell were also kindly disposed towards Denmark and wished to support her militarily. They were, however, hampered by Queen Victoria's staunch opposition to a military involvement that would put her at odds with the Prussian Crown. So from the beginning of the conflict Palmerston and Russell instead worked hard to broker a speedy peace agreement.

Shortly after the fall of the Dannevirke in February, the British had invited the warring parties to a peace conference in London. Berlin and Vienna were favourably disposed to negotiating a peace. After all, the show of support for their German brethren in the duchies, which had been their main objective, was achieved. The Austrian emperor, Franz Joseph, and minister-president Otto von Bismarck therefore readily agreed to a round of peace talks. Incredibly, the Danish prime minister, D. G. Monrad, turned down the invitation. He feared that Denmark was in too weak a position to achieve favourable terms at this point, and chose instead to put his faith in the Dybbøl fortifications and trenches.

Not until Dybbøl was near complete destruction by mid April did the Danish cabinet agree to a peace conference. For strategic reasons, Bismarck orchestrated a few delays, and a date was set for 20 April, two days after the planned attack on

Dybbøl. Delegates from Prussia, Austria and the rest of the German Confederation, Denmark, Sweden–Norway, Russia and France attended the meetings, chaired by Lord Russell and Lord Clarendon. Thirteen delegates participated in the conference's thirteen sessions.

From the beginning, unity of purpose was inordinately difficult to achieve, but the British delegates worked tirelessly to bring the parties together. The first item on the agenda was defining and agreeing on terms for an armistice. Denmark's most effective weapon in the war was her blockade of German ports in the Baltic and the North Sea; she was therefore reluctant to give in to demands from the Confederate delegates to lift it. After lengthy discussions, however, Denmark was persuaded to comply and an armistice was arranged for 12 May. Ironically it came into effect a few days after the war's only sea battle, the Battle of Heligoland, which took place on 9 May 1864. The Danish North Sea Fleet engaged the Austrian fleet and won – one of Denmark's few victories in the war.

Of course, the essential point at issue was negotiating a peace agreement, but it would prove exceedingly difficult to navigate through the parties' divergent interests. Russia, France and Great Britain each had their own agenda. Denmark and the Germans (Austria, Prussia and the rest of the Confederation) were inhibited by internal disagreements about which course to pursue. Officially, Bismarck supported Austria's suggestion for a constitutional arrangement by which the duchies were to be reinstituted in a personal union with the Kingdom of Denmark. His support, though, was more a diplomatic ploy than anything else, as he was secretly working towards a decision that would allow him to annex at least the southern part of Schleswig to Prussia. The Danish National

Liberal government, however, was emphatically not interested in re-establishing a constitutional arrangement similar to the one stipulated in the London Protocol, as the shrewd and calculating Bismarck very well knew. To complicate matters further, the Danish king, Christian IX, who, unlike his cabinet, welcomed Austria's proposal, suddenly intervened on behalf of the Danish government. His bipolar prime minister had fallen down a psychological rabbit hole, which was distorting his sense of reality to a degree that rendered him unfit to direct the negotiations.

Bedevilled by internal strife, Denmark's manoeuvrings at the peace conference, inconsistent and confused as they were, resulted in a complete failure to achieve anything but the most unfavourable peace terms. This despite the fact that Lord Russell and Lord Palmerston, with the support of France, had pushed through a compromise proposal in which Schleswig would be divided at the Schlei along the line of the Dannevirke, allowing Denmark to retain two-thirds of the duchy. Incredibly, and mostly because of the prime minister's personal difficulties and the king's continued meddling, Denmark turned down this generous offer.

Bismarck, however, was able to keep his cool and was neither greedy nor unreasonable in his demands. On the contrary, the man who would later be known as the Iron Chancellor manoeuvred smoothly and deftly through the negotiations – already proving himself a world-class realist diplomat. In the interest of becoming a sea power, it was Bismarck's key objective at the conference to obtain access to the planned Kiel Canal, where he saw an opportunity to build a Prussian naval base. He was therefore not particularly interested in gaining control of the rest of Schleswig; in fact, he once noted that annexing the Danish-speaking part of Schleswig would only result in 'trouble'. He was therefore willing to concede half of the duchy to Denmark – an offer he maintained throughout the talks. By a strange quirk of fate, the current Danish–German border, established by referendum in 1920, divides Schleswig according to Bismarck's proposal.

At the eleventh hour the British made the (for its time) radical proposal that the duchy be divided by a referendum – a suggestion Napoleon III, who had made himself a spokesman of the sovereignty of peoples everywhere, welcomed and supported. Bismarck was also favourably disposed to this approach. But yet again the obstinate Danish leaders said no, and to the great consternation of the British mediators, the talks broke down, leading to a renewal of hostilities. And this time, Denmark's situation was even more hopeless. By her own doing she was now completely isolated.

When hostilities were resumed on 25 June, Denmark still had 40,000 men under arms, but allied forces, which had occupied Jutland, had swelled to more than 100,000 troops. Also present on the front now was Prussia's later legendary chief of staff Helmuth von Molkte, who planned and executed the greatest military triumph in the war, namely the conquest and occupation of Als, which took place on 29 June, just a few days after the peace talks in London had broken down.

Under cover of darkness on this beautiful summer night, hundreds of rowing boats carrying Prussian soldiers crossed the Sound of Als. The Danish troops posted along the coast of Als were unprepared to meet the swarms of Prussian soldiers that suddenly loomed out of the darkness. Fierce but one-sided fighting ensued, and 29 June probably remains the blackest day in Danish military history.

The Danes, who were in possession of the formidable iron-clad warship *Rolf Krake*, at this time patrolling the sound, should by all standards have been able to prevent the crossing. Instead they were overrun in a surprise attack. On this bitter night the Danish casualties numbered 3,300 men, more than eight times as many as their opponent – a humiliation almost too great to bear.

No myth-making was ever able to ameliorate the devastating blow Denmark received on 29 June. Only by the skin of their teeth were the Danes able to salvage the remnants of their forces in a Dunkirk-esque withdrawal to the island of Funen, where they nervously prepared for the final great battle – a countdown to doomsday in the minds of most soldiers. Denmark was seized by panic. Copenhagen's National Guard was assembled. Denmark seemed on the verge of total disintegration. If the Prussians could take Als, which should have been impossible considering the strength of Denmark's sea power, what was to prevent them from occupying Funen, then Zealand and Copenhagen? Seemingly it was not until this moment, when it appeared Copenhagen was in imminent danger of being overrun, that the seriousness of the situation dawned on the country's political leaders. In a desperate attempt to save Denmark, the king ousted Monrad and his cabinet and installed a conservative government in their stead. But nothing could save Denmark from having to relinquish vast amounts of its territory. With all appearing lost, the king made a last-ditch effort to save the monarchy, secretly suggesting peace terms to Otto von Bismarck and King Wilhelm according to which the Kingdom of Denmark, in a personal union with the duchies, would become a member of the German Confederation. Denmark itself teetered on the edge of extinction. Bismarck, however, blankly refused even to consider the proposal. He did not want a people with anti-German sympathies incorporated in the Confederation.

The final peace negotiations took place in Vienna, in October 1864. France, Russia and Great Britain had had quite enough of the Schleswig-Holstein Question by this time and none of them attended the talks. Indeed, calling the Vienna conference a 'negotiation' is rather misleading: Denmark had peace terms dictated to her and was forced to cede all three duchies: Lauenburg, Holstein and Schleswig. Denmark's territory was thus reduced by a third, and the country was shorn of half its former population. Denmark had, at the single stroke of a pen, become a Lilliputian state.

Prussia on the other hand was beginning a new chapter in its history. The war against Denmark was the first of a series of wars Bismarck would wage which would come to change the map of Europe. A squabble between Austria and Prussia over the control of the territorial spoils from their victory over Denmark spilled over in 1866 into a full-blown war over the domination of the German Confederation. Prussia crushed Austria in a monumental battle at Königsgrätz on 3 July 1866. After this short war, known as the Seven Weeks' War, Bismarck's long-held political ambition for control of the Confederation was realised. Napoleon III looked on anxiously: Prussia was rapidly becoming one of the most powerful of Europe's Great Powers. A clash between France and Prussia seemed inevitable, and war erupted in 1870. Moltke's military genius ensured a quick and overwhelming victory. The French Empire fell within a few weeks. Emperor Napoleon III capitulated at Sedan on 1 September 1870.

This was the ultimate triumph for Bismarck and the

ultimate humiliation for France, not least because Prussia chose the Hall of Mirrors at Versailles for King Wilhelm's coronation as German emperor – an intentional and finely tuned insult choreographed by Bismarck, for whom the ceremony represented the crowning glory of his political life: the unification of Germany under Berlin's rule.

The Siegessäule (Victory Column) – a monument celebrating the three victories in 1864, 1866 and 1870–71 – was erected in Berlin. It was originally intended as a monument to the victory over the Danes, but as the construction of the monument was not yet completed by the time Prussia and the then German Reich had won the following two wars, it was decided to include emblems of these victories as well. Until the First World War, every child in Germany knew about the 'three unification wars' and could relate the dates and details of the battles of Dybbøl, Königsgrätz and Sedan.

Today the Siegessäule is located in the Große Stern (Great Star), in the Tiergarten. The barrels of captured Danish cannon that adorn its sides serve to remind us it was the forgotten war of 1864 that set in motion the string of events leading to the unification of Germany and a new order of power in Europe. Bismarck's political career, teetering on the verge of collapse before the war, was saved by Prussia's victory over Denmark. Had Prussia not won, there would have been no Siegessäule, the wars against Austria and France would maybe never have been fought, and European history would most likely have played out very differently. In that sense, the Danish–German war heralded a new era for Europe.

For many of its survivors, the war's devastation did not end with the last shot at Als or the signature of the Treaty of

Vienna. Christian Julius de Meza was found dead in his apartment in Copenhagen one September day in 1865. On his desk was an unfinished handwritten manuscript with the title *My Last and Irrevocable Opinion about the Warfare and the State*, which he had been working on for weeks. The manuscript was one long defence of the withdrawal from the Dannevirke on 5 February 1864. In it, de Meza cuts the political leaders in Copenhagen down to size, describing them as dreamers with no understanding of the realities at the front. He accuses them of blindly following the will of the people and of being informed by a ridiculous romantic sentiment which held that the fortifications built by a legendary queen were impregnable.

Had de Meza only lived a little longer he would have been gratified to discover that the leaders who came into power after the war deeply regretted Denmark's entry into an ill-conceived conflict and, in particular, their predecessors' scape-goating of the head of the Danish army. Now everyone agreed that the withdrawal from the Dannevirke had in fact been the only sound option. Too late for Denmark, and too late for her eccentric but brilliant military leader to appreciate, de Meza's reputation was posthumously rehabilitated and his strategy during the war vindicated.

After being relieved of his duties as commander of the Danish army in mid February 1864, the otherwise sociable, music-loving former general had withdrawn from the world. He lived alone and was rarely seen in public. The devastation and humiliation of his dishonourable discharge from the army took years off his life, the remainder of which he spent writing his defence – his last battle, fought only with pen and paper.

His replacement at the helm of the Danish army did not fare much better. In the last phase of the war, George Daniel

Gerlach was demoted to division general and at war's end was dismissed from the army. In light of the fact that he had obeyed every order he had been given, his dismissal seems particularly unfair. He had fought to the bitter end at Dybbøl, as ordered. The impossible situation he had been put in, which required him to defend a position that was doomed and at the same time ensure the survival of the Danish army, had of course been the main reason for his undoing. Even before the Prussian assault on Dybbøl the irreconcilable orders he had received had broken him and turned him into an apathetic leader whose inertia frustrated the general staff. After the war he too became withdrawn and spent the brief remainder of his life – he died on 7 March 1865 – on his estate, which by a strange irony was called 'Solitude'. He died, perhaps deliberately, before the one-year anniversary of the war.

Gerlach and de Meza's tormentor, Denmark's war minister, Carl Christian Lundbye, who directed the war from his desk in Copenhagen, was dismissed for his irresponsible and incompetent leadership in the last phase of the war. Prime Minister D. G. Monrad, his long-time supporter, fired him, and the mentally unstable Lundbye subsequently fell into a deep depression. As one contemporary biographer laconically wrote, 'He spent his last years in a mental fog, which prevented him from doing any work at all.'

Monrad, who had not only led Denmark into war through his refusal to revoke the November Constitution of 1863, but had also badly mishandled the subsequent peace negotiations, was so distraught and embarrassed by his failures that he emigrated to New Zealand with his family. Five years later he returned to Denmark, but never managed to regain his political footing. He died in 1887.

It would take years for Denmark to recover from the after-effects of the war. For the thousands of disabled soldiers, it would shape the rest of their lives. In a Danish medical journal from 28 October 1865, Dr F. Trier gives a vivid account of their suffering. In the eighteen months since the war he had treated 1,500 disabled soldiers and describes in his article the various types of disabilities he had seen inflicted on the men.

The most common injury, according to Trier, was gunshot fractures of the jaw. If a soldier had taken a bullet or shell fragment in the upper jaw, he had typically lost all his upper teeth and his palate. A fractured lower jaw was the most serious: 'For some the wound never heals, for others it heals but causes deformity and misaligned bite. For the majority the fractures cause lack of mobility, making opening and closing the mouth difficult.'

Such disabilities blighted the lives of many, but the families of those who had not returned at all – fathers, sons and brothers – were hit especially hard after the war. Among these families were Inger Marie Larsen, twenty-nine years old, from the Pilsgård Mill in Hellum, and her two children, three-year-old Christian and infant daughter Marie. Her husband, Niels Larsen, from the 22nd Regiment, died on 18 April.

Exactly how he died is not known, but one of his comrades later said he had seen Niels Larsen fall somewhere on the right flank of the Dybbøl position. We know, however, that he was stationed on the far left flank in the trench between Redoubts I and II, where fierce fighting took place, so this account seems unlikely. Still, perhaps he made it as far as the right flank in the wild retreat that followed the battle. His name is not on any of the official casualty lists and it seems he was forgotten in the panic up there on Dybbøl Hill.

At home, however, he was deeply missed. Their emotional response aside, his wife and children were dependent on Niels to run the mill. The army had not listed him among the dead, and as Inger Marie awaited news of her husband after the battle she fervently hoped that he had been captured by the enemy and was in a POW camp. He was not, though, among the some 7,000 Danish POWS who had been repatriated by late summer. Still, Inger Marie kept her hope alive and insisted that no one lock the front door to the house: if Niels should come home one day, she did not want him to be met by a locked door.

Inger Marie was eventually forced to leave the mill and move into a more modest cottage with her two children. As a war widow she received an annual pension of thirty-seven rixdollars, and twelve rixdollars per child until they turned fifteen. Inger Marie was thrifty and managed to get by on her meagre pension. She was well liked in her community but never remarried. She died in 1912 and was buried in the Hellum churchyard, where her large gravestone reads: 'Inger Marie Larsen, widow of Niels Larsen, who fell at Dybbøl, 18 April 1864'.

The Schau family, too, was forever marked by the war. Dorothea lost her last two sons, Ernst and Emil, on 18 April. Friede and her three small children lost a husband and father, Ernst Schau. Olufa Finsen, the wife of Sønderborg's mayor, Hilmer Finsen, met with the family in a park in Copenhagen on 19 May 1864. 'They were bowed by grief, the poor darlings. Dorothea is ill and Friede looks poorly too,' Olufa wrote to her husband that day.

Upon receiving the news that her husband was alive but seriously wounded, Friede had rushed to Flensburg a few days after the battle. There was, however, never to be a happy reunion between husband and wife. When she arrived in Flensburg, she was informed that Ernst had died shortly after they had amputated his leg.

Though the young and energetic Wilhelm Dinesen survived the 8th Brigade's counter-attack, it seems likely that a vital part of him died on Dybbøl Hill. Dinesen is one of the more colourful characters in the war. Today he is mostly known as the father of world-renowned writer Karen Blixen, but in his time he was a well-known politician and a brilliant writer (*Letters of the Hunt* being his most important work).

The war left Dinesen restless and unable to settle into normal life. His strong drive to seek out new and dangerous exploits propelled him to volunteer on the French side against his old enemies in the Franco-Prussian War (1870–71), in which he was promoted to the rank of captain and experienced the total collapse of the French army known as the 'Army of the East'. He survived this war as well, but his hunger for danger had not subsided and he volunteered to serve with the Turkish army in the Balkans in the Russo-Turkish War of 1877–8. Dinesen later travelled into the American wilderness, where he lived among the native peoples of Wisconsin for two years. After returning to Denmark he became a part of Copenhagen's social elite, but, although he married and had five children and became engrossed in Danish politics and hunting, he was a broken man, and on 27 March 1895, at the age of forty-nine, he committed suicide. Unlike so many of his comrades, he had survived the war itself; we cannot know, but like many others on the Danish side – indeed, like Denmark herself – perhaps he never recovered from the trauma of the war of 1864.

Chronology of the war

1848–51

The Schleswig crisis actually began in 1848, when it led to a three-year civil war between Denmark and the two duchies of Schleswig and Holstein (the First Schleswig War). The duchies were defeated. However, during the peace conference Denmark was forced to agree to sign a peace treaty stipulating that the two duchies remain an indissoluble union under the auspices of the Danish Crown, though without being subject to the Danish constitution (the London Protocol of 1852). The treaty proved a major hindrance to effectual policy-making, and thus when the National Liberals, riding on a wave of national enthusiasm, came to power during the 1850s with the campaign slogan 'Denmark to the River Eider' (that is, a constitutional inclusion of Schleswig), they issued a proclamation demonstrating their intent to incorporate Schleswig into the Kingdom of Denmark, thereby effectively violating the London Protocol and setting the stage for the 1864 conflict.

1863

March: In the March Proclamation the Danish cabinet once again announces its intentions to incorporate Schleswig into the Kingdom of Denmark and to allow Holstein to become incorporated in the German Confederation (a loose federation of the then thirty-nine independent German states).

October: The German Confederation is outraged and calls for a retraction of the proclamation, threatening to occupy the duchies unless Denmark complies.

13 November: Despite threats from the German Confederation, the Danish cabinet approves the new constitution, which incorporates Schleswig into the kingdom, thereby annulling the London Protocol of 1852.

15 November: The popular Danish king, Frederik VII, dies. The country is in deep mourning. On behalf of Prussia and Austria, both signatories of the London Protocol, Prussian minister-president Otto von Bismarck sends a note to the Danish cabinet demanding a retraction of what becomes known as the November constitution.

18 November: The atmosphere in Copenhagen rises to fever pitch. The National Liberal party is eager to defend Denmark's right to govern in accordance with the new constitution. The international community counsels Denmark to choose a less intransigent course of action, as they realise the little country will not be able to win a war against Prussia and Austria on its own, and none are eager to support Denmark and risk a large-scale war that could unsettle the current power balance in Europe. Denmark, however, turns a deaf ear to their counsel and proceeds with the ratification of the November Constitution, the signing of which falls to the very reluctant new Danish king, Christian IX, who would have preferred Denmark to have abided by the London Protocol and remain a multinational integrated state.

December: Danish deployment to Dannevirke commences. General Christian de Meza (aged seventy-two) is given the High Command of the Danish troops at the Dannevirke.

1864

1 February: The war officially begins. The allied troops of Prussia and Austria, by this time advanced to the River Eider, begin crossing the river, moving into enemy territory.

2 February: The Battle of Mysunde, in which 10,000 Prussian troops attack advanced Danish positions near the town of Mysunde. Despite being numerically inferior, the Danes manage to repulse the massive Prussian forces. While the victory greatly heightens morale and cohesion within the Danish troops, the Prussians are surprised and alarmed by the apparent strength of the Danish army.

3 February: Austrian troops advance on the central position of the Danish Dannevirke line. Intense fighting ensues. Losses are considerable on both sides, but Austria is clearly the winner of this battle, having taken the strategically significant ground immediately in front of the position and forcing the Danish troops to entrench.

4 February: The Prussian-Austrian general staff agree to launch the planned grand-scale pincer attack within a few days. They hope that by encircling the Danish position they will be able to crush and completely destroy the Danish army within hours. De Meza has a clear vision of his opponent's attack strategy and, realising his troops will have no chance of holding the position, he gathers his generals for a war council.

They talk late into the night and, following the lead of their decisive commander, decide to abandon the Dannevirke the following afternoon.

5 February: While the Prussians are preparing the grand pincer attack, the Danish troops begin the logistically demanding and morale-lowering withdrawal. Thousands of men and masses of equipment move out in the dead of night, right under the noses of the enemy, who are completely unaware of what is going on until several hours after the withdrawal has begun.

The early hours of 6 February: The withdrawal train is thirty kilometres long. Men with heavy knapsacks, horses, cannon, and wagons with provisions and equipment, struggle along the icy road through the heavy wind-blown snow towards the new main line at Dybbøl near the border to the Kingdom of Denmark, as well as to fortifications at Fredericia and Kolding further north.

6 February: An Austrian brigade leaves all equipment behind in order to try to overtake the retreating Danish troops. As they close in on the Danish troops at Sankelmark, the rearguard is ordered to take up the fight with the Austrians to provide cover for the remainder of the retreating Danish forces. A furious battle ensues, man-to-man combat with fixed bayonets, rifle butts and fists. The Danes succeed in staying the pursuers but at great cost to both sides. In the morning the battlefield is strewn with dead and dying men.

7–8 February: The Danish army is divided into two forces: one continues north to the towns of Kolding and Fredericia; the other is deployed to Dybbøl. In Copenhagen there is outrage. Tempers run high, and General de Meza, commander of the Danish army, is scapegoated for what is perceived as a cowardly and unnecessary withdrawal from the Dannevirke, Denmark's fabled and supposedly impregnable fort.

9 February: De Meza is recalled to Copenhagen and his actions subjected to investigation. A mock hearing follows, launched primarily to appease the angry and disillusioned Danes. Strengthening and extending the Dybbøl fortification begins in all haste and with much anxiety.

February–March: During the last days of February and the first weeks of March there is, apart from a few skirmishes and seemingly random Prussian shelling, little fighting on the Dybbøl front. The Prussians, thrown off balance by the Danish retreat from the Dannevirke, are at a loss as to what their next move should be and, fearful that the positions at Fredericia and Kolding are too strong, they dither, losing precious time. Berlin is anxious and puts pressure on its general staff to act soon.

15 March: The Prussians decide to make Dybbøl their primary point of attack and commence reinforcements here, doubling their forces and setting up more heavy artillery pieces. The siege bombardment of Dybbøl commences. The Danes return their fire with vigour.

17 March: Battles are fought over the villages of Dybbøl and Ragebøl. A Danish attempt to retake Ragebøl results in a major battle with severe Danish losses. The Prussians win an overwhelming victory and the Danes are almost pushed back to the redoubt line.

28 March: A Prussian attempt to conquer the last bit of no-man's-land in front of the redoubts is successfully repulsed by the Danes.

28 March – 2 April: Almost 20,000 Prussians amass near the Ballebro ferry berth, preparing to cross the Sound of Als and conduct a surprise rear attack on the Danish position. A hundred and sixty rowing boats and several pontoon bridges lie on the shore, ready to be launched as soon as the order is given. An incoming storm, however, prompts the Prussian commander Prince Friedrich Karl to call off the operation at the last minute.

2–9 April: More than a hundred Prussian cannon shell the Danish redoubts day and night. More Prussian cannon are installed and it becomes increasingly difficult for the Danish troops to repair damage incurred by the incessant shower of Prussian shells pouring over the redoubts. Conditions for the Danish soldiers are horrendous. The Prussians are digging their way closer and closer to the Danish line.

9 April: General Gerlach, commander of the Danish troops at Dybbøl, asks permission to withdraw from the position and retreat to the island of Als.

11 April: The Danish cabinet rejects Gerlach's request, stressing that the position is to be held at all costs. Long trains of impromptu hearses and ambulance wagons leave the Danish line every day. The Danish army is literally bleeding to death. Approximately 100 men are lost daily on the Danish side at this time. Amputations are conducted night and day at the field hospitals.

On the Prussian side, Prince Friedrich Karl and his general staff set a date of 14 April for an assault.

12 April: Prince Friedrich Karl receives a telegram from his uncle King Wilhelm I of Prussia which urges his nephew to postpone the planned storm of Dybbøl until a third parallel trench has been dug, minimising the ground to be covered by the storm columns before reaching the redoubt. A new attack date is set: 18 April.

13 April: The Danish 8th Brigade arrives on Als as reinforcements.

14 April: A battalion of Prussian soldiers conducts a raid at night on the most advanced Danish outposts on the left flank of the position. The Danes are beaten back and work on the third parallel trench can commence.

15 April: The Danish army is at breaking point – mutinous behaviour erupts and is only just prevented from spreading. Prince Friedrich Karl concludes work on his plan of attack.

16 April: Almost 40,000 Prussian troops have amassed in front of the Danish redoubt line; 11,000 have been selected to lead the first wave of attack. A desperate Danish division general named du Plat tries to convince his commander, General Gerlach, to abandon the position, arguing that taking up the fight with the Prussian forces would be suicide. Gerlach, however, does not have enough courage to go against his superiors in Copenhagen.

17 April: All is quiet on the Dybbøl front. Though the usual shelling pours over the redoubts there is no clear sign that an attack is imminent. Gerlach tries unsuccessfully to parley with the Ministry of War in Copenhagen. On the left flank of the position, 2,200 men from the 2nd and 22nd Regiments are on duty that night, and 3,000 men from the 8th Brigade are standing ready at the bridgehead, awaiting the signal to move up to the redoubt line should the Prussians attack.

18 April: During the early hours, approximately 10,000 storm troops move quietly into the third trench parallel closest to the Danish redoubt line. At exactly 4 a.m. an intense bombardment of the redoubts begins. More than 8,000 shells pour in over the redoubts before the clock strikes 10 a.m., at which point the shelling abruptly ceases. There are a few moments of quiet, then all hell breaks loose.

Acknowledgements

This book would not have been possible without the kind and insightful help of many people, including the staff at various archives and museums. I am deeply indebted to them all. While I cannot list everyone here, I would like to acknowledge the names of those who have been especially involved in the making of this book: Inge Adriansen, Annette Buk-Swienty, Peter Christensen, Lasse Jensen, Sven Reiner Johansen, Mary Kalb, Rasmus Øhlenschlæger Madsen, Knud Møller, Søren Mørch, Ervin Nielsen, Bjørn Østergaard, Dan Folke Pedersen, Dag Petersen, Anders B. Rasmussen, Lars Ringhof, the staff at the library of the University of Southern Denmark in Odense, and Louise Wolthers.

And as always, I would like to thank my family for their patience and support, not least my wife, who took on the job of translating this book from the Danish.

A note on quotation

As the wording of most of the first-hand sources used in this book – much of it in archaic German and Danish – often proves difficult for a modern reader to follow, I have for the ease of reading rewritten quoted passages in a more modern idiom. In Part 3, which recounts the Prussian assault on the Danish position, I have on occasion changed tenses in quoted passages from the past to the present, as this section is largely written in the present tense for dramatic effect.

Sources

All material quoted in this book is based on eyewitness accounts such as letters, diaries, contemporary reports and newspaper articles or memoirs written by people who participated in the war in one capacity or another. The majority of my source material consists of first-hand accounts, which provide fresh, immediate and honest renderings of how events were experienced in the moment. Conversely, memoirs, with a few notable exceptions, tend to romanticise events or actions. In order to counterbalance the inevitable inaccuracies of some of this material, I have also relied on some sources written after the clamour of battle had died down, when the author was able to gain a greater breadth of view.

One of these later accounts, written by Wilhelm Dinesen, who participated in the 8th Brigade's brave and determined counter-attack, has been quoted at some length, in part because of its high literary quality. Though his book *Fra Ottende Brigade* ('From the 8th Brigade') was written twenty years after the war, with much pathos, it remains one of the most well-written, reliable descriptions of many of the war's most brutal engagements. His depictions are furthermore corroborated by contemporary military company, battalion and regimental reports; by a report from his superior officer Captain Redsted on the battle for Dybbøl Mill, written a few days after the battle (preserved in the Danish military archive);

and by entries in the diary of Private Peder Hansen (the 1864 Archives, Sønderborg Castle Museum, southern Jutland).

It has been important to me to show the conflict from both sides. Most other Danish works on the war have been informed by Danish nationalism and a them-against-us thinking. In book after book, the feelings and experiences of the Danish troops have been described in detail and with much sympathy, whereas the Prussian forces have been portrayed as stereotypical, even cartoonish, bloodthirsty attackers. In reality, of course they were men, sometimes just boys, of flesh and blood, with as many fears and anxieties as their Danish opponents. For the Prussian soldiers leading the first wave of attacks on the Danish line at Dybbøl on 18 April, the battle was as horrific and terrifying as it was for the Danes, and many Prussian lives were lost. Based on contemporary letters, I have been able to portray the feelings and experiences of some of these men. Unfortunately, many Prussian letters and military reports from 1864 were lost when the large German military archive in Berlin was destroyed in the bombings of the Second World War. It has therefore been necessary to base descriptions of Prussian experiences on published memoirs. Though there is a good amount of romantic nationalistic pathos on the pages of these works, many of them were written within a year of the war, when events were clearly still fresh in the memory – as is obvious from the wealth of detail provided.

I have decided to forego footnotes in this book as it is not in the strictest sense a history book, but first and foremost the story of regular soldiers' experiences of being on the front and participating in the battle that came to define Denmark and ultimately influence the power balance in Europe. Letting story stand uninterrupted by tiny numbers swarming about on the page seemed the right thing to do but I would like to review the archives and archival material I have used for this book. The Danish military archives have thousands of documents from the war of 1864, which, when I researched this book, were archived in a delightful disorder. The only available index was a very old typewritten one, which no one, not even leading archivists at the State Archives, could make head or tail of. It seems fair to say that Denmark had indeed done all it could to repress the memory of the war. Since I did my research, however, much has been done to organise the material, notably by museum director Bjørn Østergaard of the Dybbøl Centre, who has made much of the material available (in the original Danish, of course) on the centre's website (www.1864.dk). The Rigs Archives have also since begun digitising their collection.

Fortunately, the thousands of personal files of the soldiers who participated in the war are in perfect order and have been of great help in the writing of this book. I have systematically gone through all letters and diaries, most of which have never been published before but are richly quoted in this work.

The Sønderborg Castle museum has a large collection of letters and diaries, not only from Danish soldiers but also including quite a few remembrances from Prussian soldiers.

The Red Cross in Geneva has also been very forthcoming with material, forwarding me their case file from the war, the first in which there was a Red Cross presence.

Finally, I have used contemporary newspaper articles from the Danish *Berlingske Tidende* (a conservative daily), the *Fædrelandet* (chief organ of the National Liberals) and the *People's Paper* (chief organ of Copenhagen residents), as well as a collection of articles written by British war correspondent

Edward Dicey for the *Daily Telegraph* and by Antonio Gallenga for *The Times*.

The illustrations in this book are from collections in the Danish Royal Library and the photo collection at the Sønderborg Castle museum.

Index